Soulful SEX

DR. VICTORIA LEE

MJF BOOKS
NEW YORK

Published by MJF Books
Fine Communications
Two Lincoln Square
60 West 66th Street
New York, NY 10023

ISBN 1-56731-198-9
Soulful Sex

This edition published by arrangement with Conari Press.

The author gratefully acknowledges permission to excerpt from the following:

> *The Shared Heart: Relationships, Initiations, and Celebrations* by Barry
> and Joyce Vissell. Copyright © 1984 by Barry and Joyce Vissell.
> Reprinted by permission of Ramira (Aptos, CA).

> *Venus After Forty: Sexual Myths, Men's Fantasies and Truths About
> Middle-Aged Women* by Rita M. Ransohoff. Copyright © 1987 by Rita
> M. Ransohoff. Reprinted by permission of Macmillan (New York).

Manufactured in the United States of America on acid-free paper

10   9   8   7   6   5   4   3   2   1

∽

To my children,
who have given me the opportunity to love fully, my heartfelt wish
that their lives may be full of passion, joy, and contribution.

For Scott,
who has the gifts of kindness, laughter, and commitment to his dreams,
may all the love he gives come back to him.

For Alex,
who opened my heart permanently on the day of his birth
and who has the courage to march to his own drummer,
may he continue to walk the path with heart.

For Angela,
who understands loyalty and the bonding of women,
in loving appreciation of wisdom beyond her years.

To my mother,
who has been my lifelong teacher, pointing me toward God.

To the memory of my father,
who believed in me and loved me from birth.

∽

CONTENTS

ACKNOWLEDGMENTS

Many people contributed to the completion of this book. Will Glennon and Mary Jane Ryan of Conari Press shared and supported my vision for this book as a work that can touch many lives. I am more grateful than I can say for the opportunity they have provided for my vision to become a reality.

In addition, I am grateful to be a first-time author whose editor really understood my message and was committed to helping me deliver it clearly and powerfully. Thanks to Mary Jane Ryan's editing skills, the book has a message of far more clarity and depth than it would have without her contributions.

As other writers will understand, writing a book evokes a unique mixture of joy and loneliness during thousands of hours of sitting alone, attempting to touch the hearts of strangers by placing words on paper. Many friends and colleagues provided support of various kinds. Some read parts of the manuscript and gave valuable feedback or made suggestions about content. Others were there for me in person or sometimes by telephone from other states or foreign countries. Some are long-term friends to whom I am always connected regardless of geography.

For contributions that were unique in each case, I am grateful to Loretta Finn, Demetrias Nichols, Patty Vance, David Sowerby, Barbara Clancy, Bob Mister, Claudia Tomaso, Jeanne Watson, Marty Klein, Mary Ellen Edwards, Lynne Wiese, David Steinberg, Vicki Traylor, Carman Gentile, Mike Harris, Nick Ross, Nancy Weyrach, Christine Lehman, and Richard Nylund.

My personal journey toward wholeness has been enhanced by many opportunities to grow. Among my mentors, trainers, and therapists, I especially thank Lila Kramer, a most supportive Jungian analyst; Marge Weimer, a compassionate therapist; and Mary Goulding, a respected trainer in my early professional development. I also pay tribute here to the memory of Robert Goulding, beloved mentor and father figure. To David Viscott, I owe appreciation for inspiring me to manifest the vision this book represents.

For invaluable assistance in healing my relationship with my parents, I thank Bob Hoffman and the staff of the Hoffman Institute in San Anselmo, California. The Hoffman Process assists participants to live in daily awareness of their spirituality, and it is the most powerful path I know of for fostering complete forgiveness and compassion toward parents. This leads to a level of self-forgiveness and self-love which in my experience cannot be reached in any other way.

I would like to express special gratitude here to some of the many authors whose books have influenced this work. Each of the following has articulated a significant building block of *Soulful Sex*.

- Harville Hendrix, whose *Getting the Love You Want* is the best explanation I've found of the couple's journey and how to heal it.

- Sam Keen, whose *Hymns to an Unknown God*, *The Passionate Life*, *Fire in the Belly*, and *To a Dancing God* inspire courageous commitment to a soulful journey.

- James Redfield, who, in *The Celestine Prophecy*, teaches us the insights that help us become full participants in the spiritual revolution that is upon us.

- Dr. Clarissa Pinkola Estes, whose *Women Who Run With Wolves* inspires all women to affirm their wild and instinctual nature and their inherent spirituality.

- Stephen Mitchell, who, in *The Enlightened Heart*, inspires us to realize the joy within.

- Margo Anand, who, in *The Art of Sexual Ecstasy*, presents a compelling vision of the blissful possibilities of lovemaking.

- Thomas Moore, who, in *Soulmates*, teaches us about the "mystery and madness" of exploring our souls in relationship.

- Joseph Campbell, who, in *The Power of Myth* and many other works, teaches us to affirm our journey into the farthest reaches of our own inner mystery.

- Bernie Zilbergeld, whose *The New Male Sexuality* does more to illuminate male perspectives on lovemaking than any other book I know.

- Lonnie Barbach, author of *For Yourself*, *Pleasures*, *The Pause*, and other books, and co-author of *Shared Intimacies*, whose works on sexuality should be on everyone's bookshelves.

- Marianne Williamson, whose book *Illuminata* offers a collection of prayers and spiritual guideposts that can powerfully assist us in opening to the reality and joy of the Light.

- David Viscott, whose *Emotionally Free* inspires us to speak our truth, affirm our creativity, and fully experience our capacity to love and give.

Preface

I was inspired to write this book because I found something missing in the popular literature on sexuality. There are many books that give the facts and teach technique. They explain in careful detail how to caress the clitoris or the penis for maximum pleasure. The best ones also talk about feelings and make it clear that emotions are a major factor in how well lovemaking goes between two people. But these practical guides to sexuality have little to say about spirituality.

On the other hand, there are books that talk about sacred sex. These books use Hindi and Sanskrit vocabulary and attribute the source of their ideas to ancient Taoist or Hindu wisdom on sexuality. A few other books do discuss sacred sexuality in interesting ways that are relevant to Western readers, but these have little to say about how people can go about actually practicing this kind of lovemaking.

I found no practical guides to spiritual sexuality addressed to a mainstream Western audience with a Judeo-Christian heritage, no books telling this audience how they can experience ecstatic lovemaking by learning to integrate it with their spirituality.

After fourteen years of clinical work with inspiring people who want nothing less than the best in their intimate relationships, I believe that it is time that millions of couples have this information. It is my privilege to provide a road map to loving couples for a journey that can bring more fire and joy than ever before into their sexual relationships.

Limitations of this Book

This book is not addressed to my gay and lesbian brothers and sisters, to whom I wish all of God's blessings. It speaks instead to heterosexual couples whose sexual relationships must deal with the very diverse socialization that males and females receive in this culture. The sexual issues faced by such couples are permeated with this difference in life experience, and couples trying to bridge the gender gap need an approach designed especially for them.

Soulful Sex is also not designed for those who have suffered sexual assault or trauma. Having assisted many such clients in my private practice, I am well aware of the damage to self-esteem and to sexual trust that results from being a survivor of such experiences. A woman or man who has been hurt in this way deserves the opportunity to work with a supportive therapist who knows the path of healing these wounds.

Those who are in recovery from addiction to alcohol or other drugs and who are committed to that recovery will find much of value here. Those who have not yet found the courage to commit to recovery may not be ready for the journey this book proposes, because that journey asks us to bring all of ourselves and all of our spirituality to lovemaking. Perhaps, though, reading here about what is possible will inspire some to understand that their greatest potential for joy in sex and in life lies in recovery.

A relationship that is foundering on conflict and unhealed childhood wounds will not be saved by better sex. However, *Soulful Sex* can help couples find more joy in lovemaking, giving a constant incentive to keep a relationship healthy.

To all readers, it is my hope that the attitudes and practices presented in this book will open your heart and strengthen your connection to those you love most and to the divine within.

Sexual union is mutual surrender to
the mystery at the heart of human
life. . . . Sexual union is an act of
profound worship and praise. . . .
—Kevin Regan

❦

CHAPTER 1

Saying Yes to Passion

A passionate sex life is your birthright. Regardless of your age, background, health, and circumstances, you have the potential for a sex life full of passion and fulfillment. This book is addressed to all women and men who would like to find still deeper fulfillment in their sexuality.

Today many of us aspire to life on a higher plane of consciousness. We try to eat for health and to exercise for endurance and strength. We try to treat others with compassion, to be well informed, and to make a contribution to the world. Many of us also have a hunger for a deeper sense of spirituality. Gradually, we are beginning to understand that what we need is to learn to experience the sacred in our daily lives.

Soulful Sex challenges us to do this—to become as conscious about our sexuality as we are about the rest of life. This precious part of our lives can become an unexpected vehicle for expressing and sharing our innate spiritual capacities.

Practice the discipline of delight—
Let no day go by without adding something to the music of your experience. . . .
—Sam Keen

What's Wrong with Our Sex Lives

According to sexology pioneers Masters and Johnson, forty million Americans are dissatisfied with their sex lives. In fourteen years of clinical practice counseling couples, I have found that once the early romantic stage of new love has passed, routine, uninspired lovemaking is the norm. Most couples have never had any way of learning something different.

Couples making love usually follow an established routine. *Sex,* we have been taught, must always mean foreplay, followed by intercourse, followed by orgasm. At best, this is bread-and-butter sex. When we make love in the same way over and over, there is little possibility that we will experience anything heart-opening or ecstatic.

Besides the limitations of repetitive sex, most couples also make love in the presence of unresolved resentments, withheld communications, lack of trust, severe bodily tensions, and shutdown emotions. Under these conditions, the best you can hope for from sex is the comfort of being held, and a few moments of orgasmic pleasure.

You and your beloved deserve so much more than this!

Together, you can learn to share more passion than ever before. Your lovemaking can become a source of joyousness and heart-opening delight. You can learn to experience a new kind of sexuality—one that comes from the depths of your hearts and souls.

Giving this great gift to yourself and to your partner allows you to experience the inner revolution of which Joseph Campbell spoke when he said: "We are at this moment participating in one of the very greatest leaps of the human spirit to a knowledge . . . of . . . our own deep inward mystery."

Soulful sex happens when you begin to see more deeply—when you see the divinity within your partner and when you respond to your beloved's invocation of the divine within you. When you contact each other's essence, you can experience transformation of your sexual experience.

Soulful Sex can help you learn how your already good sex life can become a great one. It happens through undertaking the journey of integrating your spiritual life with your sexuality. The principles and practices of this book offer you a road map for that unforgettable journey.

In referring to the divine, this book speaks often of the Light, a shortened version of the Quaker term for God or our divine essence—the *Inward Light.* If you wish, please substitute *Higher Power* or any other term that speaks to your heart. The words are far less important than being in touch with your experience of a transcendent reality and of the divine essence within yourself and your partner.

ᔫ

Explore daily the will of God.

—C.G. Jung

Is Changing My Sex Life Really Possible?

Is it really possible for this book to make a difference in your sexual experience? The answer to this question lies in your own quiet mind—in the part of you that longs for God and for wholeness. This part of you knows sorrow and despair, and it longs for sexual experience that goes beyond physical and emotional release; it longs for that which connects us to each other and to a higher reality. This part of you is also capable of ecstasy.

The message of *Soulful Sex* is that you can learn to incorporate this part of yourself into shared sexual experience. When you do this, passion and joy have no limits.

This book points you inward and upward, toward a destination that is natural to human beings. The ability to experience human touch as nurturing and fulfilling is built into our cells. As infants, we smiled when stroked. As sexually mature adults, sexual pleasure and orgasm are inevitable under the right conditions. The ability to appreciate a larger reality than that of the material world also lies at the core of human nature.

Soulful Sex guides you toward your own essential sexual and spiritual nature and shows you how to integrate them. It offers you many practices for increasing passion and accessing the sacred. Some will be simple extensions of where you are right now. Others may be quite unfamiliar to you. Experimenting with them will require courage.

Soulful Sex also encourages you to move beyond old attitudes of shame, guilt, and their contemporary equivalent—a general devaluing of sexuality so that developing it fully becomes a low priority. In soulful sexuality, you learn to experience great joy and little conflict about lovemaking, so you naturally want to experience it often.

In part, this book speaks to the many who are committed to a particular religious orientation and who have a need for an approach to sexual change that respects those values. If you are one of these individuals, this book asks you to go straight to the heart of your faith and to find there the validation of a sacred approach to sexuality. Look carefully in the sacred writings and you will find that sexuality with your beloved is meant to be regarded as a sacrament. Some wedding vows even state this explicitly: "With my body, I thee worship."

Soulful Sex also speaks to those who are not affiliated with any formal religion, but who feel the deep call of their hearts to spiritual growth and to a sexuality that honors its own inherent mystery.

Finally, this book is also for those who feel that they are "not religious" but who have found in sexuality a special joy. If you already experience lovemaking as offering unique possibilities of delight and self-expression, the sacred sex journey can teach you to deepen those experiences in marvelous ways.

> *Life shrinks or expands in proportion to one's courage.*
>
> —Anaïs Nin

Opening the Door to Spirit

In order to have a sexual relationship be all that it can be, we need to say good-bye to the fallacy that our higher selves are interested only in prayer and meditation. On the contrary, that precious part of us loves celebrating the wonder of life and love and the universe. It loves feeling its deep connection to God and all of life. It loves the divine exuberance of passionate lovemaking that expresses God's greatest gift to us—our ability to love.

The power and depth of your sexual experience matches the extent to which you can integrate sex and spirituality. When you learn to do that, you experience a deepened connection to your beloved; shared sexual experience that is far more heartfelt and powerful than ever before becomes possible. We open the door to a better sex life through mindfulness, through awareness, and through learning to stay present in each moment.

One of the great goals of most spiritual paths is to learn to experience the sacred in everyday life. The great teachers of virtually every spiritual tradition urge prayer or meditation or ritual observance such as blessing food before eating. Through these practices, ordinary daily experience is enriched.

A moment of grateful silence before eating reminds me that my food and I are part of a great universal chain of events. Sitting in meditation reminds me of my connection to a greater reality than that of ordinary life.

In lovemaking, the path is similar. When you take the time and have the courage to look deeply into the eyes and heart of your beloved, you become aware that your partner is more than a body and a personality. Looking deeply into eyes and heart, you also see a reflection of your own essence.

In this kind of lovemaking, each touch has more sweetness and more meaning. It becomes easier to keep your heart open and allow your partner into the inner spaces of your soul as well as of your body. We learn to

∽

Learn to get in touch with the silence within yourself and know that everything in this life has a purpose.

—Elisabeth Kübler-Ross

see deeply, looking behind the eyes of our beloved. We find the courage, at times, to let ourselves be seen in depth.

Does this mean we must always be conscious and "spiritual" when making love? Not at all! While soulful sexuality affirms the divine in all loving sexual acts, it does not ask us to give up anything. If exuberant lustiness is your need at this moment, take your pleasure with joy! If twenty minutes of missionary-position intercourse ending with orgasm for both participants is your pleasure, please enjoy. But along with ordinary sex, you may choose to experiment with high passion some of the time. On those occasions, you and your partner can enjoy vast new possibilities.

In soulful sexuality, you are fearless and open to ecstasy. There is no script—no list of events that must occur. *And there is no way to fail.* In this kind of lovemaking, you can never be found wanting or inadequate. Every sexual experience is prized, rather than compared to others or to a preconceived scenario. Intercourse is only one of many possibilities. When partners do choose it, it is valued partially for its symbolism of a higher unity—the oneness of God—ritually manifested on the material plane by physical union.

To know, feel and discover this in the presence of another human being, as we are invited to do in making love, is to be brought face to face with one of the great mysteries of human existence—that we are spirit embodied, and that as human beings we are partaking in this miracle.
—Daphne Rose Kingma

Opposition or Mixed Feelings

If you or your partner find yourselves resistant to these ideas, you are in good company. Western science and Western medicine are based on the scientific method of inquiry, which holds that only that which can be observed, measured, and replicated is "true."

Even those who follow a traditional religion are invariably influenced by this scientific bias, perhaps because it has demonstrated value in helping us distinguish between superstition and objective reality. It is useful to know that infection comes from bacteria rather than from evil spirits.

Western science tends to throw out the baby with the bathwater where transcendent experience is concerned, however. Many of us have been so indoctrinated by pseudoscientific prejudice that we believe to be real only that which is concrete and measurable. We have no room for the poetic or the mystical.

This is not true science, according to some of the greatest minds of our time. Albert Einstein had this to say in defense of the importance of openness to mystical consciousness: "The most beautiful and profound emotion we can experience is the sensation of the mystical . . . to wonder and stand rapt in awe . . . to know that what is impenetrable really exists, manifesting itself as the highest wisdom and the most radiant beauty."

Once you are open to it, there is also "a radiant beauty" to sexual exchange with a cherished partner. Discovering this dimension of sexual experience is both a challenging goal and a great adventure. This discovery begins with a heartfelt desire to experience it.

Who Am I?

Helping people change is my life's work and my greatest privilege. As a psychologist, sex therapist, and marriage counselor, I have extensive experience in designing the mixture of education, vision, support, and practice that enables human beings to fulfill their potential. The opportunity to impact many more lives through the writing of this book fulfills a lifelong dream.

Hundreds of images come to mind as I write these words. These memories come from the stories of my clients—men and women who learned to dramatically increase their experience of passion and of spiritual depth by using the information this book contains.

You will find in this book the lessons about sexuality which my clients have taught me. You will also find their stories—stories that illustrate the reality and the process of intimate change that centers on the sacred aspects of sexuality. The client stories presented here are masked so that

I may not reach [my aspirations], but I can look up and see their beauty, believe in them, and try to follow where they lead.

—Louisa May Alcott

no one, including the clients themselves, will ever recognize the actual people.

It is my hope that the attitudes and practices presented in this book will open your heart and deepen your connection to those you love most. For if you use these principles, you will be rewarded with a sexual relationship that is grounded in spirituality and whose joyful passion fills your heart, mind, body, and soul.

. . . go into yourself and see how deep the place is from which your life flows.
—Ranier Maria Rilke

The secret of sexual energy . . . is not only that
it is capable of begetting new generations, but
that it has a second function of much greater
importance: to lead [us] step by step up the great
Jacob's ladder of consciousness to God.
—Elisabeth Haich

CHAPTER 2

Spirituality and Sexuality
Do Go Together

Passionate lovemaking that calls forth all of your feelings, sensations, and courage can amplify your experience of the sacred many times over. Each moment in which you are conscious of the sacred sexual energy that runs through your veins becomes one in which you experience the divine. You become aware that your ability to convey love with your physical body is your personal expression of divine love.

Your sexuality can be and should be in full support of your spiritual life; at the same time, your spirituality can enliven and deepen lovemaking in ways that may cause your current sexual experiences to pale in comparison. High passion is, in part, a spiritual experience. It can lead to a deepened sense of your participation in the Infinite.

When you learn to integrate your spirituality with your sexuality, you receive two priceless gifts. First, sex becomes richer, more passionate, and more fulfilling. There is so much to see in your beloved's eyes: the essence of Man or Woman, the luminous child, flesh becoming Word. Sexual boredom is no longer an issue, because when the door to each other's depths swings wide, it becomes clear that the fascinating journey of exploration will take more time than one lifetime offers.

The second gift is that your spiritual life deepens and your feeling of sharing that precious part of life with your partner increases. This happens because you are learning to incorporate the transcendent, expansive parts of yourself into your lovemaking. You are learning to assume an attitude of mystery in sexual sharing, to experience sex as sacrament.

No esoteric practices are required on this path of sacred sexuality, though some will be offered. This approach does not require that you act like a yogi or a mystic or a saint. Instead, it asks that you simply open your heart and mind to potentialities that are inherent within you—to begin when you are ready to experience your sexual activities as precious aspects of your spiritual life.

This path invites you to move beyond the mechanistic, concrete approach to sexuality that Western culture instills in us. Large numbers of us struggle with common sexual problems such as unreliable orgasm or premature ejaculation or lack of desire. On the other hand, many of us have learned to experience intense arousal and plentiful orgasms. In either case, we tend to think of our sexuality in terms of numbers and comparisons: How often? How long? How intense was it this time compared to last time?

An invisible screen seems to lie between us and the depth of passion and sexual joy we would like to experience. In the flush of a new love, lovemaking is often intensely joyful. But when this stage of early romance inevitably gives way to familiarity, we have nothing but technique to fall

---

Most of us in committed stable relationships settle for predictability, comfort, and companionship because we fear . . . the exposure of our deepest selves. Yet in our fear of the unknown within us and between us we ignore and avoid the very gift that our commitment sets within our reach—true intimacy.

—R. Norwood

back on. All too soon, we find that technique alone cannot yield sexual fulfillment.

We struggle to re-create romance then, because it is the only remaining path we know to passion. It doesn't work. It can't work over time, because romance is based on fantasy and lack of familiarity. Although romance and fantasy can be pleasing games on occasion, they can never fill the deep soul hunger we feel.

The true answer to our need for lifelong passion lies in the depths of our hearts, in our ability to incorporate the sacred into our daily life, our relationships, and our lovemaking.

Lovemaking in the Light

Consider the radical hypothesis that passionate, joyful sexuality can lead you closer to the divine within you, to God, to your Higher Power as you understand it. To use an adaptation of the Quaker term, it can lead you closer to the Light.

Although few couples have received any assistance in this, some have nevertheless discovered a well-kept secret: *Well-developed sexuality can be a vital part of a deep spiritual life.* Just as important, lovemaking is one of the best ways to share your emotional and your spiritual life with your beloved. When these two areas of your life are comfortably integrated, both areas blossom. A relationship that includes both has unique depth and the potential to be the love of your life!

Spirituality Versus Religion

It's important to distinguish here between spirituality and religion. Many questions from clients and lecture audiences have shown me that for many people, the distinction is often unclear.

Though both remind us that lovemaking can have a larger purpose than physical release, spirituality and religion are not the same. Your spirituality is much deeper than any formal religious affiliation. It lies in the depths of your own heart. It is the part of you that responds to stirring music and evocative paintings—the part of you that yearns for and is capable of transcendence, that is profoundly connected to every living thing. This spiritual or *higher self* shines within you at every moment.

Being *religious* refers to acceptance of a specific set of values and principles; it usually means being affiliated with an organization that has a particular point of view on matters of morality, doctrine, and even politics. Being religious in Western countries usually means being a Catholic, a Jew, or a member of one of the Protestant denominations.

Whether or not you are religious, you were born with an innate ability to appreciate the spiritual dimension of life.

You can be in touch with your spirituality whether or not you are religious. When you stare at the stars in the night sky and feel awed by their magnificence, you are being spiritual. When you feel your connection to every other living creature, you are in touch with spiritual reality—a reality larger than that which you can see and feel.

Another way of understanding spirituality is to think of it as getting beyond ego—beyond the limitations of our minds. When we open our hearts to God, to love, to our own and our partner's inner beauty, we soften, we forgive, we become more willing to give and to receive. We also become less fearful. A kind of divine exuberance can fill our hearts and our bodies in such a way that we can allow a depth of passion we've never experienced before.

That's why spiritual consciousness intensifies sexual exchange in wonderful ways. Lovemaking can become an experience of spirit manifesting through the body, transcending time and space, temporarily blurring the boundaries between self and other. It can put us in touch with a dimension in which there is no sadness, *only joy.*

Raising Our Consciousness About Sex

Our experience of lovemaking changes when we come to understand that the desire for sexual union is fundamentally a spiritual one—we long for wholeness, for transcendence of our separateness through merging with another. These profound needs cannot be satisfied merely through sexual arousal and orgasm. Nothing short of ecstasy fully satisfies these longings.

The Uncommon Integration of Sex and Spirit

Why is it that we are so unaccustomed to this integration of sex and spirit? Why is it that the idea of sacred sexuality does not come naturally to us?

Part of the answer lies in our Western dualistic heritage, particularly our puritanical roots. This history influences most of us in one of two ways. Some of us grew up in religious households in which our sexual education was determined by the teachings of our parents' faith. The rest of us may not have attended church or synagogue as children, but we still grew up in a culture where everything sexual was viewed through the filter of Puritanism: that the body is something to be overcome in order to be good or to reach God. We are all deeply influenced by this legacy, whether we grew up in religious households or not.

In childhood, most of us learned that our bodies and our spirits are completely separate. In some families, we were taught that our bodies and spirits are enemies who oppose and threaten each other. Our bodies, we gathered, are fundamentally unclean. They get disgustingly dirty and have terrible odors which must be sanitized with deodorants. Our bodies also eliminate waste—a smelly, distasteful function which must be done in private and never discussed.

We learned that our genitals were the impure opposites of that which was valuable, holy, and beautiful. The words used to refer to our genitals carried clear messages of distaste, embarrassment, or sin: *twat, dick, pussy, rod, cunt, prick, private parts*. These words told us not to be proud of these parts of our bodies. We were never told that desire itself is a gift from God.

When passion burns within you, remember that it was given to you for a good purpose.
—Hassidic saying

We learned to fear unbridled sexuality. Our families taught us that impulsive sexuality could dishonor the family and ruin our lives. Sex can be a good thing, we learned, under sanctioned and perhaps procreative conditions. Otherwise, sex was trouble. At best, it was suspect, earthy, a part of our lower natures. If we grew up in conservative religions, we were taught that it was potentially dangerous, wicked, and sinful.

At some point in childhood or adolescence, we began to be aware of stirrings in our own bodies. We learned that touching our own bodies brought us pleasure. For most of us, it was not long afterward that we learned that the adults around us felt that those pleasures were vaguely shameful at best—something to be hidden from others. At worst, if we were especially unlucky, we were adamantly told that touching ourselves was wicked and would lead to dire consequences.

At puberty, our genitals started calling us to behavior that we learned to regard as necessarily secretive or even sinful. If male, our bodies began to produce embarrassingly frequent erections and "wet dreams." Pleasuring ourselves, we learned, was "jerking off," or "beating the meat." We began to understand that the parts of our bodies that seemed to give us the most pleasure were to be kept hidden and not discussed. In conservative families, we were supposed to keep their needs on hold indefinitely until some distant time when we would marry.

If female, we menstruated, which in our own or our mother's childhood may have been called "the curse." This new phase of our development was not celebrated. We were led to believe that this was the first of many experiences that were the painful lot of women. If we grew up in conservative religious families, we were told that painful menstrual cramps and childbirth were the result of the sin of the first woman—Eve's legacy to us. We were to bear these unfortunate feminine realities with grace. This was our introduction to the functions of our bodies, and even though most of us "know" better now, those early messages are deeply ingrained.

As adults, we found partners and learned that sexuality could be delicious. If we married in a church or a synagogue with our families in attendance, we got the message that our sexuality was now sanctioned and acceptable. But it was still separate from and in opposition to our spiritual lives.

Priests in eastern Canada in the early part of the twentieth century are said to have taught married parishioners to have intercourse fully clothed, through holes in sheets draped over each partner's genitals. This is a vivid metaphor for a view of sexuality that has influenced millions: Well-controlled sex between spouses for procreative purposes is acceptable, at least until the next baby is conceived. But what if these two married lovers were to throw off their sheets and their clothes? Presumably, the marital bed would become a setting for sin.

Family Influences on Sexuality

The attitudes in your family may have been less dramatic, but probably took their toll nevertheless. Whatever your introduction to sex, it set the tone of your experience.

Here are some of the stories my clients have shared with me about their early introductions to sex:

- *Thirty-six-year-old female teacher:* "When I had my first period, I thought I was bleeding to death. It was two years later in health education class that I learned about menstruation."

- *Fifty-two-year-old male scientist:* "My father caught me touching myself once and told me I would go crazy if I kept doing it."

- *Forty-year-old female attorney:* "My mother left a pamphlet on menstruation on my bed when I was ten. She never talked to me about anything related to lovemaking."

- *Twenty-six-year-old male musician:* "My parents never said one word to me about sex. It was understood that I'd find out for myself."

- *Seventy-three-year-old female retired nurse:* "When I married at twenty, I knew absolutely nothing about sex or how babies were made."

- *Thirty-four-year-old male engineer:* "Sex was not bad in our family. It just wasn't important like education or making money. I learned early that my sexuality was never to interfere with those priorities."

- *Twenty-nine-year-old male minister:* "My father took me aside when I was thirteen and told me that God would punish me if I ever got a girl pregnant before marriage."

- *Seventeen-year-old female high-school student:* "My mom told me she hoped I would become a nun like my aunt, because then I would 'never have to use [my] body for sin.'"

Through early conditioning like this, we learned to distrust our bodies and to treat them as though they were separate from us. Through addictions or through carrying habitual muscle tension, we learned to deny our bodily sensations. Eventually, we even became capable of sexual acts in which we are not fully present.

Most of us have internalized this separation of parts of ourselves. We learned to believe that our bodies and their needs are antagonistic to spiritual life. If we are religious, we probably value what we call "spirit" far more than we value our "animal" natures. If we reject religion, we often identify with our minds and may be just as out of touch with our bodies as are our religious peers. In both cases, we devalue our bodies and their potential for connection with the sacred. As a result, we feel less integrated, less whole.

Cautious Lovemaking

Even if we grew up without heavy negative messages about sex, we learned early that sexuality is a kind of wild horse that must be trained, broken, disciplined. Lovemaking in its natural state is "lust," desired by our animal natures. It must be sanctioned and sanitized in prescribed ceremonial ways before it can be fully acceptable. And even when we marry, we have no clear guidance. We still have to be careful—to be "normal," not to be "kinky," to want the "right" amount of sex, and to please our partners or else.

Given this background, it's no wonder that most of us make love in limited, cautious ways. Perhaps we do it in the dark with our eyes closed, often fantasizing about someone other than our partner. We worry about whether we're doing it "right," or whether our partner is satisfied. When worrying about our acceptability, it's difficult to feel really close to our partner. We have thoughts and feelings that we think we must conceal, and this withholding produces distance instead of closeness.

We follow our mind's ideas of how to be pleasing and how to be skillful. We strive for orgasm or for lasting longer. We worry about whether we are having as much sex or as many orgasms as other people do. We worry whether our body parts are big enough or small enough.

I invite you now to affirm and explore soulful sex. It is a journey that can take you far beyond these concerns into a sexual arena of unlimited passion and absolute fearlessness—where you can reclaim your God-given

∽

Fear is a warning that a rule is about to break.

—Linda Riebel

right to the full development of your capacity for sexual pleasure and passion.

Soulful Sexuality Is Your Birthright

Through sex we enter the timeless, boundary-less moment. We partake of the one experience above all others in life which allows us the bliss of true union.

—Daphne Rose Kingma

The journey of soulful sexuality invites you to rethink any assumptions you may have about your sexuality and its seeming conflict with the higher, "better" parts of yourself. Through coming to view your sexuality as sacred, you may come to understand lovemaking as one of the most precious means by which you can affirm and enjoy spirituality in every-day life.

You have a priceless, God-given body, and you can experience the infinite preciousness of that body and all that it can do and feel. You can learn to accept your own body and to see its beauty regardless of how it does or does not reflect our culture's stereotypes of what is beautiful.

Affirming Sexual Joy: The Song of Solomon

Western men and women may find inspiration for joyful sexuality in the Old Testament. Consider these verses from the King James Version of the Song of Solomon. Are these words meant as metaphors describing the search of the soul for God? Or are they meant to teach us to feel love and passion in the depths of our hearts? Look into your own heart for the answer. Meanwhile, perhaps these verses from chapters 1 through 8 will touch you:

> *Behold, thou art fair, my love; behold thou art fair . . .*
> *My beloved is mine, and I am his; he feedeth among the lilies.*
> *Thy two breasts are like two young roes that are twins, which feed among the lilies.*
> *By night on my bed I sought him whom my soul loveth . . .*

Thou hast ravished my heart . . . thou hast ravished my heart with one of thine eyes . . .

How fair is thy love . . . how much better is thy love than wine! and the smell of thine ointments than all spices!

. . . honey and milk are under thy tongue . . .

His mouth is most sweet: yea, he is altogether lovely. This is my beloved, and this is my friend . . .

Thy navel is like a round goblet, which wanteth not liquor· thy belly is like an heap of wheat set about with lilies.

How fair . . . art thou, O love, for delights!

I said, I will go up to the palm tree, I will take hold of the boughs thereof: now also thy breasts shall be as clusters of the vine, and the smell of thy nose like apples;

And the roof of thy mouth like the best wine for my beloved, that goeth down sweetly . . .

I am my beloved's and his desire is toward me.

Let us get up early to the vineyards; let us see . . . whether the tender grape appear, and the pomegranates bud forth: there I will give thee my love.

Set me as a seal upon thine heart . . . for love is strong as death . . .

My Own Sexual Journey

As a young girl, growing up in the '50s and '60s, sex both fascinated and frightened me. My church taught that sex was a dangerous thing, especially for girls. "Show interest but never give in," we learned. We kept the choices we actually made secret, and we condemned ourselves whatever they were. We felt we were "too" innocent or "too" daring. We internalized the idea that "nice" girls were those who *didn't*.

I was passionate by nature, but throughout my teens I was devoted to the ideal of premarital virginity I had been taught. There have always been ways to enjoy loving touch, even without intercourse. During the next two decades, I participated in many of the experiences of my generation—the challenges of marriage; parenthood and stepparenting; the loss, pain, and disruption of divorce; the uncertainty of being single again at an unexpected time of life. Many times, I experienced the invisible screen that seemed to lie between my vision of my sexuality and how I actually experienced it.

... have patience with everything unresolved in your heart and ... try to love the questions themselves as if they were locked rooms or books written in a very foreign language.
—Rilke

I've been privileged in many ways. I have known the deep pleasure of new love, the comfort of a long relationship, the great depth of passion that can occur when two people deeply love and open to each other, the joy and laughter that two passionate rebels can create together. I have felt valued, admired, and cherished. Over time, I have become more and more able to contact my ever-present Source of inner joy.

I have also known anxiety over my own sexual abilities, feelings of being judged and found wanting by a partner, grief over a relationship gone awry, and sexual boredom. I have experienced deep loneliness during intimate moments and times when something seemed to be missing though I could not have said what it was. There were many years when I was not capable of even guessing that it was my contact with my own spirituality that was missing.

I have been privileged to be able to study the principles and practices in this book. I have learned that lovemaking can be an endless source of sharing and of joy.

The Path of Fully Developed Sexuality

For most of us, mature sexuality is the path that gives us the opportunity to best express all the love we are capable of feeling. It is only when we love ourselves fully that we can love another well. And it is only when we can love another human being, that we can love all humankind.

Coming to love and accept yourself as a sexual being is key. When you accept and love your sexual urges, your sexual energy, your sexual needs, you are affirming the divine plan as it is expressed in your body and your heart. When you understand lovemaking as sacred, you begin to treasure bodily sensation and physical expressions of human love.

You Are Capable of High Passion

In directing you toward sacred lovemaking, words and concepts have limited value. The experiences I want to invite you to open to are anything but intellectual. Our minds, in fact, cannot lead us to these possibilities. Perhaps that is why people who are highly developed intellectually sometimes seem the least able to experience high passion.

It needn't be that way. Intellect is no barrier to passion, except when there is too much attachment to the mind and to the control that most intellectuals have learned to expect. Joy emerges when we surrender that control. For it is in a state of openness that the most joyful experiences of life occur.

I write these words in a state of reverence for the open-hearted love I have been fortunate to share in my life. With joy, I recall peak experiences that left me changed for life. I remember my first intensely passionate, long-postponed lovemaking experience with my first love. I also remember spiritual experiences when my awareness of God's love overwhelmed and filled me with indescribable peace and joy. Most of all, I remember experiences in which I was filled with passion for God, for my partner, and for myself all at once. I described one of these experiences this way in an old diary of mine:

> We stayed up all night, touching, hugging, joining our bodies as closely as we could as many times as we could. We were underneath the stars, and we were part of them. We were stars too. God's love shone out of his eyes–it was unforgettable!
>
> I knew that he was Man–all men. He was every man I ever loved

or hoped to love, all rolled into one. He was also a precious child of
God. He was all the vulnerability, all the passion, all the joy that
Man is capable of being. Our bodies and every touch seemed perfect.
I wanted to make him part of me, to join our bodies together so that I
could never lose him.

*And those who
come together in
the nights and
are entwined in
rocking delight
perform a
solemn task and
gather sweetness,
depth, and
strength for the
song of some
future poet...*
—Rilke

The opportunity for profound connection that sexual sharing offers is
unique and should be prized as a sacred gift. Face to face, open-hearted
physical intimacy provides an opportunity for closeness unlike any other.

The Interdependence of Sex and Spirit

The path of sacred sexuality offers a new vision of shared spirituality
and sexuality that are in full support of each other. One of the keys lies in
coming to accept that our own and our partner's spiritual lives are in-
exorably intertwined.

Barry and Joyce Vissell, in *The Shared Heart*, offer a radical view of
spiritual growth for couples. Whether or not you agree with all of it,
their vision of growing toward the divine hand-in-hand with your beloved is powerful:

> The greatest need that exists in a relationship is the spiritual need...
> it is when a couple, after many tests and initiations, comes to the
> deep inner knowing that they cannot realize God separate from each
> other. There comes a time along the path of love when we are faced
> with our own selfishness.... As long as our own dreams and goals are
> more important to us than those of our partner, we prevent ourselves
> from experiencing Divine Love. Unconditional love is attained the
> moment we forget ourselves and truly desire to help another on this
> journey of life.

When we learn to express sexually our attempts at unconditional love, we will have begun to integrate these two most powerful forces. But how do we learn to integrate sexuality and spirituality? The answer is that although you can learn some of the lessons here, that fundamental integration is a divine mystery whose unique character must be discovered by you and your beloved together. It evolves as you learn to manifest the most unconditional love you find in the depth of your heart.

Human Touch Has the Power to Heal and to Nurture

Many religions teach this lesson. In the early Judeo-Christian tradition, for example, the laying on of hands was central to healing.

Your body's capacity to feel pleasure is one of the great gifts of being human. Fully affirming and accepting that gift opens your heart to more and more joy and assists you in letting go of any guilt you may have associated with self-pleasuring or with the enjoyment of another person's touch.

It is unfortunate that so many of us have been taught to feel guilty about pleasurable bodily sensations. Even self-pleasuring, which in fact is a healthy, often comforting gift from God, has been maligned by so-called "authorities" who fear passion or who want to control even solitary behavior.

Perhaps you are one of the millions who was taught to believe that self-pleasuring is dirty and might make you crazy or cause some other malady. Woody Allen's retort is apt: "Don't knock it. It's sex with someone I love." Contrary to Grandma's prediction, of course, the green hair that was supposed to grow on your palms never materializes.

Rather than being racked with guilt, it's more likely that you simply believe that self-pleasuring is an inferior or immature form of sexual expression. Not so! Pleasuring your own body is an expression of the sexual relationship you have with yourself throughout life. It can also be a divinely given way of taking pressure off a sexual relationship. When you affirm and practice self-pleasuring, you don't need sex with your partner for sexual release. You can then approach your beloved out of a desire to share sexual joy rather than to get something.

Learning to find joy in solitary self-pleasuring is a good starting point for integrating sacred sexuality, as well as for solving many common sex problems. Learn to look at or touch any part of your own body in such a way that you are reminded of the precious gift that it is. Thank God for the exquisite pleasure potential of your genitals and erogenous zones.

Learning to reclaim your right to enjoy your own body alone requires thinking for yourself. To find out the moral truth about masturbation, pray and meditate on the value of solitary sensual pleasure. Why did our Creator make our bodies so that they could feel pleasure alone? The answer lies within you.

Perhaps masturbation was condemned in ancient times because those civilizations needed to direct all their citizens toward sexual activities that increased the birth rate. Modern sexologists of all theological persuasions, however, believe that self-pleasuring is good and useful. It helps you learn about your own body's sexual functioning and is a valuable tool in the solution of common sexual problems.

Celebrate your sexual relationship with yourself!

Sexual Longings Often Mask Spiritual Hunger

In his compelling book, *We*, Robert Johnson writes of the spiritual hunger which is often hidden beneath sexualized longings. In Western, scientifically based cultures, the experiences of falling in love and passionately merging with the beloved may be the only transcendent experiences we acknowledge and accept.

Passionate lovemaking and intense orgasm can seem like the only healthy paths to extraordinary experience—the only times we get to let go of ego and intellect. (Chemical addiction is the other, less healthy path that masks the same inner need for experience that is larger or more pleasurable than everyday reality.)

As Johnson suggests, looking honestly and deeply at our romantic and sexual longings is a heroic journey. It can lead us to a new understanding of deeper sides of ourselves. It can lead us to joy.

Vanessa's Story: The Transformative Journey

Most chapters in this book tell the unfolding story of Vanessa, a long-term client of mine now in her fifties, and her husband, Ben. They have personally lived through most of the stages of sexual development this book proposes. As a means of helping others to develop an understanding of sacred sexuality, Vanessa generously shares her story with us.

Vanessa is tall and has a well-proportioned, slightly stocky build. She has green eyes and curly, shoulder-length brown hair lightly touched with gray. She teaches English at a small college and is the mother of two grown daughters. The following story is in Vanessa's own words.

Faith is the opening of all sides and every level of one's life to the divine inflow.
–Martin Luther King

Spiritual sexuality has made all the difference in my life. I'm finding so much joy now in my sexual relationship with my husband that it's amazing to me. In a way, I thank my mother for this, because she is the one who taught me two great lessons—that sex is a divine gift and that spirituality should be the center of life. I know that my mother's teachings helped me to accept the ideas of sacred sexuality.

I was raised in a Baptist family of four in the Midwest. My father was a high-school teacher, and my mother did what all the wives in our church did—stayed home and took care of our food, clothing, and housing as well as carefully managing my younger brother and myself. We went to church three times a week or more—twice on Sunday and every Wednesday night.

When I was nine, my mother told me how babies were made. We were sitting outside on the backyard swing on a summer night. My brother was already in bed and my father had gone to some kind of business meeting. Mom acted like she had a secret to tell me and she seemed happy about it. I already had seen my dad and my brother naked, and I had started the conversation by asking her why Billy "looked so funny in front."

She told me that God made little boys different from little girls and that it was all part of His plan. "What plan?" I asked. Mom said that boys had a penis so that when they grew up they could help their wives to start a baby. She said that men and women who were married to each other liked to get really close to each other when they were naked, and that the man put his penis inside the woman's vagina. She had already taught me these words earlier.

After a while, some "liquid seeds" came out of the man's penis, she said, and they went swimming inside the woman's body until one of them met a tiny baby egg and went inside it. Then, if God blessed them, she said, this tiny egg started to grow and grow until it became a baby human that got born after nine months.

It may not have been perfectly accurate biologically, but it was completely thrilling to me. I had never imagined anything like it. The best thing was that Mom seemed to like to talk about it. I got the idea that making a baby was a really great thing to do, as long as you were married. She made a big point of that. These things were only good to do if you were "married in the sight of God." But as long as you were married, she really got across the message that these things were wonderful.

Remembering my nine-year-old perspective on the world, I feel grateful again to my mother. By now I know that most little girls (and boys) are not this lucky in how they first hear about sex.

When my husband, Ben, and I were starting out, we weren't

even open to ideas of sacred sexuality. The idea of sex as a means of increasing and sharing spiritual growth never occurred to us. Spiritual growth itself wasn't of much interest to us then anyway, because we were still thinking the way our culture had taught us to think about sex. It was a romantic adventure once in a while, and a simple comfort the rest of the time. We knew we wanted to have children soon, and so the reproductive possibilities (and risks) of sex were always on our minds.

We were busy growing up and trying to find out who we were. The only thoughts we had about sex then were about how to make it more passionate, because as we got more and more familiar with each other, our passion seemed to decrease.

We were lucky when we had just been together a few years to find a very enlightened family doctor. One time I told her that Ben and I were having some sex problems, and she recommended that we see a sex therapist. It was something we never would have thought of ourselves. The therapist helped us get better at communicating with each other about sex, which we had never done before. He also helped us negotiate our differences about how often we wanted to make love. The things we learned from him helped us for quite a while.

Two children later, though, we had started feeling discouraged about our sexual relationship again. It was feeling pretty repetitive and mechanical to us. It was about then that we started reading every book we could find about all aspects of sexuality. But the best thing we did was to attend a seminar put on by a church near us. It was called "The Spiritual Aspects of Sexuality in a Committed Relationship."

Learning to see our sex life as sacred changed everything. We both responded to the idea as soon as we heard about it. It just felt right to think of our sexual relationship that way, especially when the workshop leader told us all that we could still enjoy plain old earthy sex when we wanted to. The seminar leaders read various scriptures and quoted clergy and theologians from all the major faiths, including ours. The message that sex was sacred and sacramental was consistent.

The leaders set up some meditation processes where we went into deep silence and asked for divine guidance to give us wisdom about our sexual relationships with our spouses. What really came through to me was that sex is holy and that everything my partner and I do together is part of our mutual journey toward spiritual growth.

We left Ben's Episcopalian guilt and my Baptist guilt at that seminar. We had plenty of guilt between us and we were unaware of a lot of it. We really were not sure that anything sexual could be fundamentally good.

The way we expressed that idea was by feeling that we were allowed to make love in only one of a very few ways. Of course, that led to sexual boredom.

In the years since that seminar, our sex life has gone from night to day! We've had some just incredible experiences together. We've been so passionate at times that we just couldn't believe that we could experience so much after all our time together. We've had other times when we just lay together joined for a long time and touched each other only gently. Those times have been just as wonderful because we have felt unbelievably close—close to each other and close to God.

Almost every time, I feel deeply how precious Ben is to me and how much our lovemaking has a spiritual purpose and spiritual meaning for me. And now and then, it's just plain sex—often a "quickie." And that's great, too. I feel really blessed.

Ben was always by best friend, but now he's also my true part-ner—my lover and my beloved.

∽ Practices for Beginning the Journey ∽

1. *Share your early sexual history.*
Write a summary of your sexual history and share it with one other
person. Where did you first get information about sex? Was it accurate?
How did you feel about it? What were the underlying messages? What
were your earliest sexual experiences? Include masturbation experiences,
"playing doctor," and other childhood experiences. What was the overall
effect of the experience you had prior to puberty?

> ∽
>
> *The big ques-*
> *tion is whether*
> *you are going to*
> *be able to say a*
> *hearty yes to*
> *your adventure.*
>
> —Joseph Campbell

2. *Get in touch with early influences.*
Write down all the names you know for male and for female genitalia.
What do these names suggest? Share this list with a partner. Write and
discuss your earliest memories of sexual messages given to you by a
clergyperson or some other authority figure other than your parents.
What were the unspoken messages about sexuality?

3. *Contact your higher self.*
Find a quiet time when you can be undisturbed for at least twenty minutes. If you wish, put on some soft, emotionally evocative, instrumental
music. Have someone read these directions aloud, or audiotape them, or
familiarize yourself enough with them that you won't have to read them
while you're in deep meditation.

Take several deep breaths and consciously relax your body, focusing
on the muscles in your feet, legs, hips, and so on throughout your body.
Tell the muscles to relax. Breathe deeply.

Now take yourself in imagination to the most sacred place you have
ever been or can imagine. Let it be a place of worship or some beautiful

outdoor place you know or wish to know, a place where you can feel the wonder of the universe. Ask for support and guidance now in whatever way is meaningful to you.

Relaxing there in that sacred place, allow a new aspect of your being to emerge in your awareness. Visualize or imagine your higher self now coming into awareness. It is a radiantly beautiful part of yourself—a part that is peaceful, loving, and wise. It has always been a part of you and it will always be a part of you. This part of you connects easily to God, to the Source, to the universe. It is untroubled by ego or by fear. It wants only your highest good and the highest good of those about you.

Spend a few minutes getting to know your higher self. Admire and talk to this part of yourself. Thank it for its love and guidance throughout your life. Promise your higher self that you will be in daily contact with him or her. Feel your gratitude at this marvelous gift.

When you're ready, come back to the room and where you're seated. As you return to normal awareness, consciously retain your awareness of your inner, ever-present higher self.

4. Share sexual education and wishes

Write the answers to the following questions and then share them with your partner. Alternatively, answer the questions verbally while your partner listens.

This is not meant to be an interrogation of what your partner may have experienced before meeting you. Later on, if you would like to know more than you already do, and if you are capable of hearing nonjudgmentally whatever is reported, you can let your partner know that you welcome any sharing that she or he is comfortable with.

It's not fair or wise to demand any sharing except that which is necessary to protect yourself against disease. See Appendix B if yours is a new relationship or if there is any doubt about your or your partner's monogamy.

Otherwise, invite your partner to offer you the gift of sharing freely, but be willing to accept his or her unwillingness to do so right now.

Answers to the following questions will give you new insight into each other's sexual realities and into any religious influences which may be affecting either of you.

- *How did you first learn about sex? What is your earliest memory of having sexual feelings?*

- *If you were taught a religious orientation, what did you learn about that religion's attitude toward sexuality?*

- *Did anything sexual that was scary or painful happen during your childhood? During adolescence or since?*

- *How did you feel about the sexual feelings you had as a teenager? How did you express them?*

- *Please name one difference you would like to make in our sexual relationship now.*

- *How do you feel about the idea that our sexual relationship is sacred and that we are meant to fully enjoy it?*

End these times of sharing with a few minutes of prayer or meditation. Affirm your gratitude for the opportunity to share this precious journey with your beloved partner.

Until now most human beings
have remained quite ignorant of
their own potential . . . we are often
disappointed after lovemaking. Why?
Because most of us are like owners of
a precious Stradivarius violin that we
have never learned to play.

—Jolan Chang

CHAPTER 3

Opening to the Miracle:
Deeper, Better, More Fulfilling Sex

Just as it's possible to take violin lessons at any age, it's never too late to decide to love yourself and your partner better. Deepening your experience of lovemaking is as natural as learning to grow in music appreciation. Mastery in the dance of love requires no special talent. It does not require that you be beautiful or young or athletic. It does require a change of mind and heart as well as dedicated practice in a safe learning environment with a trusted partner.

Attitude Change Is the First Prerequisite

Begin by becoming willing. Sex as a pleasant routine can change to frequent passionate celebrations if you are willing to risk changing your mind about how you approach lovemaking. All personal changes begin with intention and a decision. The decision needed here is the willingness to move beyond habit, routine, and duty, *beyond your comfort zone* into a state of receptivity.

> *Life shrinks or expands in proportion to one's courage.*
>
> —Anaïs Nin

If you already enjoy your sexual experiences, opening to the idea of change may be particularly challenging. Why fix what isn't broken?

On the other hand, if you face unsolved problems in your sexual relationship, your mind may want to focus on problems and specific solutions, rather than on a global change of attitude toward sex. Why think about spiritual sexuality when you're concerned about orgasms or erections, or conflicts about frequency of lovemaking?

The answer to both of these questions lies in the results you will experience if you develop a spirit of openness to new attitudes, experiences, and feelings. Specifically, if you open to the idea of integrating your spirituality into your lovemaking, you will plant the seeds of joy, of overwhelming passion, and of solutions to any present or future sexual problems.

Loving partners can assist each other in these important goals:

- *Becoming aware of the sacred potential in all human touch.*
  Through affirming the sacred in sexual touch, we increase the meaningfulness of every sexual behavior.

- *Increasing your own and your partner's self-acceptance.* With self-acceptance, I appreciate my imperfect body as a sacred gift; I offer it to my beloved without apology. I accept my beloved's imperfections in the same spirit.

- *Deepening each partner's courage.* This opens many doors. With courage, I approach lovemaking with a willingness to let go—I can make noise, lose myself, scream with laughter or pleasure, become more aroused than ever before.

- *Strengthening your mutual imagination.* The possibilities are limitless.

- *Learning to laugh more.* With humor, I can lighten up about sex. I can be silly, outrageous, and playful. We don't have to do it "right."

The Cultivation of Deep Trust

Trust is the foundation for all these choices. I must trust you to accept me when I laugh or scream or share my feelings. I must trust you to welcome and share my letting go and my intention to be imaginative rather than predictable.

Many couples find it necessary to work on building trust before trying to solve specific sex problems. Ideally, we learn to trust in our first year of life. If we have loving and supportive parents, childhood offers us repeated lessons that we can trust others and that those we love will not knowingly hurt us. The more our backgrounds were like this, the more easily we trust our beloved.

Most of us, of course, did not have ideal family histories. Our parents did not fully love themselves, and therefore could not fully love us. Our parents hurt us, whether or not it was intentional. So we learned not to trust those closest to us. As a result, we must learn trust as adults, small step by small step, in a relationship with someone who is committed to our well-being. When we do learn to trust deeply—and only then—we become able to experience the full heights and depths of sexual love and joyful passion.

∽

Being guarded, armored, distrustful and enclosed is second nature in our culture. It is the means we adopt to protect ourselves against being hurt.
—Alexander Lowen

This kind of trust can develop only to the extent that partners become expert at creating safety for each other. When we become skillful at creating safety, heart-opening experiences begin to occur and to encourage us to continue. Trust in God and ourselves then grows.

What does it mean to *create safety* for your partner? It means giving up criticism and the seductive illusion of being "right." Rather than saying, "I hate that" or "Not so hard," it means saying, "Yes, just like that!" when your partner is doing something right, or "More gently, please," when that's the change you want. Creating safety means offering your partner the great gifts of acceptance, affirmation, and understanding. It means being, as much as possible, the one person in the world who can be counted on to listen lovingly.

Learning to do this well is a lifelong challenge. It is inevitable that the most loving couples sometimes find themselves in periods of stress, frustration, and estrangement. In the part of my work that focuses on marriage counseling, I have seen hundreds of couples experience distance from each other when they are in the throes of common stress situations such as a new baby, financial problems, illness, house-building or moving, or a new job.

With such couples, my goal is to remind them of their bond. When I remind them of their opportunity to provide a safe harbor for each other, committed couples usually respond. When I teach them the tools I offer you in Chapter 8, they learn to rethink their impulse to assign blame for their stress to each other. Instead, they become skillful in affirming their commitment during times of stress. As their bond grows, a couple's sexual connection can flourish and comfort them even during difficult times.

A Trust Exercise

This adaptation of a classic trust exercise can help you to become aware of and increase your level of trust toward your partner. Set aside at least an hour when you can be alone together and uninterrupted. Allow your partner to blindfold you. For about ten minutes, allow yourself to be led around your living space, going outside if possible. Experience relying on your partner for direction, leadership, and safety. Notice how you feel. At your partner's direction, now spend a few minutes in some form of physical touch, still blindfolded. Choose a back rub, kissing, or whatever appeals to you.

Then switch roles for another ten or fifteen minutes. Afterward, sit together and discuss the feelings you had during the exercise. Tell each other what might help you feel more trusting.

We must learn love like a profession. . . . Those who love must act as if they had a great work to accomplish . . . .
—Rilke

Building Trust Solves Sex Problems

Lovers who feel profound trust for each other solve intimate problems more easily. When deep trust is lacking, lovemaking will be less fulfilling than it could be. Here's an example of a couple for whom this was true.

Kip and Celia were quite embarrassed about seeing me for sex therapy. Neither was aware that the problem that was troubling them was one that millions of couples share.

When Celia made the first appointment with me, her voice trembled on the phone. "Our sex life is so disappointing now. I seldom have orgasms and that's really embarrassing. I'm afraid to even talk about it with Kip, because he puts so much pressure on me by constantly asking me about it—'Did you come?' 'Why didn't you come?' 'Did you come with your ex-husband?' The questions are almost as bad as the problem!

"I could tell him some things about how to help me come, but right now, I can't stand to talk about it with him. What's even worse is that our lovemaking seems to be all about orgasm now. I want to have orgasms, but it's even more important to me to feel close and in love with Kip. I guess I want both."

During their first appointment, it was clear that Kip was also unhappy about discussing their sexual troubles with a stranger. "I'd rather have a root canal, if you want to know the truth," he said. However, he also admitted to a great sense of loss about the active sex life he and Celia had enjoyed early in their marriage.

"The funny thing is," he said, "I love my wife more than ever, but the excitement we both seemed to feel in the past just seems to be gone most of the time. Every time she doesn't come, it makes me feel more and more like she's lost interest in me."

This couple's issue was trust, not sex. Celia was an orgasmic woman who feared discussing her sexual needs with her partner. Kip was a considerate lover whose anxiety about his own competence caused him to grill his wife in a way that discouraged trust rather than enhanced it.

Celia and Kip solved their problem when they learned to create safety for each other regarding their sexual communication. My first assignment to them was to create a lovemaking environment where no mistakes are possible. Specifically, I advised scheduling some lovemaking experiences in which they would have no goals other than enjoying the emotional and physical closeness—no orgasm, no intercourse. As with many sex problems, the first objective here was to get the couple back to enjoying each other intimately, instead of allowing sex to become a time for evaluation and possible failure.

Two weeks of lovemaking without intercourse helped Celia and Kip rediscover their pleasure in massage, pillow talk, and intimate touch. When I prescribed some of the exercises in this book, they began to experience more joy and depth in their lovemaking. As they learned to communicate clearly and with trust, Celia and Kip soon discovered ways to bring Celia to orgasm when she desired it.

For both of them, it was even more rewarding that they got much closer. They began to treasure the bond and the commitment they shared. Sex became an opportunity for closeness, not a performance.

Transforming Your Sexual Experience

Many people whose sex lives lack fire and joy believe that they (or their partners) are just made that way. Not so! Great sex is effortless when you master the principles of soulful sexuality. In addition to a changed attitude and deepened trust, the principles involve communication skills, information mastery, and specific tools and techniques.

Passionate sexuality requires a good sexual vocabulary and the courage to use it. Communicating clearly about sex starts with acceptance of the necessity of doing so. Many lovers seem to believe that love itself results in the ability to read minds. Thoughts like the following influence thousands: "If he really loved me, he'd know I need more foreplay." Or: "If she really cared, she'd give me the oral sex I long for."

The truth is that no lover can know our inner experience unless we communicate it verbally. We occupy separate bodies, minds, and personalities, and even in our most intimate moments with another, we have separate, different experiences. When we accept this profound reality, we become more able to act on the fact that communication is our only hope of having our deepest sexual desires understood and honored. Chapter 6 describes the holy work of sexual communication and offers you a powerful set of tools.

For now, be aware that any hesitation you have toward talking freely about sex is a holdover from your childhood. Most of us got lots of messages about keeping our sexual questions and feelings under wraps. Our parents may have wanted to protect us or they may have been uncomfortable talking about sex. As an adult, though, you may choose to

∽

Your assignment on this planet is to enhance the part of the world you were put in charge of. You keep that world free by living and speaking the truth.

—David Viscott

make your own, new decision: I choose to talk freely about sex so that I can have more passion and more joy.

Learn to Play and Experiment in Bed

This simplest of principles goes against our usual oh-so-serious attitudes toward sex. Playfulness is a God-given attribute which fully supports human beings in enjoying each other more and therefore loving each other more.

For many couples, sex is deadly serious. This leads to sexual boredom, frozen smile muscles, an out-of-shape sense of humor, and often a limp penis or clitoris. Lovemaking was not meant to be one more place to evaluate yourself ("Was I good, honey?").

There are so many ways to play with your lover! Begin by creating a context for play and imagination. This means creating safety—a no-lose situation. It means sending a clear communication that *I won't condemn or reject you if you try something new*, and *Experiments don't have to turn out any particular way*.

Here are some ways to experiment and have fun with sex:

- *Have a lovemaking session in which you use only positions or locations that you've never tried before. How about making love in a swimming pool or the bathtub?*

- *Take turns being blindfolded.*

- *Wear a hat or shoes next time.*

- *See how many bad jokes, knock-knock jokes, or puns you can squeeze into your next intimate time. ("Mabel, when Irving was still alive, did you have mutual climax?" "I'm not sure; I think we had Mutual of Omaha.")*

- *Take turns wearing costumes requested by the other.*

- *Meet each other in a strange bar or restaurant; enjoy some kissing in the parking lot before going home.*

- *Have a lovemaking session in which you agree in advance that neither of you will have orgasms. Instead, have fun seeing how aroused you can get in new ways.*

- *Take advantage of the games, toys, books, and videos available for lovers. Make friends with a vibrator. Stock up on and use fragrant massage oil. (See Chapter 12 for sources of sex toys, games, and instructional materials that are respectful of sexuality and relationship.)*

- *Lighten up!*

Most important of all, avoid one of the biggest deterrents to relaxed and pleasing lovemaking—the "sex as performance" mentality. This often involves silent lovemaking, followed by a report-card session: "So . . . how was it?" It's better to talk while making love ("Yes! Just like that!") and to stay in such clear communication throughout that it's unnecessary to ask for evaluations at the end.

Master the Fundamental Facts of Anatomy, Technique, and Emotional Response

Chapters 4 and 5 offer you detailed guidelines about each gender's sexual reality and needs. For our purposes here, consider the following:

- Constantly deepen your perception of your partner; look deeper than appearance and personality *and communicate that.* "Your inner beauty touches me most of all," you could say if it would feel sincere.

- Understand that there is absolutely no reason for "sex" to be over when the man ejaculates. Ending lovemaking abruptly because the man has ejaculated first is one of the most common reasons for sexual dissatisfaction and lack of sexual interest among women. If the man comes first, he can use his fingers, mouth, or a sex toy to continue stimulating her after his penis has softened. To do this, a man must be or become comfortable contacting his own body fluid.

Love is letting go of fear.
—Gerald Jampolsky

Expand Your Consciousness About Sex Role Behavior

In sex therapy, Art, a forty-four-year-old father of three, objected to continuing to make love after his orgasm. "I just don't feel interested in doing anything sexual after I come. Leslie usually takes longer than I do to climax, and I try to really arouse her before intercourse, and then I try to prolong the act as long as I can. But sometimes it just doesn't work. I come first, and then as far as I'm concerned it's all over. We just have to wait for another time."

Leslie, age forty-two, looked sad as she listened to Art. She rolled her eyes at his last sentence, and then stared silently at the floor.

I knew from private sessions with both Art and Leslie that they were one of the thousands of couples for whom this issue is a long-standing source of conflict. Although Art was usually a considerate man and Leslie was a responsive woman, they were limiting themselves with stereotypic thinking about lovemaking.

Art, like many men, viewed sex as performance. He felt that he had nothing to give when his penis was soft, and nothing to enjoy once he had climaxed. Leslie was a woman who believed her role was to take care of her man's ego and wait passively for her own needs to be met. She did not let her partner know how important orgasm was to her and she rarely took the lead in being sure it happened.

One of the crucial changes in a spiritual orientation to sex is that sex becomes an opportunity to share intimacy rather than to perform. It's all about experiencing the deep connection between two people, rather than trying to reach a goal—to "get somewhere." We learn to give up having a goal. Instead, we focus on sharing whatever experience develops.

The great paradox is that the most fulfilling sexual experiences occur when we stop trying to "get somewhere." When we surrender our goals and focus on pleasuring our beloved, we experience the greatest pleasure ourselves. We may even experience ecstasy, not by making it a goal, but by being fully present in the moment and fully willing to experience our beloved deeply.

Though reluctant at first, Art and Leslie were exceptionally open to learning new sexual habits; they needed only a few sessions to solve their problem. Lovemaking *without* intercourse taught them how many other pleasures are possible. Art learned that a "soft-on" can provide a unique stimulation for a loving partner. He learned that he could find great delight in pleasuring Leslie, whether or not he was aroused himself. Just as he had always enjoyed giving her a massage, he found that so long as he was not worried about having an erection, he enjoyed his ability to arouse her and to please her.

When it turned out that Leslie was easily orgasmic with oral sex, both of them were delighted. Art found it was a different but still delightful pleasure to bring Leslie to orgasm orally on occasions when he came first (and sometimes before he entered her). Leslie, for her part, was so touched by Art's willingness to take care of her needs, that she became much more giving in her own efforts to please him. She also became interested in making love more often.

Leslie also learned some other new attitudes. She learned that it was okay to assert her needs and to initiate what she wanted. She learned that she didn't have to feel pressured to come as quickly as Art did and that she wouldn't end up frustrated.

Leslie helped Art understand that there were rare occasions when she didn't want to climax during lovemaking. Sometimes, when tired or preoccupied, she had learned that she could enjoy giving to Art even though she was not very aroused herself. Like most women, however, it was very important to Leslie that she be the one to choose these occasions. She let him know that most of the time, orgasm was just as important to her as it was to him.

Art and Leslie learned that delightful things happened when one of them became even a little more willing to move out of his or her comfort zone and sexual belief system. Each time this happened, their mutual trust grew, and they experienced more love and appreciation for each other. Such loving gifts alter the image each lover has of the other—they announce that there is a greater, deeper experience of love available now, in this moment.

Sharing the Responsibility for Sex

Nina, a thirty-two-year-old attorney, complained in sex therapy that her thirty-one-year-old husband, Mitch, wouldn't make love as often as she wished. "I must be the only woman around who wants to make love twice as often as her husband does," she said with sadness and frustration.

When Mitch had his turn to speak, he surprised Nina. "I get tired of Nina's agenda," he said. "Her idea of sex involves hearts and flowers and me doing all the work. She wants me to make dinner and then flatter and seduce her. I'm supposed to make her forget her hard day at the office by lots of romance and foreplay and figuring out just what she's in the mood for. Sometimes it feels like another job after my usual ten-hour day. Why doesn't she take the responsibility if she wants sex so much?"

In sex therapy, Mitch and Nina both learned that they had many more options than they were exercising. Mitch actually enjoyed making love as much as Nina did, as long as it didn't seem like one more responsibility. Mitch learned that he could turn the tables and ask for nurturing and for whatever pleasuring he wanted at the moment. He could be passive at times. He could say no at times. It was not necessary for him to assume the role of responsibility for sex.

Nina learned that being a full sexual partner meant sharing the responsibility as well as the pleasure. She was surprised to learn what fun it could be to take charge of lovemaking. She could initiate much more than she did. When she learned to initiate touch and contact without having an agenda, the frequency conflict dissolved. Mitch was almost always willing to have his back or feet rubbed, and to reciprocate.

Nina and Mitch also gained a new attitude toward their relationship. One assignment I gave them was to sit together in silence for ten minutes a day for a week. They were to spend this time recalling their early connection and remembering why they were together.

They experienced a breakthrough on the fifth day of sitting together, when Nina began to cry. She was remembering their early love and how much Mitch meant to her. Mitch responded in kind. He had been feeling like a servant rather than the object of her love. As this couple began to experience opening their hearts to each other, their conflict seemed to dissolve.

> ∽
>
> *The loss of spiritual ecstasy in Western society has left a void that we fill in the only way we know how: with danger and excitment.*
>
> —Robert Johnson

The Only Rules Are Safety, Mutual Consent, and Staying True to Yourself

Partners in soulful sexuality adventures are committed to mutuality and to protecting each other's health and well-being. Never engage in any sexual behavior that feels wrong or painful. A loving partner will not ask you to do so. You must be able to say no if you are to be able to say yes.

On the other hand, if you stay open you may find that practices that once seemed unappealing now are very pleasing. Many people have this experience about oral sex, for example. Staying true to yourself means acting on your answer to the question: Do I really want to do this? It also means allowing yourself to change your answer as trust in yourself and in your partner grows.

If you believe that touching any bodily part with a finger is morally superior to touching it with a mouth, you suffer from the false-rules syndrome. Here are some examples of "rules" my sex therapy patients have expressed to me:

- *Forty-five-year-old man:* "She lets me touch her pussy with my penis but not with my hands or mouth."

- *Twenty-eight-year-old woman:* "I don't like him rubbing his penis against my backside during the night. It makes me feel used."

- *Thirty-six-year-old man:* "I like her to do oral sex on me, but I never do it to a woman."

- *Twenty-six-year-old woman:* "People of my nationality think oral sex is too mechanical and not clean."

- *Forty-four-year-old woman:* "I've never had an orgasm with him in twenty-three years of marriage. The important thing is that he comes. I take care of myself later."

- *Forty-seven-year-old man:* "I believe that women don't like their breasts touched."

- *Sixty-year-old man:* "Your sex life is pretty much over after fifty."

- *Eighteen-year-old woman:* "I can't stand the thought of touching semen. It's nasty."

All of these people are limiting themselves unnecessarily. There are thousands of ways to arouse sexual desire, and endless ways to achieve your own and assist with your partner's orgasm. Whole books have illustrated the way two bodies intent upon intercourse can arrange themselves. One of the pleasures of a long marriage is the exploration of the limitless possibilities for sexual pleasure. Doing so takes an experimental attitude and a willingness to look foolish.

Medical Safety

Medical safety must be a prerequisite to all sexual behavior today. No sexual pleasure is worth risking your life through exposure to the AIDS virus. You can express your sexuality in ways that are risk-free. Risk-free acts are the *only* appropriate sexual behaviors when you lack reliable information about your own or your partner's medical status.

The principles and practices in this book assume that you have taken care of the need for medical safety. *Abstinence from any sexual activity that exchanges bodily fluids offers the only 100 percent guarantee against transmitting a sexual disease.* Otherwise, unless you have a partner you *know* to be monogamous and disease-free, you must choose any partner carefully and practice safe sex even then. Appendix B tells you what you need to know about sexually transmitted diseases and how to protect yourself from them.

Overcome Sexual Myths and Claim Sexual Pleasure as the Birthright of the Magnificent Human Being You Are

If any early experience is interfering with that birthright, seek out counseling with no more hesitation than you would have about seeking out a dentist if you had a toothache.

Janet, a high-powered businesswoman, wrote to me after hearing me give a lecture on sacred sexuality at her church. She writes:

My husband is not very interested in the idea of bringing more spirituality into our sex life. I, myself, at forty, am just beginning to open this door, and I'm at a loss as to how to even explain what I'm talking about to him. He's a science teacher, and a wonderful man, but he says our sex life has been fine for twenty-one years, so why try to change it? I understand that there's something more, but I'm not sure how to get closer to it.

Here's my answer to Janet, and to you if you are in a similar situation:

You are on the brink of some thrilling discoveries, and it's up to you to be the leader as you start this journey. Once your partner understands that this means he will receive more love, have more fun, and experience more passion with you, he's likely to get interested. For now, just ask for his support and let him know that this doesn't mean he needs to agree. You just want him along for the ride.

> *Whereas the romantic relationship operates in time, the spiritual union has timeless infinity as its context.*
> —Daphne Rose Kingma

I suggested that she introduce him to some of the practices that are outlined in Chapters 8 and 9, especially the "night of service," believing that when he has new experiences that open his heart, he may become more receptive.

Learning to Receive

Vanessa describes a time when her partner gave her a night of service. It allowed her to learned what it means to receive. Both Vanessa and her partner experience great healing as they separate the roles of giver and receiver.

Naked, I lie on the large white bed with its sheets pulled back. A single red rose has been left on the pillow beside me.

My beloved smiles down at me as he caresses my whole body. He strokes my hair, my eyelids, my cheeks. He continues until he reaches my toes. Gently, he squeezes each one.

For a long time, he strokes and kisses me all over. Eventually, his fingers enter my vagina and begin to massage what I've just learned is my sacred spot. For hours, he continues to awaken me with a hundred varieties of inner touch.

I laugh and I cry. I scream with joy and pleasure. I lapse into fear that he will leave me, fear that giving me this much will make him resent me. To receive so much, I need to be impeccable. I am not.

With touch and with presence, he teaches me that I am worthy after all. Not impeccable, but lovable. Our eye contact is never broken as the sea of unfamiliar emotions washes over me. He is with me through each peak and valley.

He laughs with me, and becomes even more tender when I cry. He declares his love over and over. He breathes deeply, mirroring my rhythm. He sighs loudly along with me.

On this night, by agreement, I do not reciprocate. I simply receive, drinking in his love and his touch.

Vanessa has learned what it means to receive, and, because of this, she and her partner experience more and more joy each time they separate the roles of giver and receiver.

Barriers to Receptivity

What keeps us from opening fully to our beloved?

Fear and lack of self-acceptance are the primary answers. We feel we are unworthy to be fully seen and deeply known; we believe we earn acceptance only by a polished image or a good performance.

For most of us, there has never been a time when we felt safe to fully reveal ourselves to another. When we approach an opportunity to share ourselves sexually with our beloved, we may feel drawn to our old self-protective patterns.

When we begin to acknowledge and express the pain our sense of unworthiness brings us, our partners can help us. A simple example might be, "Sometimes I feel I don't really deserve you and everything you give me." As soon as we become able to take a risk like this, we begin to heal our self-doubt and self-criticism.

Another barrier to receiving is the fear of loss of control. Giving comes naturally to many of us. Givers initiate. They determine what touch will be given and for how long. When intensity builds too much for their comfort, givers can slow down or withdraw emotionally.

If, like Vanessa, you allow yourself to fully receive, you will experience loss of control. When we open fully to sexual touch, we may feel emotions that seem unfamiliar or even dangerous.

Three simple experiments will help you deepen your ability to receive:

- *Agree with your partner to have times when you separate the roles of giver and receiver. When you receive, do not reciprocate. Simply stay present with whatever feelings arise. Begin with ten minutes and work up to an hour or more.*

- *Whether you are receiving or giving, breathe deeply and frequently. This allows more flow of energy and emotion.*

- *Allow sounds to accompany each exhalation. Moving beyond silent lovemaking allows the building of more intense feeling.*

But only some-one who is ready for everything, who doesn't exclude any experience, even the most incomprehen-sible, will live the relationship with another person as some-thing alive and will himself sound the depths of his own being.
—Rilke

Sexual Receiving Is Ultimately a Spiritual Act

Receiving has the potential to heal our fears and our feelings of unworthiness. It is our nature to experience love most fully when a trusted human being offers it. Through receiving, nurturing, and even adoration from our beloved, we experience the reality of divine love, expressed in the most human of acts.

When lovers meet with respect for the mysteries
of their separation, they may, in coming
together, suddenly experience lovemaking as a
sacramental dance.

—Sam Keen

❧

CHAPTER 4

Feminine Mysteries Unveiled: Increasing Female Passion Through Emotional and Spiritual Connection

M astery of gender-based information about sex is crucial to the full development of soulful sexuality. This is because so much sexual misunderstanding occurs between men and women that love-making often becomes an arena of confusion or alienation, or even a battleground. How can two people focus on the spiritual aspects of their lovemaking when they are battling over gender-based conflicts?

She nags him to be "more romantic" and lets him know he doesn't satisfy her need to feel courted. *He* continually pesters her to make love more often, and makes no secret of the fact that he doesn't "get enough."

This is one of the battles of the sexes. It recurs because men and women have different biological, emotional, and sexual realities, and because most couples have not developed their sexual communication skills well enough to gently teach and graciously learn from each other.

If this mutual learning process doesn't happen, couples remain un-enlightened about each other's sexual reality after years of living together. In order to bridge the gap, this chapter articulates what women feel and long for in lovemaking. If you are female, share this information with your partner and add your own comments.

If you are a male who would like to unlock the mysteries of female biological processes, read on with an open heart. It can be difficult to allow yourself to seek out and take in information about something so fundamental to male identity as skill at lovemaking.

Take nothing you read here to mean that men are any less vulnerable about sex than women; often they are more so. Men bear more than their share of responsibility for lovemaking. They also grow up with an unfair dilemma—that the ability to be a good lover is vital to a man's identity, and yet his culture tells him that he should not need to ask for information.

In this chapter, we will shine the light of understanding on women and their journey. Willingness to learn that which you cannot know from your own experience is one of the qualities that allows you to make a quantum leap in the sexual joy you can give *and* receive. Mastering these principles makes great lovers out of good ones.

Women's Sexual Anxiety

In spite of limitless potential, most women have pain and anxiety about their sexuality. That pain is the result of millennia in which women have been treated not as full partners in relationship, but as objects or possessions.

Men have difficulty understanding what it's like for women to live in a culture that bombards us with messages that we must *qualify* to be sexually desirable. We must be young, thin, attractive, fertile, and sexually responsive. And if we do achieve such states, we must maintain them permanently, regardless of the influences of pregnancy, illness, or aging. Loss of any of the crucial traits disqualifies us as the objects of male attention and consigns us to the realm of sexually invisible women.

Women internalize these painful messages and, throughout their lives, bring them to the bedroom. The effects show up in lack of sexual courage or disinterest in sex because it may result in increased feelings of inadequacy.

Connection Is the Aphrodisiac

The overriding principle that illuminates female sexuality is that a woman's arousal *and* her satisfaction are determined primarily by her feeling of emotional and spiritual connection. *Connection is the aphrodisiac,* not technique, not flowers and candlelight, not doing everything her way. Learning to connect means learning to open your hearts to each other. A man who looks deeply into a woman's heart will see archetypal Woman, the eternal feminine.

For many men, it is difficult to understand that the first thing his partner wants is neither an action nor a technique. Men are trained to be problem solvers—to seek concrete solutions. Once a man has learned which sexual behaviors arouse and bring his partner to orgasm most quickly, he may want to engage in those behaviors as soon as possible after lovemaking begins.

Women, however, tend to feel that this is a cookbook approach to lovemaking and they want something different. Although they may not yet be able to say so, they also long for emotional depth and intimate connection *prior* to intimate touch.

∽

The especial genius of women I believe to be electrical in movement, intuitive in function, spiritual in tendency.

—Margaret Fuller

How then can two lovers get the sexual process going, if not through intimate touch? The answer, from a woman's point of view, is *through intimate emotions*. The behavior each woman prefers at the beginning of lovemaking is individual, but it almost always involves taking time—time to connect prior to any touching. Beginning intimate times with a quiet, unhurried exchange of feelings and affection will go a long way toward helping a woman open to her partner sexually.

Most women also long for touch that is meant to express love rather than to arouse. Once she feels close, she is likely to want him sexually. And once you *both* feel close, you are likely to have a better sexual experience.

Women Need to Feel Safe in Order to Be Fully Aroused

Joanne, forty-three, wondered why she couldn't bring herself to make love more often with her forty-two-year-old husband. Roland regularly threatened to leave the marriage, saying that he didn't get enough sexual satisfaction. He also complained that she had gained ten pounds since their marriage. Joanne loved Roland and wanted to maintain the marriage. But when he approached her sexually, it was all she could do to respond. It seemed to both of them that Joanne no longer felt attracted to Roland.

Actually, Joanne was feeling unsafe and unaccepted. Both of these states are great deadeners of passion, especially in women. Women need safety and stability before they can fully open to their sexual potential. A partner whose loyalty or commitment is uncertain is anything but safe.

What Joanne most longed to hear was, "I love you just the way you are." She also needed to be sure that Roland was not going to leave her, that he was committed to the marriage even though his needs were not always met.

Fortunately, Roland was in fact committed to Joanne in spite of his threats. This emerged during a touching therapy session in which Roland cried and told Joanne that he wouldn't want to live his life without her. Joanne and Roland experienced a great blossoming in their intimate life when they succeeded in learning to create safety for each other. Roland became more emotionally expressive, and Joanne became more sexually free.

Orgasm Is Just as Important to Women as It Is to Men

Del, twenty-eight, believes that his wife, Lana, doesn't care much about sex or orgasm. "Lots of times, it seems like she just doesn't feel like coming. Not me—I always feel like it!" he exclaims. Lana often turns Del down when he wants to make love. Del feels bad about this, but comforts himself with a belief that Lana has a "lower sex drive" than he does. He does not know that she pleasures herself several times a week.

As their therapist, I know that this couple has many sexual misunderstandings. Both Del and Lana think that there's something wrong with Lana, but the truth is that there's something wrong with their assumptions and with their lovemaking style. Lana tires of lovemaking that regularly arouses her but fails to bring her to orgasm. She is one of millions of women who rarely or never come during intercourse.

Like many men, Del tries to last as long as he can during intercourse, but once he ejaculates, he feels that the lovemaking is finished. "I do my best," he says, "but I can't help it that she takes so long."

Two myths account for the fact that this kind of misunderstanding is extremely common:

Myth 1: *Intercourse is the ultimate sexual act, and a sexually mature woman "should" come to orgasm this way.*

Myth 2: *The natural end of lovemaking is male ejaculation. When this occurs, the lovemaking session is over, and no man should be expected to do more.*

Empowered women are healthy women connected to other lives by hundreds of sturdy bridges.

—Jeanne Englemann

These two myths reveal a destructive ignorance of sexual potential. The first ignores the reality of female anatomy and assumes that women should be like men. The second myth devalues men as lovers except when their penises are erect. Both myths lose sight of the profound potential of openhearted lovemaking to foster an ever-growing soul-to-soul connection between two lovers. They also ignore a very simple biological fact—a majority of women do not reach orgasm through intercourse without some other kind of stimulation.

Although mainstream sexology claims that all female orgasms result from clitoral stimulation, many women disagree. A few women come to orgasm with no clitoral contact at all. Nipple stimulation, sacred-spot ("G-spot") or other vaginal stimulation, or even thoughts alone can set off the orgasmic response in some women. Females, like males, can also have orgasms while asleep and dreaming.

In spite of these facts, it is still true that most women need good clitoral stimulation to reach orgasm. In many positions, intercourse does not provide adequate stimulation to the clitoris or to the most sensitive areas of the vagina. In some positions, such as entry from behind, it provides almost no clitoral stimulation; it may or may not stimulate the sacred-spot area of the vagina. Even in the popular man-on-top ("missionary") position, unless the man learns to ride high and make conscious clitoral contact, a woman may receive relatively little clitoral stimulation.

The woman-above position offers the best possibilities for female orgasm with intercourse, because the women can control pressure, angle, and rhythm better if she is on top. But, as many couples can attest, a position change is often not enough.

Indeed, most of the traditional intercourse positions favor male stimulation at the expense of female needs. Achieving the mutual satisfaction that most couples want requires a recognition that many women enjoy other sexual acts more than intercourse, and that female arousal and satisfaction may be quite independent of intercourse.

What is confusing to many men is that their partners seem to enjoy intercourse so much. And, in fact, most women do enjoy it, for its sensations, for its ability to please their partners, and for the sense of intimacy many women say that intercourse provides. Nevertheless, a majority of women reach orgasm more easily in other ways.

On the other hand, a vocal minority of women come to orgasm *only* through sustained and carefully positioned intercourse. These women are capable of learning other ways, but many need encouragement to do so.

Because there are so many different ways a woman may feel about intercourse, detailed communication is key. What is more or less certain is that *a man can and should offer more stimulation to his partner after reaching his own orgasm.* Pleasuring her is different in this state, to be sure, but it can be enjoyable. It is the enjoyment of giving and the satisfaction of building sexual trust.

Strange as it may sound, *a penis with a "soft-on" can still give great pleasure*—a different, more subtle pleasure than when erect. A man can also give pleasure with his mouth, his hands, a knee, or a vibrator. It's easy to be creative if you're not worrying about it.

A woman may need help in learning to receive this kind of attention. Since most women have been left unsatisfied many times in their lives, this kind of offer can be overwhelming at first. She may need help in believing that she is worthy of it.

A man should take his cues from his partner. She may actually *prefer* not to come this time, or she may feel unable to. He should accept that with grace, but never take it to mean that next time she won't care whether she comes. A pattern in which he comes and she doesn't will inevitably lead to resentment and/or less frequent sex in the long run.

∽

When sleeping women wake, mountains move.

—Chinese proverb

He Should Take the Time to Allow Her to Wish
for Any Touch Before Providing It

"I can't stand it when Mack goes for my breasts the minute we get into bed!" exclaims Brigette, married ten years. She echoes the feelings many women voice. *A woman wants touch to express what she is feeling right now, and perhaps to invite her to go just one step further.* A touch that aims to get her to feel what her partner wants her to feel is much less pleasurable.

Ancient texts on sexuality teach five modes of touch: stroking, tapping, pinching, scratching, and squeezing. Each can vary from soft to hard and from fast to slow. Experiment with the many modalities of touch that come from combining mode, speed, and pressure. An "almost touch" in which you get close to contact but never quite actually touch can be very exciting, too.

A woman often wants gentle stimulation of the whole body before her partner focuses on her breasts or vulva. He can fondle, massage, scratch gently all over her body, perhaps concentrating on different areas than last time. He can try tapping on her inner thighs, for example, prior to touching her genitals.

Women often feel that patience distinguishes a great lover. "Men are always in a hurry," complains Sally, a young attorney. "Before marriage, they pressure you constantly about sex. After marriage, they want to hurry all lovemaking—let's get to bed, let's get to intercourse, let's get to orgasm, let's get to sleep! I want more time for all of it, but my husband can't even understand why I'm dissatisfied. 'You always come, don't you?' he says, as if that were the whole story."

Sally's husband was regularly rushing through lovemaking with results that threatened the sexual relationship he valued. In therapy, he learned to pay attention to Sally's cues and to let her wait just a little longer for each touch. Rather than focusing on her breasts or genitals the moment he felt like making love, he learned to tease and wait a little, and then a little more. When he finally did touch her intimately, she was eager for the touch.

Expertise in Arousing the Breasts Is Fundamental

Many women feel about their breasts the way a man may feel about his penis. In a unique way, breasts seem to represent femininity, as a penis represents masculinity. For some women, their breasts are the most sensitive parts of their bodies. If a woman feels this way, receiving just the right touch on breasts and nipples can open her heart like no other touch.

For many women, a great deal of emotion is associated with allowing breasts to be touched or nipples sucked. It is an act of love and trust, and brings up feelings of great vulnerability. On the other hand, other women are lukewarm or even dislike breast stimulation.

It's crucial, then, that a man be well-informed about what's true for *his* partner, because his reactions to and treatment of her breasts may be very important to her. He should ask her to tell him exactly how she feels.

Women voice several common objections to the way men treat their breasts:

- *"He doesn't give me the feeling that he likes my breasts. I'm afraid they are too small, and his silence about them makes me worry that I'm right."*

- *"He reaches for my breasts the minute he starts thinking about sex. I need time to get ready for such an important touch."*

- *"He goes for my nipples and pays no attention to the rest of my breasts. I want him to massage, squeeze, and enjoy the whole breast."*

- *"He acts as if my big breasts are the most important thing about me. Sometimes I feel it's my breasts he loves, not me."*

Women, as those quoted show, long to feel that their breasts are completely accepted and enjoyed by their partners. At the same time, women want to feel that they are loved independently of their breasts or any other part of their bodies. If this seems difficult, or as if there's no way to do it right, a man can make it easy by talking to the woman in his life about her needs and following her lead.

Unless his partner tells him otherwise, he should approach her breasts with gentleness. It's important not to zero in on her nipples the moment he approaches her breasts. This conveys the feeling that his only purpose is to arouse her, and may cause her to feel pressured. Instead, she wants him to celebrate and enjoy her breasts, as a way of celebrating *her*. He can touch each breast all over; stroke it, squeeze gently, massage it. If he likes and enjoys her breasts, he can express that over and over.

This is one of the times when it's valuable to consciously give up a goal orientation. Instead of one minute on the breasts before going for penetration, if he actually takes time to enjoy the experience, undoubtedly she will, too.

Beauty comes from the spirit. It is the spirit that 'dresses' the body, not the clothes that are added to it.
—Margo Anand

Honoring the Genital Organs of Femininity

Even a skilled lover can learn from the way the ancients taught men to honor the vagina and the clitoris as the ultimate symbols of feminine essence. Even though a man may already be knowledgeable about touching his partner intimately, the suggestions here can offer variety and a deepening of passion.

To *honor* means just that—to admire and pay tribute to this beautiful aspect of the female form. *Honoring* suggests that intimate touch conveys respect and love, not just the intention to arouse.

When a man has established true and deep trust with his partner, and when he knows that she welcomes it, he can examine her clitoris and vulva in detail both visually and by touch. He can make it a goal to know

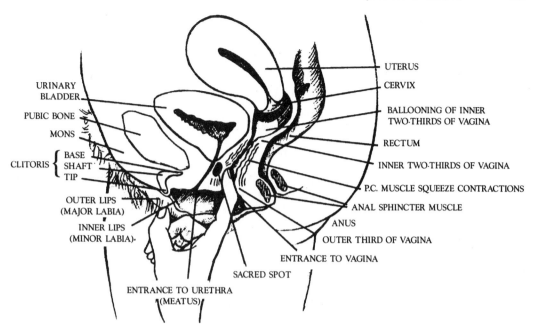

UTERUS
CERVIX
BALLOONING OF INNER
TWO-THIRDS OF VAGINA
RECTUM
INNER TWO-THIRDS OF VAGINA
P.C. MUSCLE SQUEEZE CONTRACTIONS
ANAL SPHINCTER MUSCLE
ANUS
OUTER THIRD OF VAGINA
ENTRANCE TO VAGINA
SACRED SPOT
ENTRANCE TO URETHRA
(MEATUS)
INNER LIPS
(MINOR LABIA)
OUTER LIPS
(MAJOR LABIA)
CLITORIS { BASE / SHAFT / TIP
MONS
PUBIC BONE
URINARY
BLADDER

it like the palm of his hand. He can ask her to show him how she touches herself.

If she is comfortable stimulating herself in front of him, he can watch and learn how she likes the touch to change as she gets more and more aroused.

∽ Caressing the Clitoris and the Vulva

Most women love the caresses a man can offer with his lips and tongue. He can try licking the sides of the clitoris with his tongue and try gentle, rhythmical sucking right on the clitoris when she is well aroused. Many women will reach orgasm this way, and almost all will greatly enjoy it.

Chuck, according to his wife, is a "certified great lover." This fifty-year-old man says, "I spent years learning to know everything I could about the clitoris. It's an incredible and beautiful tiny structure, with as many nerve fibers in it as the penis. I love her beautiful vulva too. I tell my wife I can 'stay down here for hours' just looking at her and touching her in a hundred different ways. I always spend plenty of time on her that way before I ever enter her."

When Chuck's wife, Jan, told her women's group about Chuck's attitudes and expertise, the group spontaneously applauded!

ᴄ᷈ Focusing on the Vulva

When he does approach her genitals, he should begin with a light, feathery touch, teasing and fondling the whole genital area first, circling closer and closer to the clitoris without actually touching it. He can then spread the lips or labia and stroke them lightly, using the soft pads of his fingers to stroke. (When using his fingers on the vulva, he should have short, smooth nails and no hangnails.)

Well-Informed Lovers Use Lubricants

Many men and women are uninformed about the necessity of using lubricants when touching the vulva. Lubrication is essential to avoid pain in the exquisitely sensitive tissues in the clitoral and vaginal areas. The amount of natural lubrication can be influenced by hormonal swings and other factors, and is not a negative reflection on the woman's arousal level or the man's technique. A woman of any age may need additional lubricant at times, both before and during intercourse.

Have a water-based lubricant such as Astroglide, KY Jelly, or Probe available at your bedside at all time and use it freely. If you do not use condoms, a diaphragm, or other latex barriers, you may use natural oils as lubricants. *Oil-based products (including baby oil and petroleum jelly) can damage latex within sixty seconds.*

When she has begun to respond, he can try to duplicate any strokes she has shown him. He can also experiment with dozens of strokes and speeds—side to side, around the edge, up and down, carefully observing her breathing, words, and other responses.

Gently stroking the sides of the clitoris often produces a better response than touching it head-on. Experiment with a head-on approach to the clitoris only when she is clearly aroused. Use two or three fingers together; using only one can be irritating. Try a push-release-push-release touch in a slow rhythm at first, gaining speed only if her response indicates that she prefers it. Many women will reach orgasm in five to fifteen minutes of this rhythmic stimulation, but this is not the goal. The real goal is connection and deep contact.

> ✄
> *The first duty of love is to listen.*
> —Paul Tillich

Welcoming Feedback

If a man truly wants to be his partner's personal expert, he should encourage her to overcome any fear of giving him feedback. Most women believe that it's their job to help their partner feel that he's a good lover, even at the expense of their own satisfaction. He should let her know that he's open to feedback, if he is. "A little to the left"; "Suck harder, please," she might say; he can then take in and act upon these requests. Such open communication will foster an improved feedback system that will serve both of you well in learning to pleasure each other more and more.

What's in all this for him? The answer is the opportunity to become a great lover to this particular woman and to have a deep experience of love and passion with her. Eventually, ecstatic response is possible, too. Just making the effort makes it much more likely that she will be enthusiastic rather than reluctant about sex.

Women respond to a man who shows an understanding of the nature of the sacred feminine and a willingness to honor it. When a woman's essential spiritual needs are honored in relationship, many seeds of conflict are transformed into fertile blossoms of deepening love. This is nowhere more true than in lovemaking.

In love and sex, as in everything else, what you give comes back to you. As he honors the eternal feminine in his partner, he will experience more deeply this aspect of himself.

Hygiene Affects a Woman's Feelings of Safety and Arousal

This section will discuss matters of hygiene that are a given to many men. As a couple therapist, however, I have heard complaints about cleanliness and grooming from women whose partners are attorneys and professors and from every other kind of occupation. Many women hesitate to bring up this subject, even when it is affecting their level of sexual interest.

It is not always obvious to men that there is a connection between grooming and their partner's feelings of emotional safety. Women feel that a man who comes to bed unwashed, unshaven, or without brushing his teeth is making a statement to her, saying, essentially: I don't care enough about your feelings to bother with cleanliness. I shower and shave for work, but not for you.

Women are often embarrassed to tell their men that there is an unspoken etiquette for partners in an intimate relationship. It involves keeping our bodies, mouths, and genitals clean and fresh. For men who shave, doing so before kissing or oral contact is crucial to the woman's comfort. Many women suffer in silence rather than voice the criticism they feel. Here are some examples from a women's sexuality group:

- *Jane, age thirty:* "My husband never shaves at night. He likes oral sex, but he doesn't realize it makes me sore for days sometimes."

- *Estelle, age forty-five:* "Jack showers, but he doesn't always clean under his foreskin. I hate it when he's dirty, but I can't say anything. Uncircumcised men should clean themselves carefully!"

- *Maria, age twenty-three:* "Lester eats garlic and onions at lunch a lot. His breath is still bad when he comes home, but he gets insulted if I say anything. It makes me not want to kiss him."

- *Sarah, age fifty-six:* "Mel says he likes to 'smell like a man,' so he doesn't use deodorant. Sometimes his body odor makes me want to sleep in another room. He thinks I'm losing interest in sex, but I'm really just losing interest in making love with someone who smells. I know he'd be insulted if I said anything."

Even in such mundane matters as this, spiritual awareness helps. When we view our bodies as the temples of our spirits, it becomes clearer that every aspect of body care is important. This includes nutrition, medical care, exercise, and cleanliness. Cleanliness is a gift to your partner—one that symbolizes your respect for the sacred nature of lovemaking. Partners on the journey of soulful sexuality have a right to ask this thoughtfulness of each other. Both should make it a habit to come to bed clean and fresh.

It's a good idea to bring the issue up yourself once in awhile. A starting point could be: "Is there anything about my grooming you'd like me to improve?" Make an agreement that you will bring up any problem that occurs. It should be agreed that saying, "Could you please brush your teeth (or shave or wash)?" is a gift.

Cleanliness of the vulva and vagina are also important. Men can be turned off by odors from an unwashed vulva or from such conditions as tampons left in too long. A woman who knows that she is clean and naturally fragrant can relax more easily. Contrary to advertising campaigns, healthy women have no need for douching and vaginal sprays. Gentle soap and water are all that's needed.

If a woman uses spermicidal cream and a diaphragm for birth control, she should try showering *after* inserting the diaphragm. Then, if he wants to pleasure her orally, her labia will be free of cream or jelly.

Bridging the Differences

The many men I have worked with in counseling and sex therapy have convinced me that most of them truly want to provide pleasure and fulfillment for their partners. The path, though, is sometimes mysterious to them. The next section addresses some of the most frequent concerns men express.

How to Get a Woman to Want Sex as Much as a Man Does

Simone de Beauvoir has said . . . that a woman's sexuality hardly ever ends and that it flows like waves through peaks and valleys into infinity.

—Jolan Chang

The truth is that plenty of sexually mature women want a lot of sex. But many men feel that their partners just don't want to make love as much as they do. "No matter what I do," says forty-eight-year-old Luke, "my wife is just not as interested in sex as I am."

What Luke and many other men fail to realize is that what they call "sex" is a series of events that are best suited to *male* arousal and *male* orgasm. What Luke's wife may like is "being intimate." She defines this as cuddling, sweet verbal exchanges, massage, and pillow talk, with intercourse only if it turns out that both of them feel like it.

A woman may prefer oral or hand stimulation instead of intercourse. If she is one of the majority of women who does not reach orgasm through intercourse, constant pressure on her for "sex" as conventionally defined may feel to her like continual invitations to waltz when she prefers to tango.

Communication is the road to resolution of conflicts like this. Couples who learn to talk freely and clearly about all aspects of their sexuality have a wonderful adventure before them. Once you learn to skillfully create pleasure and safety for each other every time you make love, frequency conflicts evaporate.

If the question is, "Would you like to get close, be touched in ways that you choose, have fun, and have me tell you how wonderful you are?" the answer will rarely be "No."

How to Get a Woman to Want to Experiment

Males in our culture are encouraged to be assertive and even to take risks when it comes to sex. Women, especially in their formative years, are encouraged to be conservative and cautious.

The result of these cultural patterns is that millions of couples have conflict about experimentation. It is usually, though not always, the male who wants to try new sexual options. One husband, a twenty-nine-year-old teacher, said this when he consulted me: "My wife is only twenty-eight, but she has lots of closed doors when it comes to lovemaking. She doesn't like oral sex, anal sex is out of the question, and any position other than me on top is unacceptable to her. I've tried to get her interested in sexy videos, sex books, and even sexy jokes, but I'm getting nowhere. I feel frustrated and bored. What can I do?"

I told this man that a woman of less than thirty has barely begun to explore her sexuality, so time is on their side. Women (or men) with such restrictive attitudes about sex usually have many fears about their adequacy. She may feel that she's sexually unskilled, or that she won't look attractive doing the new behavior, or that she won't know how to react to something new.

The way to help a woman who is afraid is to help her feel safe. Invitations to play are less threatening than criticism or demands for performance. Very small steps toward any goal are best. For instance, he can try kissing her everywhere she encourages and then push the limits just a little, very briefly. Work toward your goals by millimeters!

When Romance Is a Dirty Word

Most married men can relate to Elliot when he says that "*Romance* is a dirty word in our house. My wife always wants it and never seems to feel satisfied with how much she gets from me. She says she wants things to be the way they were nine years ago, before our son was born. Why does she expect me to act like a college kid when I'm a man with a mortgage and a few gray hairs? I wish I had a partner who wanted sex with me without my having to earn her favors with flowers and candy."

In therapy, Elliot learned that pleas for romance often reflect a desire for lovemaking to be deeper, more powerful, and more meaningful. If a man learns to incorporate the spiritual aspects of himself into his interactions with his wife, he may find that the result pales in comparison to experiences that begin with him straining to be "romantic."

Women and Hormonal Changes

Anthony was one of those unusual men who had been in a men's group. When he came in to talk about some problems in his marriage, he said that his group included men whose wives were pregnant, nursing, suffering from PMS, or in menopause. "We all agree that our women are strange and unpredictable when these things are going on. We don't know how those hormones affect sex, but we all seem to hold back from approaching our wives when they're showing signs of the effects of one of these conditions. How can we find out how we should treat them?"

I told Anthony that it was great that he and his fellow group members were trying so hard to understand their partners. It's a fact that female emotions and libido are affected by hormones and reproductive processes. It's reminiscent of what men say about being sixteen and having erections surprising them in all kinds of situations. Big changes going on in your body do affect how you feel!

When a woman is facing mood swings and unexpected emotionality, the man in her life can help her remember the fact that her reproductive capabilities are a divine gift, or that each stage of life has its gifts. When PMS is the issue, his reminder may help her with what can be overwhelming, hormonally induced moodiness. When mood swings are associated with important losses as they are at menopause, his support can be even more valuable.

Communication, again, is the answer. When couples learn to talk freely about the bodily events they both experience, they each get an education. Most women feel supported if their men ask friendly questions about PMS, for example. Women want to be listened to and accepted, of course, not advised.

Supporting a Menopausal Woman

Women dealing with menopause may feel as embarrassed to discuss it as if they had leprosy! Many see it as admitting that they are over the hill, or they fear that others will see them that way. A partner's encouragement to talk about it will probably be greatly appreciated.

Understanding the many varieties of menopausal experience takes reading and study. This is a wonderful gift a man can offer the woman in his life if she is experiencing or approaching this important change. Consult Appendix A for sources of information.

∽ Recovering the Miracle: Vera and Morris

Vera first came to me when her eighteen-year marriage to Morris dissolved over sexual issues. Her husband, a history professor, had pleaded for more sex. When pleading failed, he demanded it. Finally, he left, saying that he wanted to find a woman who shared his desire for an active sex life while he was still young. Vera was crushed. She had taken her marriage vows seriously and had believed that they had made a lifelong commitment. For a year and a half, she remained celibate, licking her wounds, and fearing to risk closeness with anyone.

Nineteen months after he left, Morris showed up on her doorstep. Vera was flabbergasted when he announced, "I love you. I always have

∽

If we imagine ... the individual as a larger or smaller room, it is obvious that most people come to know only one corner of their room, one spot near the window, one narrow strip on which they keep walking back and forth. In this way they have a certain security.

—Rilke

and I always will. I've learned that sex isn't everything. For starters, it's not love. I made a commitment to you almost twenty years ago, and I want to come back and fulfill it no matter what. I still hope you can get into sex more, but if you can't, I want you anyway."

Two days later, Vera and Morris came to see me for marriage counseling and sex therapy. The first month of counseling focused mainly on Vera's anger at being abandoned. She screamed at him while violently hitting pillows in my office. She also had a great deal of rage which had begun to accumulate long before their separation. Morris had anger of his own, which he also had a chance to express and defuse in the safe counseling environment. Finally, they were ready to communicate.

"How *could* you leave me after all we went through together?" Vera demanded.

"How *could* you reject me sexually time after time all those years when you knew how much I needed you?" Morris retorted.

"Because it was always for *you* and about *your* needs—hardly ever for me," she sobbed. "We did it when *you* wanted to and the way *you* wanted to. You never asked me what I liked, or how I felt, or whether I was satisfied. I started to hate you whenever you hugged me, because I knew what you wanted."

Morris was dumbfounded. He had always felt that he was a reasonably good lover. He took pride in having never been "one of those hair-trigger guys," and he had always made sure to caress his wife's breasts and genitals for a while before he entered her. He had never embarrassed her by asking whether she came or not. He had always kept in shape by jogging. He had usually remembered to tell Vera he loved her before or after sex. So *what* was the problem?

Vera had to be convinced that he really wanted to know. She was afraid of hurting his feelings, and she needed the protected environment of counseling to even be able to begin discussing the feelings that had never been communicated in all their years together.

Finally, she began. "I wanted more depth," she said. "More close-ness, more meaning. It never mattered to you whether we were getting along or not; you always wanted to do it, and you wanted to do it in the same way—you on top or me on top, same sequence of events. You always had an orgasm, but you seemed oblivious to whether I did or not. After-ward, you'd say, 'I love you,' in exactly the same tone of voice every time. I felt empty!

"I got tired of your ABC approach to sex. What I wanted was to have some deep emotional and spiritual experiences with you. I wanted to feel really close and really loved. I wanted to feel that you cared about my pleasure as much as your own, but I wanted more than pleasure. After all our years together, I wanted to feel that our love was deep and unique, that we had built something together. But your idea of love was a quick hug after sex and then getting up and making a sandwich.

"I didn't know how to say all this, so I just avoided making love a lot of the time. You thought I didn't like sex, but you were wrong. I just preferred to let you think that to avoid having to tell you that it was sex *with you* I didn't like. I did love you and I still do, but I don't know how we can get together sexually."

Morris then shared his withheld feelings. "I was really hurt when you started turning me down so much. You knew how important sex was to me, but you said no to me anyway, over and over. At one point, I had no sexual confidence left.

"As far as whether I cared about your pleasure and your orgasms, there was nothing I cared about more. I just didn't know how to talk about it. I tried to show you by my behavior that I cared, but I thought it would embarrass you to talk about it directly. For instance, I always thought it was rude to ask a woman whether she came or not.

"By the time I left, I had given up on both of us. I felt that your turning me down so much was a sure sign that you didn't love me. I also felt that it was impossible for me to go through life without someone who really shared my interest in sex. It took all that time apart for me to realize that living my life without your love was even worse."

This couple's healing began with this first honest exchange.

My suggestions for Vera and Morris included the following, which would help any couple have a more meaningful sex life:

Until we accept the fact that life itself is founded in mystery, we shall learn nothing.

—Henry Miller

- *Learn to complete the expression of accumulated anger and resentment so that feelings of love for each other will be more accessible.*

- *Become skillful communicators about sex.*

- *Learn what the other really wants when making love.*

- *Open the door of spiritual sharing and bring those experiences into lovemaking.*

I also gave them some "home-play" assignments with the following goals:

- *To recover their pleasure in and to increase the amount of non-goal-directed affectionate touch.*

- *To find out how to facilitate Vera's orgasms.*

- *To separate the roles of giver and receiver at times, so as to more fully enjoy each of these.*

Vera and Morris were among the few fortunate couples who got the assistance they needed to reestablish their relationship. Their belief in the sacred and permanent nature of their commitment paid off in providing the motivation to seek help and do the necessary work to recover the marriage. When they finally succeeded, their appreciation for each other knew no bounds.

Vera said: "I never realized how much Morris really loves me. During our first eighteen years, I didn't love *myself* enough to believe that he could care so much. Until we came to therapy, I didn't have the skills or the courage to talk to him about the misunderstandings we had. When

he came back after our separation, I saw that he was truly my holy partner, and that my job was to learn to love him as well as I could. As I
committed myself to that, our sexual problems seemed to dissolve."

Morris had his own perspective: "It's strange how my sexual needs
got filled only after I became willing to give them up. Vera was never the
cold fish I imagined—she loves touch and she loves passion and she loves
me! She's the greatest gift God ever gave me, and I know now that I will
never leave her no matter what."

Vanessa's Experience: Helping Ben Understand

Vanessa now shares some of the ways she and her husband Ben learned
to bridge the gender gap.

It took about five years for my husband, Ben, to start to understand
me sexually. When we were first married, he often used to approach
me for sex when we had been fighting. We'd exchange some very
unpleasant words—even insults—and then he'd expect to make up in
bed. I hated it when he would try to touch me sexually while I was
mad at him!

He just didn't seem to get the message that I wasn't interested in
sex if the feelings between us weren't right. He used to accuse me of
"holding out" on him to get my way. I found out in my women's group
that a lot of other women's husbands said the same thing to them.
But I really wasn't doing that. I missed our lovemaking a lot, and I
longed for it, but I just couldn't do it when there was bad blood
between us. I did try it a few times and it was awful. I'd feel bad for a
few days afterward.

I guess it was the letter I wrote to Ben that finally got through to
him. We were separated for three weeks one year, because I had to go

home and help my mother take care of my father when he had heart surgery. I missed Ben while I was gone, and I wrote to him.

One day I wrote him a long letter about our sex life. I told him all about how I felt, and what I wanted to change. I wasn't ready then to discuss specific sexual acts, but I told him about a lot of feelings I had never expressed. For instance, I told him that making love when we were mad didn't work for me.

I also told him how much I valued our sex life and how much I appreciated him as a lover. I told him that I thought we had a holy relationship and that he was the love of my life and my spiritual partner in life.

I spent a long time explaining that I needed to feel close before I could really get into making love. I said that I wanted to be as close to him as possible. I even asked him to forgive me for the times when I had rejected him. I told him how I had tried to go along those few times and how bad I had felt afterward.

It was clear as soon as I got home that Ben had finally started to understand me better. The big change I saw in him was that he stopped trying to rush me into sex. He started spending ten or fifteen minutes talking first, touching me a little while we talked. That made such a difference to me! I felt so loved every time it happened, that I could just feel my heart opening to him. Our lovemaking got better right away, and we started to realize how strong our bond is.

To know what you prefer instead of humbly saying Amen to what the world tells you you ought to prefer, is to have kept your soul alive.
—Robert Louis Stevenson

The stories of all the couples in this chapter illustrate two great lessons that soulful sexuality teaches. First, most couples have to go through difficult times on their way to true understanding of each other. The second lesson is even more fundamental: *We can always come back to love.*

*A man who has followed the
precepts taught by his parents,
the mass media, teachers,
coaches and other authorities is
now in the very strange position
of hearing that everything he
learned is wrong.*
—Bernie Zilbergeld

CHAPTER 5

Honoring the Masculine: Spiritual Perspectives on Male Sexual Reality

In this chapter, you will learn what men tell their counselors about sex. If you are a woman who has ever struggled to understand your man's attitude toward sex, the stories in this chapter may open your heart to male sexual vulnerability. If you are a man, share this with your partner, and tell her what's true for you.

What Sex Means to Men

The essence of what most women fail to understand about male sexuality is this: Sex is a man's primary source of nurturing and contact; it is also a proving ground—the arena in which he evaluates himself and in which he must feel successful if he is to feel good about himself as a man. To the extent that a human expression of love is the most powerful experience of divine love that most of us encounter, man looks to woman as the vehicle for that expression.

A spiritual approach to sexuality can be a priceless gift to a man, because it offers a kind of lovemaking in which there is no way to fail. On the path of soulful sexuality, the only evaluation we can make of ourselves is that we are precious children of the divine, sharing our love with another treasured being. All forms of sexual encounter, then, are in some sense moments of worship, never of critical evaluation.

If you are a woman who longs to fulfill the sexual needs of the man in your life, it's very important to communicate acceptance and to give him the nurturing and contact he needs. Then you must help him to *be* and to *feel* successful as a lover. This happens not through pretending to like what you dislike, but rather through honest communication of your preferences and through practicing together.

Learning to really see into your man's heart and soul is one of the spiritual challenges of loving a man. Doing this starts with making it your intention to learn to see him as your treasured companion on the path of spiritual growth, not a means to the ends of social status or financial security.

We as women miss out on the opportunity to share a profound, spiritually based love, exactly to the extent that we insist on seeing our men as financial or social objects. As women, we often fail to understand that men are hurt by being seen this way. It is the counterpart of the pain women feel when judged by our appearances alone.

> *To have a spiritual relationship is to conciously acknowledge that above all we are spiritual beings and that the process of our own spiritual refinement is our true undertaking in this life.*
> —Daphne Rose Kingma

Penis Size Still Worries Many Men

Any woman who has ever worried that her breasts are less than perfect can understand how men worry about penis size. It's no joke to say that "penis envy" is best understood as the way that men compare themselves to each other.

It is one of the effects of our culture's mechanistic approach to sex that many men still believe that their partners would prefer someone with a bigger or differently shaped penis. Women who have not yet come to understand the soulful approach to sex may actually feel this way.

Let it be said once and for all that *penis size is unrelated to the amount of joy couples experience in their lovemaking.* A woman may need to convey this truth to her man. Yes, you can acknowledge, some few women may feel that a large penis feels better during intercourse, just as some men feel that holding a large breast is more exciting than a small one might be. But women and men who seek fulfillment at a soul level do not think in those terms.

Both men and women can grow beyond such limited thinking. Loving partners have an opportunity to give each other valuable reassurance about concerns like this. A woman should let a man know that it is his heart and soul that really turns her on. When attached to a man with a big heart, a penis of any size and shape can give immense satisfaction.

Frequency Arguments May Not Be What They Seem

Greg looked sad and embarrassed during a sex therapy session with his wife, Lucy. The subject was sexual frequency, a subject of disagreement for millions of American couples. Usually, though not always, it is the man who feels he is "not getting enough."

"Lucy has a hundred excuses," Greg said. "She's tired, she has to get up early, she has a cold coming on, the kids upset her today, she's worried about money—you name it. It all adds up to no sex tonight again. And none of those problems get any better because we don't make love. I suspect she holds out on me to get even for every little thing she gets mad at me about."

When Lucy had her turn, she said, "Greg wants to make love every night, no matter what. If we were having a hurricane and both of us were sick with tuberculosis, Greg would still want to make love. Lots of times, after a long day of juggling my job and three kids, I just want to read at night, or go to sleep early. Greg makes me feel that sex is just another chore and obligation, and the time he wants it is after I want to be off duty! But when I say that, Greg gets mad."

When I asked Greg why sex was so important, his apparent anger turned to sadness. When I asked who else he was close to besides his wife, he admitted that there was no one. "I have friends," he said, "but we talk about work and sports, nothing personal. I work hard, and I worry a lot about my kids, my job, and our future. When Lucy isn't there for me, I've got no one.

"Last year when my father died suddenly, I felt so alone. Lucy was good to me at first, but then she withdrew again. I've been depressed about it all year, and I have no one to talk to." Greg's eyes were full of tears, which his wife had never seen.

As therapy continued, Lucy and Greg both learned that Greg's deepest need was for contact and acceptance, rather than for intercourse. Like most men, he had no other source of emotional intimacy. While women usually have girlfriends or relatives they talk freely with, men rarely have real sharing with anyone other than their mates.

Greg came to understand that there were many forms of intimacy that could satisfy his needs. He began to learn that Lucy was almost always responsive when he asked her for cuddling and pillow talk. Some of these occasions led to intercourse, and others led to times of sweet affection. Both Lucy and Greg felt closer and more satisfied than before.

Lucy learned that Greg's needs for intimate connection were not unlike her own. She began to feel more loving and more sexual toward him. As they learned more ways of connecting, they ended up having more sex, not less.

⌒

The only thing you have to offer another human being, ever, is your own state of being.

—Ram Dass

This story shows that frequency issues often conceal other issues that are difficult and may feel risky to talk about. If you and your partner experience similar conflicts at times, your goal should be to defuse the power struggle by getting to the deeper needs underneath it.

Male Self-Esteem Depends on Being Fully Accepted Sexually

Understanding how much a man's self-esteem depends on his partner's sexual acceptance of him can illuminate some of the common disagreements men and women have about sex. If you're a woman whose partner persistently asks for sex at times when you feel the mood or circumstances are not right, he may not be simply demanding to have his way, as you imagine. Instead, he may be reaching out for your comfort, your kindness, and your acceptance.

Most men long to hear "I want you, baby!" spoken in no uncertain terms by a loving partner. Many, unfortunately, never do.

Rejection, instead, is what men experience often throughout their lives. A man who is often sexually rejected by his mate may feel much like a woman would feel if her man told her, "You've gotten so fat that I don't even look at you anymore." Either of these is an ego blow that cuts deeply into self-esteem. For a man, sexual rejection is more painful than most women can imagine.

The solution never includes doing something sexual that you resent or dislike. It doesn't require forcing yourself to make love when you absolutely don't want to, while telling yourself that you are protecting his ego. Being untrue to yourself never works in the long run. Instead, the solution probably involves offering some kind of touch, cuddling, massage, and intimate contact most of the times that your partner approaches you.

If your mood is right, you may even offer to bring him to orgasm manually or orally, even though you yourself are not aroused. When approached, ask yourself what you can honestly give from the heart, without

The best way to hold a man is in your arms.

—Mae West

resentment. Offer that. Often, as in the case of Greg and Lucy, what you can willingly give will meet his need.

Learning to communicate honestly about your mutual needs goes a long way toward making it possible for those needs to be met most of the time. It might go like this:

He: "How about it tonight, sweetheart?"

She: "Well, if you mean would I throw you on the bed and lick you all over and then let you have your way with me, I don't think I'm up to it. But if a nice back rub and a chance to see if anything develops would do, I'd be up for that."

We learn to do something by doing it. There is no other way.
—John Holt

Most Men Love Partners Who Love Fellatio and Semen

Although oral sex is not every man's favorite sexual act, many men do love it. Giving her partner enthusiastic oral stimulation of his penis and

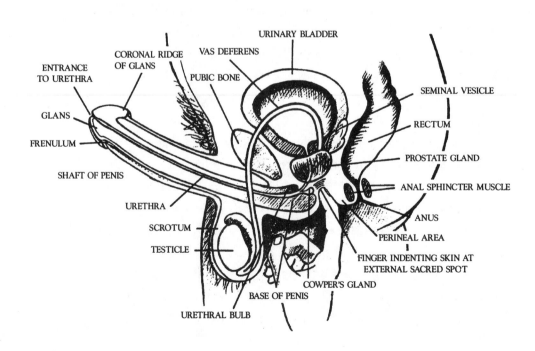

acceptance of his semen is one very important way a woman can communicate acceptance. It can seem like the ultimate way to say: "I treasure your body and all its functions as divine gifts. I love your body and everything about it because I love *you*."

If such a statement seems unthinkable now, do not condemn yourself. Most women feel anxious or queasy about behaviors such as this until we consciously work to change those attitudes. If you're a woman who hates semen or finds it disgusting, realize that you have been influenced by attitudes that are not consistent with a sacred view of our bodies.

The truth is that semen is not a waste product, *it is the life force in action*, a precious, life-giving fluid which has a mild taste. It contains, of course, the miraculous ability to fertilize an ovum and to determine human gender. It is a divine and natural gift, just as are menstrual blood and vaginal secretions.

This does not mean a woman must swallow semen when she orally stimulates her partner. She needn't swallow if the idea is disturbing. She can just ask him to let her know when he is about to come so that she can switch to manual or other stimulation before his orgasm. On the other hand, she may learn over time that swallowing need not seem unpleasant if she is in touch with the sacred nature of the acts she is sharing with her beloved.

As a woman, how do you come to this point of view, if right now you find semen unpleasant or worse? Gently, slowly, with time—have patience with yourself. Discuss your desire to make this attitude change with your partner and ask his help. He can help to create safety for you and encourage you to go at your own pace. Very small steps made systematically over time are best. If you dislike oral sex now, for example, you might start with twenty seconds of dry kissing of the sides of the penis and add tiny increments as you become comfortable.

... men's lack of skill in foreplay and their failure to understand its meaning, almost certainly substantially reflects the lack of tactile experience that such males have suffered in childhood.
—Ashley Montagu

Men See Sex as a Measure of Their Competence

Men fear failure as lovers, and many of their behaviors reflect this fear. Because women see sex primarily as a means of connecting, it can be difficult for them to appreciate a man's feeling that sex is an arena in which he can easily fail. Constant concern about evaluation follows naturally from our mechanistic approach to sexuality. When we think about sex in terms of numbers (How long? How often? How big?), we inevitably grade ourselves and expect that our partner will do the same.

Performance anxiety is rampant because we define "sex" as "intercourse until the man and (hopefully) the woman reach orgasm." If this is "sex," a man has to perform well or fail.

Here are some quotes from men:

- *"Sometimes, I just can't get it up, and it ruins everything."*

- *"When I lose my hard-on, I feel frustrated and embarrassed like a helpless schoolboy."*

- *"I was taught that sex was a sin, and even after twenty-one years of marriage, I still worry about that enough to get impotent often."*

- *"Whenever I start worrying about it, my erection is out the window. That makes me want to hide with shame."*

Women have difficulty understanding men's perspective on sexual failure. It's hard for a woman to know what it feels like to bear the executive responsibility for sex. Men feel that *they*—not their partners—are responsible for the success or failure of the sexual experience.

Whereas the woman's role is simply to show up, look good, and respond, the man's role is to "perform"—to get hard, stay hard, and direct activities until both he and she have had the requisite orgasm. Anything less than this means failure—and the person responsible for that failure is the sexual activity director, the man.

Erection Problems Make a Man Feel Incompetent

If the man is responsible for sexual "success," any event that qualifies as a sexual problem is his *fault*. Failure to get erect and stay erect long enough to satisfy his partner can feel like the worst of deficiencies.

A man who feels like a failure is *more* likely to lose his erection or his control over ejaculation; he is *less* likely to be able to improve in these areas if he feels anxious. A vicious cycle is set up because anxiety is one cause of problems with erection and control in the first place. More anxiety leads to more erection failures or more difficulties with control.

The remedy may lie in reducing anxiety. Give a man more confidence along with the tools for change and there will be fewer problems. Getting rid of the report-card approach to sexuality is the key.

As a couple, you can learn from adopting a crucial attitude about lovemaking: *No mistakes are possible.* Every sexual encounter has the potential for heart-to-heart connection and for some kind of pleasure. These can both occur easily regardless of erections or orgasms.

As a woman, there's a lot that you can do to help your man give up his feeling of executive responsibility for sexual success:

- *Communicate that he can give you pleasure whether or not his penis is hard.*

- *Learn to have orgasms in more than one way, and accept the idea that the orgasms he gives you with his fingers or mouth are just as good as those you have through contact with his penis. Touching yourself during or after intercourse is another completely acceptable option. The principle here is that a woman can be responsible for her own orgasms.*

Love keeps no record of wrongs.

—Apostle Paul

- *Help him remember the deeper purposes of lovemaking, such as
  affirming your sacred commitment, becoming closer emotionally
  and spiritually, and experiencing divine love in human form.*

Criticism Is Destructive

Feeling criticized is a most common problem, and one that can have
insidious effects. Hank and Janey, a couple in their forties, consulted me
because they were having many arguments about sex. Janey felt that Hank
was cold and unresponsive to her. Their lovemaking, she said, was "mechanical and routine." She rarely said anything to Hank about their sex
life that wasn't critical.

When I invited Hank to say what he felt about their problems, he
said, "What Janey doesn't understand is that every time she criticizes me,
I feel less like taking risks. I feel bad already that she's unsatisfied with
our sex life. I hate myself for being a man who can't even satisfy his wife."

One of the results of this impasse for Hank and Janey was the common situation in which Hank tried to make sex as quick as possible, to
his partner's distress. He wanted to get it over with before he could get
hurt again by her criticism. A lot of quick sex happens because the man
feels or fears sexual rejection.

The solution for this couple began with learning to communicate
mutual acceptance. Janey learned to take responsibility for her sexual
desires by communicating them without criticizing Hank. As Hank felt
more accepted, he became a more creative lover.

Men Need Encouragement to Be Passive at Times

Bill, age thirty-five, said this in a sexuality workshop: "I get so tired of
being in charge all the time. I run my office, I have most of the responsibility for supporting our family, and most of the time I feel like I'm

expected to be a take-charge guy when it comes to our sex life too. Sometimes I wish my wife would take over and just let me lie back and enjoy the ride." The men in the workshop agreed unanimously that they would like to feel less burdened with sexual responsibilities.

The message is: *Women, take over sometimes.* Teach your man that you can both enjoy having you be the more active partner. Offering him a chance to lie back and be taken care of is a way of inviting him to partake of divine love expressed through you.

The "night of service" described elsewhere is one of the best ways to experience the joys of being passive as well as of being the lover in charge of this occasion. Separating the roles of giver and receiver allows focused concentration on each role, its pleasures, and its potential for growth.

Your body is the harp of your soul, and it is yours to bring forth sweet music.
—Kahlil Gibran

A Man Needs to Be Taught That He Can Be a Superb Lover Whether or Not His Penis Is Hard

It is often within a woman's power to rescue her man from performance anxiety by learning to enjoy the pleasures of a "soft-on." Allowing him to feel that he is sexually useless without a hard penis is destructive for both partners. Viewing a partner in terms of the state of his or her body parts or biological responses misses the chance to give and receive love freely.

In an intimate relationship, a woman can give her partner the experience of being valued for his innate worth, rather than for what he produces. Making love with your beloved can be a new and unique dance each time, and there is no particular state your bodies must be in to enjoy it. It's more a matter of having an open heart.

A woman who communicates to her beloved that he is precious to her in every state—sexual arousal or no arousal—offers him a priceless gift. She can do this by allowing herself to experience the pleasure that he can give when his penis is soft, and then letting him know about that pleasure.

As a woman, you can enjoy his "soft-on" if you learn some new ways of interacting with it. Hold his soft penis gently and rub it against your clitoris. Play with it, stroke it, kiss it, suck it. Expect no particular response.

Share with your partner all the ways you can think of to experience physical pleasure from touch, such as kissing, massage, stroking, scratching, sucking, tapping, squeezing. Experimenting with lovemaking by agreeing to have no goal other than enjoying each other is the royal road to expanding pleasure options and decreasing anxiety about the state of his penis. Enjoy these experiences.

> *The words that enlighten the soul are more precious than jewels.*
>
> —Hazrat Trayat Khan

A Woman Can't Know What a Man Enjoys Unless He Tells Her

Each man, like each woman, is unique in his choice of sexual pleasures; a woman is very unlikely to *guess* the deep desires of his heart. To find out what they are, she must ask. She must ask in a context of acceptance in which he can feel that she is receptive to hearing what's true for him.

Vincent, a thirty-nine-year-old musician, explained his unique attitude this way: "The main turn-on to me in my sexual relationship with my wife isn't oral sex or any other particular sexual act. It's the rush of feeling connected and accepted and in touch with the woman I love. Sometimes I want to just do it with no talk and a lot of energy. Other times, I want to share some of the deep feelings we've built in our years together. What I like best is when she and I are in sync while we're making love. The particular things we do aren't nearly as important to me."

In contrast, twenty-four-year-old newlywed Ross shared his frustration in a counseling session: "I always wish that my wife would give me oral sex a lot and be enthusiastic about it. Shouldn't a woman who loves you know how to please you?"

The answer is no, whether you're twenty-four or seventy-four. Two myths account for the idea that your beloved should somehow be able to read your mind when it comes to lovemaking.

Myth 1: Being in love mysteriously enables lovers to know what their partners desire in lovemaking without being told.

Although it is true that lovers in the early romantic phase of a relationship often sense each other's feelings and desires, many people think that it follows that their sexual desires and preferences will always be sensed rather than need to be explained.

This myth ignores the fact that male and female anatomy and social conditioning are very different from each other, and certain aspects of these differences are very hard to appreciate from the other side of the fence. They are different enough that they must be explained to be appreciated, and even then understanding is often difficult.

No woman, for example, can know exactly how it feels to reach the point-of-no-return after which a man *must* ejaculate feels. No woman knows how it feels to have or to lose an erection. None knows what penile penetration feels like. A woman must be taught by a man how these events affect their lovemaking.

Myth 2: A sexually knowledgeable person will automatically be able to please and satisfy you.

This myth implies that all men or all women are alike, when the fact is that each person is sexually unique, and one's needs and desires can vary greatly from one lovemaking episode to another.

This means that however experienced a man may be, he still must learn his beloved's unique needs and preferences. He will learn these most effectively if she verbally explains them to him.

As a woman, it is your responsibility to tell your partner all of the following:

- *What kind of mood you need to be in to be receptive sexually.*

- *What he can do to help you get there.*

- *What kinds of touches and stroking are most enjoyable and arousing to you.*

- *What kinds of touches you dislike, for example, stroking the labia without lubrication.*

- *What your preferred way or ways of reaching orgasm are.*

- *What fears you have, or what traumas you may have experienced, that affect you sexually.*

- *How you feel about birth control and how you want him to assist.*

- *What kinds of sexual experiences bring you the most joy.*

∽

Inspired sexuality makes the burden of individuality bearable, and increases each person's momentum toward conciousness, compassion and communion.

—Sam Keen

Learning these answers and more about another person is a lifetime process. Accept the challenge and enjoy the journey!

Losses Can Influence Male Sexual Response in Unexpected Ways

Desmond had lost contact with his own young son and daughter through divorce. He tended to withdraw when Margaret's girls overwhelmed him with their needs for his attention. He also withdrew sexually from Margaret at times, and she had no idea why.

In therapy, Margaret learned how profoundly sad Desmond was over the loss of his own children. "When I spend a lot of time with your girls, I remember my own kids and how I miss them. I know my kids miss me too, and the closer I get to your kids, the more it reminds me of my loss and how it's never going to be repaired. I'll never get to read bedtime stories to my kids, and it tears me up." Desmond began to sob at this.

Margaret was touched when she had this experience of Desmond's reality. She knew what losing her children would have meant to her. She found compassion in her heart for Desmond, and became willing to assist him with the healing of his loss. Over time, as Desmond learned to mourn his loss, this couple experienced renewed closeness.

What Do Men Want?

How men really feel about sex is often a great mystery to women. In order to give a better picture of male sexuality, I asked men to describe their best and worst sexual experiences and to say what they wish women understood about male sexuality. Here are two revealing responses.

Every time you don't follow your inner guidance, you feel a loss of energy, loss of power, a sense of spiritual deadness.

—Shakti Gawain

～ Jason: A Long Road to True Passion

Jason, a thirty-three-year-old physician who works at an AIDS clinic, answered this way:

"My first wife, Sophia, and I had what I guess was my worst sexual relationship. She had been raised Catholic, and at first I thought that was why she was uptight about almost everything related to sex. I went along with her insistence on waiting until we got married to make love without restrictions. I'm Jewish, and was very young at the time. She convinced me that she wanted to wait because she was a woman of high moral standards.

"After the wedding, it turned out that she was really a woman of incredible anxiety about sex. Masturbation was horrible to her, oral sex was 'kinky,' and even foreplay was dubious to her if it involved anything that had the potential to get her really excited. I could barely touch her below the waist with my hands. 'Below the waist,' I had to touch her with my penis even though that often didn't seem to excite her very much. Putting my mouth on her vulva was unthinkable, and having her give oral sex to me couldn't even be discussed.

"She was young and beautiful, and I thought maybe it was just natural that a girl who was a virgin would take a while to get comfortable with sex. In other words, I thought she would grow out of her uptight attitudes. I was wrong.

"We stayed together six years, and thank God we never had children, even though she refused to use birth control. I bought sex books and videos, and I even went to talk to a priest once about how to get through the wall she had up about sex. Nothing worked.

"Sophia had bought into her mother's message that sex was basically dirty, except for procreation. She would show a shred of interest sometimes when she thought she was in her fertile time, because then sex was okay.

"The priest I went to told me that the sexual relationship of married people was a holy sacrament, and that since we were trying to conceive, it was okay from the Catholic point of view to have sex anytime, not just when we thought she was fertile. He said conception was supposed to be up to God. He was very understanding, and I came away feeling that it wasn't really the Church that was the problem, it was more Sophia herself and the way she had accepted her mother's teaching.

"The longer we went without conceiving, the less interested in sex Sophia became. I was really upset. Here I was a man in my twenties, feeling sexy most of the time, and my wife just seemed to have no interest. We went to a couple of counselors, but Sophia would never keep going to them long enough to get anywhere. She found something wrong with each one and refused to go back after the second or third visit.

"Finally, I gave up on the marriage. I had realized by then that I'm a highly sexual man and I just couldn't face a lifetime of the poor excuse for a sex life we had. I knew it could be a lot better and, as it turned out, I was right.

"I met my current wife, June, at the clinic where I work. I was slow to warm up to her because her physical appearance didn't quite match the picture I had in my mind. She was a little bit heavier than the ideal I used to imagine—not fat, just not bony and lean like I was used to. It's strange to remember that now, because now she seems exactly right to me.

"June is a nursing supervisor at the clinic, and she has a Jewish background like mine. I think that helps. Most of the time, it seems to make it a little easier for us to understand each other.

"Also, I've learned since my first marriage that Judaism has always had a very positive attitude toward sexuality. In celebrating the traditional Sabbath, for instance, Orthodox Jews are required to make love. Being sexual is part of being an observant Jew, which I'm not, but the attitude has probably influenced both of us. Maybe we have a little less built-in guilt than people from the more conservative Christian faiths—I don't know.

"I was very lucky to find June. She also has very strong ideas about sex, but they're *positive* ideas! Before I met her, she had experienced a lot of classes and read a lot of sexuality books.

"June said from the first that sex had to be 'more than just fucking.' Sophia would never have even used the word, so I really paid attention after June said that. She said that she wanted to have a 'spiritual bond' with her sexual partner. This was a whole new idea to me.

"It was even more amazing to me to find out that June was crazy about making love. She never seemed to get tired of it. And she liked everything! She loved oral sex—not only receiving, but giving it to me. She even lets me come in her mouth sometimes, and amazes me by saying she doesn't mind at all.

"Nowadays, I know what a spiritual bond is, because I have one with June. Most of the time, our lovemaking is a lot more than just sex. It's

One must . . . have one's own creative work and a sex life with oneself in addition to the sex in the relationship.
—Margo Woods

love and joy and a lot of closeness and treasuring of each other. It may sound strange, but sometimes when we make love, I feel really close to God. I've probably been influenced, too, by my work with dying people here. You start to feel closer to the Source of things when you see as many young men die as I have.

"I guess you can tell that I'm pretty excited about my wife and our sex life. This has been going on four years now and shows no signs of cooling off. Maybe it will when we're older, but even if that happens, I think I'm incredibly lucky!"

∾ Rusty: Learning the Value of Self-Pleasuring

Rusty, age forty-nine, is a high-school gym teacher and coach. He has been married to Tina, a grade-school teacher, for twenty-nine years. When asked about his best and worst sexual relationship, he said:

"I think my worst sexual relationship is the one I used to have with myself, if that makes any sense. I used to feel that my love of masturbation was a sleazy secret that I should hide from the world. Growing up as the son of a Methodist preacher in the South in the '40s and '50s, I learned that 'playing with yourself,' as we called it, was a nasty habit. It was 'the devil's work,' and my grandfather whispered to me once that it could 'ruin a fine mind.' My father even alluded to it in his sermons sometimes. He called it 'self-abuse.'

"So that was the official position of all the adults and church people I knew. The actual life of boys in our part of Alabama was a different story. By the time I was a teenager, we even had 'circle jerks' sometimes, where a bunch of boys would sit in a circle, masturbate, and see who could send his come the farthest. I enjoyed these times, but I felt guilty too, and I sure didn't talk about them.

"My guilt got worse as I got farther along in my teens and got into more masturbation. I was horny all the time and fantasizing about a different girl every day. I was jerking off almost every day, and really worrying that I was a wicked sex maniac. In spite of my guilt, I never could stop, but I made plenty of those vows to God that seem funny now: 'I'll never touch myself again if you'll just get Judy to say yes about Saturday night.'

"I married Tina when I was only twenty. Her mother taught health and sex education in another high school. Maybe that had something to do with how interested in sex and how passionate Tina seemed to be. I loved her, and I had high hopes for getting enough sex at last. We did make love a lot the first few years, and I really enjoyed it.

"Early on, I felt awful when I realized that I still wanted to touch myself sometimes. Pretty often, I did. Sometimes Tina wouldn't want to make love for a week at a time, especially during and after her period. That was too long for me. And then when she got pregnant, she wasn't interested for weeks at a time. I didn't want to cheat on her, so I would 'take care of myself,' as I thought of it, and then I would think about what a bad person I was, how I was sinful, and then I'd get quiet and sort of depressed.

"All this time, I kept my little secret from Tina. I was sure she'd be really upset with me if she knew I masturbated three or four times a week sometimes. A friend had told me that he'd had a major blowup with his wife when she found out about him doing the same thing. She thought it meant she didn't turn him on anymore and that the marriage was over. My friend said he'd decided that masturbation was something for kids, not for a married man.

"After he said that, we never talked about it again. I didn't feel like telling him I was doing it regularly, even though I was just as married as he was.

"For about three years, I made sure that Tina didn't find out about me. But things always seem to come out, don't they? One Saturday morning when I thought she had gone to the store, Tina walked in on me touching myself in bed. I was so close to coming that I couldn't stop, and she saw exactly what I was doing.

"What could I say? I was so much in shock, I didn't say anything. I just lay there waiting for her to start yelling at me.

"She didn't yell. She didn't say anything at first. She just smiled and came over to the bed and sat down by me and kissed me. 'I guess I interrupted something,' she said. What she said next really shocked me even more. She said, 'I do that too, you know. We should try it together sometime.'

"I was speechless. I didn't even know that women did it. I'd always thought she had a lower sex drive than I did, so why would she want to masturbate? And as far as doing it together was concerned, I had never heard of or thought of such a thing. I was a twenty-three-year-old Methodist kid from Alabama, and mutual masturbation was not on my list of possibilities.

"At that point, Tina and I had never talked a whole lot about sex. We weren't particularly shy about sex talk, but we were still young enough to believe that things were more romantic if you didn't discuss them. But now that the cat was out of the bag, we had to talk.

"That discussion was when I first realized how blessed I had been when I picked Tina to marry. Thanks to her God-fearing, Methodist, sex-education-teacher mother, Tina had healthy attitudes toward everything sexual. Especially masturbation, which she taught me to call 'self-pleasuring.'

'Mother says it's a *good* thing to do,' said Tina, 'a healthy thing. She says that counselors who help people with sex problems tell them to pleasure themselves so that they can get educated on how their bodies work. Mother also told me that almost all men and a lot of women pleasure themselves whether they're married or not. I just thought you were one of the few who didn't, because you never said anything about it.'

"I started feeling much better about myself after that. I realized that

Be content with what you have; rejoice in the way things are. When you realize there is nothing lacking, the whole world belongs to you.

—Lao Tzu

my self-pleasuring was just fine, that it was a gift from a loving God just as much as other kinds of sexuality are.

"My sexual relationship with my wife really took off after that, too. It was already good, but it started getting better and better. She's amazing and she's been my teacher and my cheering section all through our marriage. Thank God for my mother-in-law too, because I don't think Tina would be as open and sexually healthy as she is if it hadn't been for her mother."

"Impotence" as a Normal Variation

Lance was a thirty-seven-year-old engineer who consulted me just once. He had been "impotent" the night before for the first time and was terrified. His attractive wife had been understanding, but he had been unable to stop thinking about "the disaster."

"It never happened to me before, and I thought it never would. I've always been able to count on my interest and my ability where sex is concerned. The idea that I might be going downhill when I'm not even forty scares me something awful. If this got to be a habit, I couldn't stand it."

Lance was the occasional easy patient every therapist enjoys. It was a one-session cure.

I was not surprised to find out that "the disaster" happened after Lance had had several drinks. All that was required of me was letting Lance in on some fundamental facts about male sexual experience:

- *Every man has an occasional disappearing erection. Reaching thirty-seven without having this experience is unusual.*

- *Alcohol is very often a contributing factor. Because it lowers inhibitions, it may seem to stimulate desire, but it actually depresses many body functions for both men and women and has a negative effect on sexual response.*

- Losing an erection once (or several times) doesn't mean a man is becoming impotent; it may just mean he's having variations in desire.

- Anxiety is the main factor in turning a variation into a "disaster." A man can simply learn other ways to satisfy his partner, so that he knows that having an erection just at the moment his mind wants it is not crucial.

- The gift of this alleged problem lies in the invitation for a man to open up communication with his partner and find out what she actually feels and wants.

Lance came back the next day just to thank me. He and his wife had experienced a breakthrough. Erections and orgasms had taken care of themselves. His wife had told him that what she cared about most was feeling close to him. They began to talk about their love, their family, and their commitment in new ways.

So far as their lovemaking was concerned, Lance had found that when he stopped worrying about his erection, it usually came back. More important, his willingness to be vulnerable with his wife had opened the door to greater intimacy and mutual sharing.

Ben Speaks About His Life With Vanessa

The following story comes from Vanessa's husband, Ben. He is a dark-haired, olive-skinned, slender man of about Vanessa's height. He is a business executive whose hobby is coaching soccer in the inner city.

I was always a man who cared a lot about sex. When I was in my twenties, it was one of the main things I thought about. When I got married, sex was one of the most important reasons for taking the plunge. I wanted a sex partner who would always be there and, of course, I hoped she would love me too.

For the first ten years or so, sex was pretty good, but not fantastic. It was really great at the very beginning, but after a few years of living together and having kids, it started to get a little less terrific. We were tired a lot and always busy. The kids always seemed to need us, especially at times when we might have been able to get together. I sure remember those years when making love in the morning was almost sure to be interrupted by a kid's knock on the door or a scream for 'Mommy!' We both loved the kids, but raising them took its toll on us, especially while they were little.

As Vanessa told you, the biggest changes started when we went to that seminar on spiritual sexuality. This way of thinking about sex was completely new to both of us. I'm glad there were couples there who talked about their experience with it, because it helped me to believe that changing our attitudes in that direction could make a big difference.

It was hearing the discussion in the men's sessions that really got to me. They talked about how their sexual relationships had gotten so much better. They talked about things I'd never heard about.

The guys educated me. They told me that I could enjoy everything about sex more when I was the master of my sexual responses, instead of them running me. They told me that if I wanted my sex life with Vanessa to be more exciting and more satisfying, I had to learn some completely new ways of operating. One of the men, a big, burly executive who looked like a football player, surprised me by saying that since he had started to treat his sex life like a spiritual practice, it had changed completely and that he was in love with his wife again for the first time in fifteen years. I was skeptical, but intrigued.

When I began to open up to these ideas, our sex life really started changing. Vanessa started trying a lot of new things, too. She

✺

There are many advantages to making love without ejaculation. For men, you can enjoy making love more often, and you will not feel depleted. When you do ejaculate after containing your energy longer, your orgasm is stronger. Because you maintain an erection for a longer time, you can satisfy a woman more completely. . . .

—Margo Anand

got really good at touching me in some new ways and new places—it was great! We started feeling like kids again, except we knew a lot more than we knew then. We could laugh ourselves silly sometimes and then go on to make love in a way that felt amazing to us, considering how long we'd been together by then.

But the best thing was how close we got and have stayed. I'm not a poet or a big talker about things like this, but I will say that I love my wife more than I ever could have imagined when I was in my twenties, and the experiences we've had in bed in the last ten years make those early ones look like the warm-up they were.

A Few Final Words to Women

Your man is your window into the masculine aspect of the divine. His personal and sexual realities are very different from your own. If he loves you, his sexual desires are precious attempts to connect with you and to understand you.

You can learn to be with him sexually in a way that delights him *and* is true to your deep self. This evokes joy. Nothing less should be your goal.

Unless we are willing to explore the un-
known in ourselves and
in the other, and in the relations between
us, we will never
advance very far along the path of love.
—John Welwood

❧

CHAPTER 6

Sexual Communication: The Basis of Sexual Bonding

Communicating about sex takes courage. It is a priceless gift to give your partner, for it offers a window into another soul's intimate reality. It comes easier if partners understand that they are sharing a spiritual as well as a romantic journey.

Things change when you feel that your partner sees and cherishes your innate preciousness, your essence. When you understand that sexual communication is the holy work of relationship building, it becomes easier to find in your heart the willingness to learn to do it skillfully. That skill enables you to build a foundation for the relationship of dreams.

On a practical level, good sexual communication requires ease in using the specific words of sexuality; it's important to be able to say "penis" or "clitoris" or "orgasm" as easily as "toast, butter, and jam." Ease in making specific requests is also crucial: "Please suck hard right there!" or "Gently, gently!" or "Please do that again—oh, yes!" Because few of us grew up learning to communicate our needs, we must learn these skills as adults.

When I teach human sexuality and sex therapy to graduate students who are learning to be therapists, I sometimes challenge my students with a strange assignment. They are to use twenty-five "embarrassing" words about sex in conversation every day. My students are easy to spot on campus—they are the ones who sit in the student lounge talking about masturbation, testicles, the vulva, and the clitoris!

Of course, you don't need to be a graduate student to enjoy this experiment. Start now using the vocabulary of sex with someone close. Then branch out until you can talk about orgasm as easily as aerobics.

Men and women frequently tell me that their partners just won't talk to them about sex. Cary, a forty-six-year-old professor, consulted me in frustration. "My wife talks about everything from politics to religion to the details of the lives of every one of our relatives. But when I bring up our sex life—anything at all—she clams up. I can't get anything out of her, so I have no way of knowing what she wants, what she likes, or what she hates. I know she must have some complaints because she's not exactly chasing me around the house."

In a separate private session, Cary's wife Gena, an attractive, successful accountant, agreed that she disliked discussing sex. "It was absolutely never spoken about when I was growing up," she said. "It makes me very uncomfortable to have Cary quizzing me all the time. In the first place, I've told him I don't want to talk about it. Besides that, I don't know how to talk about it or what to say. And the worst thing is that if I did start telling him all my feelings about our sex life, I think he'd be devastated. How can you tell a man you've been married to for fourteen years that he doesn't know how to kiss you?"

Like many men and women, Gena grew up in a home where sex was not discussed. In her childhood home, any use of words referring to sex or intimate body parts was disapproved of or even punished. Gena is being asked to change a lifelong habit of silence on this very personal subject. She does not realize how damaging a no-talk rule like this can be in an intimate relationship.

When Cary let Gena know how deeply he wanted to please her sexually, she softened in her willingness to let him know what she liked and disliked. With my guidance, this couple learned to create a safe atmosphere for communication practice. Cary agreed to take the lead in verbalizing things, and Gena agreed to be an accepting listener.

When Gena had her first experience of finding out that her partner welcomed her comments and opinions and considered them a gift, she felt encouraged in her ability to let him know her feelings without being hurtful. When she finally was able to tell him her real preferences about kissing, he responded so well that they ended up deciding to study and experiment with "kissing as an art form." Gena and Cary learned the truth of a statement once made by pioneer psychologist Carl Rogers when he said that "The one thing that you think you *can't* discuss with your partner is the one thing you *must* discuss."

> *Only when you are fully able to say no will you become able to say yes! from your whole being.*
> —William Ashoka Ross

Letting Your Partner Know How You're Responding

The crucial question is this: When making love, does your partner know how you are responding at any given moment? Are you communicating your responses *constantly* either though sounds, words, breathing, or in some other way? Conversely, do you know how your partner is feeling about your lovemaking at any given moment? Is your partner communicating with you? Unless all the answers to these questions are in the affirmative, the feedback loop necessary to good lovemaking is not operating as it should.

Marlene, a thirty-three-year-old nurse, sat in my office with her thirty-four-year-old attorney husband, Norm. She had told me privately that she was not happy with the way he touched her when they made love. "He's too rough," she said. "When he touches me between my legs, it hurts."

I asked Marlene and Norm to do a short exercise. I asked Marlene to give Norm her hand and allow him to massage it.

When Norm was stroking and squeezing her hand, Marlene made no sound most of the time. Her facial expression did not change. At one point, she asked him not to press so hard. Otherwise, she said nothing. Within two minutes, the nature of this couple's communication problem was clear.

Marlene and Norm did not have an effective method of giving and receiving feedback when they touched each other. Marlene gave practically no feedback at all, unless something painful occurred. Norm did not ask her what she wanted. As a result of both choices, this man had little idea how to please his wife.

When Marlene learned to be more vocal and Norm learned to ask when he wanted to know something, things improved. They both had to learn to speak up when it was easier for them to be silent and imagine that the other knew their thoughts and feelings. Marlene learned that she could communicate just by sounds if she didn't feel like saying words. Norm learned that it was not so difficult to say "Does this feel good?" when that's what he wanted to know.

I invite you now to consider your communication with your partner. Whether the two of you discuss sex freely already, or whether you have never done so, please consider taking a giant step now. In your sexual relationship with your beloved, resolve to communicate more honestly, more clearly, and to say it all.

Few of us learned as children that developing our sexual communication abilities would someday become a way that we could grow spiritually. Few, if any of us learned that loving partners become more bonded if they discuss sex explicitly. Few of us learned to say "vagina" and "penis" along with "Goldilocks and the three bears." That would have been the ideal early training for the needs of an intimate relationship and for the sacred path of creating a lasting love.

Here are quotations from some of my clients. They show that if you're not used to communicating about sex, you're not alone:

- *Marvin, age thirty:* "My parents never said a word to me about sex. It was understood that I'd figure things out for myself. As a kid, I got the idea that in a religious home like ours, sex was an unmentionable subject."

- *Letty, age forty-nine:* "My parents were leaders in our church. They gave me the idea that talking about sex might lead to doing things you shouldn't do. My husband and I have never talked about sex in our twenty-nine years together."

- *Paul, age twenty-five:* "My little boy wants to know about babies, but I just give him kids' books because I don't know what to say. No one ever talked to me about sex, either. It comes naturally, doesn't it?"

- *Lilly, age fifty-three:* "My spouse and I talk about sex quite a bit, but there are important things I've never shared, because I'm scared I might hurt his feelings."

- *Cal, age thirty-six:* "My father said a few words to me as a teenager about being sure I never got a girl pregnant. He never said anything about making love. My teenage daughter used to ask me questions about sex, but I think she stopped because she could see how embarrassed I'd get."

- *Elsbeth, age seventy-one:* "Every time my husband touched me it felt like rape. We didn't even know enough to be sure that I was moist before sex. It hurt terribly every time, and after our third child was born, I stopped it permanently. We never discussed trying to make it better."

• *Armando, age twenty-one:* "I don't see any reason to talk and talk about sex. I prefer to do, not talk."

These men and women, like most of us, had no role models for sexual communication. While growing up, they had no practice in giving and receiving sexual information. No wonder it's difficult.

Accepting Explicit Sexual Communication as Holy Work

If you grew up in a family in which there was little or no discussion of sexuality, you may find yourself resisting the idea that specific sexual communication is necessary. It is not easy to accept that we must communicate our deepest sexual desires and fears, when we don't really know how to do so.

Once you understand how greatly male and female sexual realities differ, however, the necessity of putting your wishes into words becomes clear. A woman who wants fifteen minutes of pillow talk and caressing of her whole body prior to any touching of her breasts or genitals, may have a husband who thinks that touching her breasts and genitals as quickly as possible is the way to give her the greatest pleasure. Until this difference is put into words, they will be offending each other when trying to be physically close.

A man who longs for vigorous stroking of his penis may have a partner who finds firm pressure on her own genitals painful. She is unlikely to understand his need unless it is carefully explained to her. Unless he does that, she will almost certainly not understand that vigorous stroking communicates love and nurturing to him, whereas a gentle

There is something so inspirational about any relationship entered into with the acknowledgement of a higher dimension, that with just a little preparation most people can be taught to touch this new level of experience.
—Richard Moss

touch similar to the one she prefers makes him think she's lukewarm about lovemaking.

When you honestly acknowledge where you are now and begin to improve your skills, your sexual communication starts to flower. If you find it difficult to speak plainly about sex, begin by communicating that. Acknowledge your fears and discomfort. You might say, "I really don't know how to do this. I've never talked about these things, and I don't feel comfortable talking about them. But I'm willing to try, because I want so much to be closer to you."

If life and the soul are sacred the human body is sacred.
—Walt Whitman

Communication Safety Is Key

Because deep down we do not accept certain aspects of ourselves, we find it almost impossible to believe that our beloved can accept these disowned parts of us. It is extremely difficult to reveal yourself fully even when you have years of positive, loving experiences with someone.

It is safety that makes the difference. Safety is the foundation of open communication. Without perceived safety, you can be sure that your partner will not risk full self-disclosure.

Out of respect for the risk your partner takes when communicating openly, be sure that you are never a destroyer of confidence. We are all deeply vulnerable to the person whose bed we share. Criticism of technique, body parts, or anything unchangeable is detrimental to the safety good sex requires. It's also likely to come back to haunt you.

Intimate criticism is especially devastating—telling your partner that his penis or her breasts are "too" big, "too" small, or poorly formed is cruel and cannot be justified as "just being honest." It's really "just being hostile."

Safety means that each of you can be confident that communicating about your sexual feelings or wishes will not result in rejection or withdrawal by the other person. When you demonstrate that most of the time you can be accepting, your partner learns to feel safe revealing more.

Your goal here is to create such safe conditions in your relationship that each of you will be able to fully reveal your sexual needs and desires. This means getting across this message: *You can tell me anything. I want to hear about your sexual fantasies and your dreams. I want to know exactly what you like, what gives you the greatest pleasure, and how you'd like to experiment. I won't criticize you when you share these secrets with me. Definitely tell me what you like and don't like, and you don't have to justify your preferences. You can count on me not to criticize you or reject you because of anything you share with me about your likes and dislikes.*

What Gets In the Way of Communication?

Most likely, any hesitation you have toward talking freely about sex is a holdover from your childhood. Most of us got lots of messages about keeping our sexual questions and feelings under wraps. Our parents may have wanted to protect us or they may have been uncomfortable talking about sex. As an adult, though, you may choose to make your own, new decision: I choose to talk freely about sex so that I can have more passion and more joy.

Besides family influence, fear and a lack of experience are the main barriers to free expression. We fear what we may hear or what may come out if we engage in full communication. Nell, for instance, fears that her husband might ask her to disclose her past sexual experience, which she feels he would not approve of.

This concern can be put aside when you both agree that, at least in the early stages of deepening your communication, you will discuss only the present, not the past. Make exceptions to this only if you both feel completely comfortable doing so. Instead, limit your discussion of the past to childhood and early adolescence.

Once you have made a mutual agreement to listen without judging, each of you must make good on your promise. Your goal is to establish and maintain safety at all costs, because you know that if safety is compromised, communication will be undermined.

The Vocabulary of Sex

Here's a short list of words you should know and be comfortable using freely: *nipples, vulva, labia, clitoris, vagina, penis, testicles, anus, perineum,* and *orgasm.* Some teachers recommend the Sanskrit words for *vagina* and *penis*; they are *yoni*, which means "sacred space," and *lingam*, which means "wand of light." These words do not have the associations that the English words have for many of us, and so may be easier to use freely.

Have fun with this. It's good to laugh about sex and about ourselves. Try agreeing to exchange one verbally explicit message about sex with your partner at every meal. Mealtime conversation can take on new interest!

It's fine to use slang or other informal words so long as you mean no disrespect and your partner is not offended. "Ramming" a "rod" into a "pussy" may better capture your mood at times. Be sure, though, that you are allowing yourself to use tender words just as freely as lusty ones. It's important to develop a vocabulary extensive enough to communicate all that you want your partner to know.

Learning to Enjoy Communicating About Sex

Mel and Edith had never told each other what they wanted sexually. During their counseling, they accepted the idea that it was necessary and that it could be enjoyable.

When they began to practice "sex talk" at every meal, they frequently broke up in laughter. At dinner, when Edith said, "How was your day?" Mel replied, "I've been thinking today that I'd like you to stroke my penis harder—not so gently—when I start to get an erection." This was more interesting than the comment on rush-hour traffic Ruth had been expecting.

At meals when their children were present, Mel and Edith continued the exercise in modified form. Over Saturday lunch, Edith said, "I wonder if most people understand that the clitoris is the main organ of pleasure for women." "Yeah, it's the only organ in the human body that has no function except pleasure," Mel replied.

"You guys are weird!" their twelve-year-old daughter exclaimed, as their teenaged son added his agreement. Mel and Edith used this opportunity to tell their children that they were practicing sexual communication and trying to get comfortable using sexual words. Over time, what had at first seemed "weird" to the kids became normal.

A by-product of this couple's new communication skill was that they were much more equipped to teach their children the sexual information and values they wanted them to have. One of the most important of these values was the idea of a sexual relationship as holy and not to be entered into lightly. Being comfortable using a larger sexual vocabulary made it much easier to discuss sex and sexual values with their children.

Quantum Leaps Through Systematic Practice

Mel and Edith's story illustrates the importance of beginning to use a rich sexual vocabulary. The next step in achieving significant improvements in skill is systematic, regular communication practice.

Practice talking about sex until discussion of the vocabulary and concepts and values of sexuality becomes a regular part of your life. Talk about sex in concert with talk about spiritual goals and growth. This will reinforce the integration of these two precious areas of human experience. For example, you might tell your partner about some insight that has come to you through meditation or prayer in the same conversation in which you discuss something sexual.

Make an agreement to talk about sex several times a week. Five minutes in the morning and five minutes at night will do if that's all the time you have.

He (at breakfast): "How are you feeling about sex today, honey? Tell me what you'd like tonight if you could have anything at all."

She: "Tonight, I'd like you to spend fifteen minutes apiece on my breasts and nipples. I want you to touch every part of both breasts, gently and then harder. I want you to stroke my nipples with your fingers for a long time, squeezing the nipples gently. Then I want you to suck them for five minutes each."

After conversations like this at breakfast, partners start looking forward to coming home at night!

Reflective Listening Is a Vital Tool in Sacred Communication

Reflective listening, also called "mirroring" or "active listening," is the most vital communication skill you can master, particularly when discussing sex. It is a discipline whose practice demonstrates to your partner that you treasure his or her feelings and needs and want to fully understand them.

The essence of reflective listening is that after your partner tells you something, you paraphrase it and repeat it back, showing that you really heard the message. You then ask, "Did I get it right?" and "Is there more about that?" and listen to the answers. A reflective-listening transaction is complete when your partner acknowledges that he or she has been completely heard.

This technique short-circuits many arguments. If your partner makes a point of asserting that chocolate is better than vanilla and you say,

To be properly expressed a thing must proceed from within, moved by its form: it must come, not in from without but out from within.

—Meister Eckhart

"I understand that you like chocolate better," the conflict is over before it begins. You have not given up your preference for vanilla; you have simply heard and understood that your partner's preference is different than your own. If instead you begin to recite the many ways in which you feel vanilla is superior, a fight that is unlikely to accomplish anything has begun. Here's an example of reflective listening:

Irene: "I enjoy our lovemaking so much most of the time. But when you stop touching me right after you come, I feel disappointed and as if you don't care whether I'm satisfied too."

Charles: "What I hear you saying is that you enjoy our sex life most of the time, but you get disappointed when I stop doing anything as soon as I come. Is that right?"

Irene: "Yes."

Charles: "Is there more about that?" (Charles has just asked the crucial question that will reveal whether he got the whole message.)

Irene: "Yes, I also said that when you do that I feel as if you aren't interested in my satisfaction."

Charles: "So you're saying that not only do you get disappointed, but you start feeling that I'm only interested in my satisfaction, and not yours. Is there more about that?"

Irene: "No, that's it."

Harville Hendricks, in his outstanding book, *Getting the Love You Want*, about the healing of couple relationships, has added a valuable step to reflective listening which he calls "mirroring." After the process just illustrated in the example of Charles and Irene, Hendricks suggests *validating* your partner's viewpoint to show empathy. So, for example, after your partner has confirmed that you have heard the message correctly, you say something like, "I can understand how you would feel that way. It makes sense."

It's crucial to understand that *validating another person's point of view is not the same as agreeing.* Once you understand that, it becomes much easier to validate any viewpoint your partner wants to express. Hearing your partner out and validating his or her views will prevent or shorten many conflicts in your relationship.

In the example of Charles and Irene, Charles needs to add validation after he has heard Irene out. He could say, "So I hear that you feel disappointed and not cared for when I come first and don't do anything more for you. I can understand how you could feel that way."

Charles and Irene must now go on to address the behavioral change Irene is preparing to request. They have laid a good foundation for problem solving, by making sure the initial message was clearly received and by giving the sender a chance to feel understood. Irene is now more likely to want to hear and understand Charles when he sends a message about his side of this issue, and they are more likely to come up with a solution.

Reflective listening is a vital skill. Practice it until you achieve mastery, because it can turn fruitless, hurtful conflict into true problem solving and relationship building. In sexual matters, it enables you to send and receive crucial information without getting sidetracked by conflict or hurt feelings.

⌁

Love is what you've been through with somebody.

–James Thurber

Commonly Asked Questions About Sexual Communication

Learning to be verbally communicative about sex is a true challenge for many of us. The following questions are often asked by my clients and lecture audiences. They address some of the concerns that people often have when they begin to let their partners know about their sexual wishes and worries.

⌁ Fear of Hurting Feelings

Q: I'm afraid that my husband's feelings will be hurt if I let him know how much I wish he'd change some of the ways he makes love to me. He really wants to feel that he's a good lover, and I don't want to take that away from him.

A: Good lovers want to know how to please their partners. Chances are your husband really longs to know exactly what you like. The more he meets your needs (and vice versa, of course), the better the sex will be for both of you.

The key is learning to be skillful about how you tell your partner about your desires. There are three things to consider:

1. Choose your timing carefully. The best times are usually *not* while you are in bed or about to make love. For any complex relationship issue—including sexual ones—it's best to establish the custom of making an appointment to discuss a problem. Say, "When you have time, I have a problem I'd like to discuss." Or, "Are you available now to discuss a problem?" The answer to either of these questions, by agreement, is either "Yes" or "No, but I'm willing to do it . . .", finishing in the statement with a designated time within the next few days.

2. Give positive rather than negative messages. Talk about what you like rather than criticize him or her. Instead of saying, "Don't touch me that way," say, "Stroke me really softly right there, please; it feels so good that way." Or say, "I like fifteen or twenty minutes of cuddling and making out before we have intercourse," rather than, "You always start intercourse before I'm ready."

3. Realize that it's a gift to let your partner in on how you feel about any aspect of your intimate life. *Protect your partner from your resentments* by being sure that you have clearly communicated your wishes. If you allow him or her to touch you in ways you don't enjoy, you will accumulate a bundle of resentments that will come out one way or another. Better to risk saying even that which seems difficult to say.

✎ Partners Who Refuse to Talk About Sex

Q: I can't get my partner to talk about sex. When I ask questions like, "Do you like this position?" the only answer I get is, "Whatever you like, honey." When I ask what I can do to give more pleasure, the answer I get is, "Everything you do feels good." What can I do about this? I think my partner is happy with our sex life, but how can I know for sure?

A: Your partner probably grew up in a family in which sex was absolutely not discussed. Using the principles in this chapter, convince your partner that you will not punish, criticize, or reject if you are told something that may seem like a complaint. Be especially alert to be accepting and encouraging after the first few attempts to start communicating.

Encourage your partner to start with very small, nonthreatening steps, such as giving a one-sentence answer to some easy question you ask. Add small steps slowly.

These suggestions ask a lot of you—in a way, they ask you to function like a therapist with your partner. If this seems too much to ask, consider a few sessions with a professional who can teach while both of you practice.

✎ The Difficulty of Discussing the Spiritual

Q: I find it more difficult to communicate about spiritual things than about sex. Talking about orgasms or genitals is easy, but talking about God or anything I can't see or touch is really hard for me. I'm not sure I believe in any of this stuff. Maybe it's just wishful thinking. I do have deep feelings that I think of as spiritual sometimes, usually when I'm out in nature alone. It's not something I feel comfortable talking about, and when my partner asks me to, I can't think of anything to say.

A: Your feelings are shared by many women and even more men. Many of us have no experience talking about our spiritual feelings. For those of us who place strong value on appearing to be competent and in control, speaking honestly about that which we know little or nothing can be intimidating. Two keys to beginning new journeys are: Start small and set yourself up to succeed.

Starting small could mean beginning by talking about your fear and discomfort. You might say, "Talking about this stuff really makes me uncomfortable." Later, if you can bring yourself to acknowledge your longing to experience something greater that ordinary, concrete reality, that will be the first step in actually having spiritual experiences. The Light will come to you if you welcome it.

⮂ Difficulties with Sexual Communication

Q: Why should an educated person have so much trouble talking about sex? I have a master's degree and I've taken sex education. I know the formal words for parts of the body, but it doesn't seem to help much; when I'm actually trying to explain something to my spouse, I get tongue-tied. I don't know why this is so hard for me.

A: You are not alone. It's doubtful that the Ph.D.s of America are any more skilled than the sixth-grade graduates when it comes to talking freely about sex. It takes attitude change, practice, and the good sexual vocabulary we've mentioned.

All journeys begin with small steps. Set the goal of talking about one easy aspect of sexuality with your partner. Say that you need support as you practice. Then go for it: Say your piece, ask for feedback, answer any questions. Acknowledge your own courage. The next time, choose a slightly more difficult topic.

⮂ Saying It Once Isn't Enough

Q: My husband doesn't seem to get it when I finally work up the courage to tell him something about my sexual likes and dislikes. I told him a couple of times that I don't like it when he grabs for my crotch when we've barely begun to touch each other. But before long, he did the same thing again, as if I'd never said anything. This discourages me from trying to risk explaining things to him. What should I do?

A: Expect that many lessons need to be repeated over and over before they are really assimilated. Trying to communicate these sexual subtleties across gender lines is something like Americans trying to convince Asians that potatoes are better than rice—the audience has no experience that validates the unfamiliar viewpoint.

Repetition is key when you are learning a foreign language. Repetition is also crucial when learning the other gender's sexual reality. If he still ignores you after several repetitions, make plans to lovingly confront him about it.

You might say, "I love making love with you, and there are so many things I appreciate about our sexual relationship." Then express your feelings honestly. For example, "I feel hurt and angry when you ignore something I've told you several times about our lovemaking. I start feeling like you don't care how I feel when we make love, even though I know that isn't true. I want to tell you again, and then I want to hear you say it back to me, so I know you got it." Then use the reflective-listening technique described previously.

∽ Fear of Secrets Coming Out

Q: I have a secret that I'm afraid might come out if my spouse and I started really talking. I did something I'm not proud of and I don't think my partner could forgive me for it.

A: Establish a mutual agreement that you will open up channels of communication about the present. The question of past secrets is a separate issue. It's best to be skilled communicators before you consider opening this door.

Much has been written on the subject of whether you should disclose past behaviors that may not sit well with your partner. Some counselors

When the modern mind reduces sex to a gross bodily function or to an animal instinct, it engages in a form of sacrilege. . . . We cannot fully appreciate [sexuality's] transformative quality unless we connect with our elemental wild spirit. In this mystery lies the awakening power and sacredness of sex.
—Sam Keen

take the position that telling your partner about an affair, for instance, involves dumping your suffering on your partner, rather than handling the guilt and tension yourself. Others assert that emotional intimacy cannot coexist with secrets.

Spiritual sexuality asks you to seek divine guidance toward the highest path when you are faced with a decision such as this. No other person—not even an "expert"—can decide this for you.

You don't have to settle this issue to begin opening up the channels of sexual communication with your spouse. Just agree from the outset that you both will be focusing on an exchange of present feelings, thoughts and wishes.

∾ Confessing Faked Orgasms

Q: I've never told my husband of ten years that I don't have orgasms with him. I learned to be a skillful fake when we were first married, and he's always assumed everything is fine. How can I tell him now?

A: I have counseled a number of couples in this situation. Wendel and Lea were one example. They had been married for twelve years when Lea finally revealed to Wendel that she never had orgasms when making love with him, although she did have them when she pleasured herself.

Wendel was very upset at first. He felt deceived and "like a failure as a lover." He softened when Lea let him know that she had anticipated these feelings and because of them had not revealed herself before. She also told him that she had kept this secret because she had felt bad about herself. She felt that she was inadequate as a woman, that there must be something wrong with her.

Opening up their communication was the key to solving this couple's problem. I helped them to understand each other's position and then to forgive themselves and each other. Then Lea was able to teach Wendel how she needed to be touched in order to come to orgasm. Soon their problem was solved and both were much more satisfied with their lovemaking. An important bonus was the increase in their feeling of understanding each other. They also felt more confident that they would be able to solve any future problems that came up.

⟶ Revealing Rape

Q: I have reason to suspect that my wife was raped when she was in high school, though she's never said anything about it. If we start really communicating, it might come out, and I don't know if I could handle it.

A: If your wife was in fact raped, it would be a good thing for it to "come out." The isolation rape survivors feel is made worse by the fact that may feel they can't discuss their pain with loved ones. Family members are sometimes more concerned with protecting themselves against guilt or the pain of empathizing than with supporting the one who was victimized.

Regardless of whether or not she talks about it, if your wife was raped, you can be sure the effects are very much with her. Being unable to discuss it with her sexual partner cannot be good for her. Having a no-talk rule about this is not good for you either. It means that an important barrier to emotional intimacy lies between you.

Your concern about being able to handle it is understandable. However, the way you put it seems to imply that you should be able to make everything all right for her. That isn't possible.

Rape survivors need treatment by a counselor who specializes in sexual assault. They need to fully express their hurt, rage, fear, and guilt, as well as to mourn the loss of trust they feel. They need to forgive themselves, because victims almost always blame themselves deep down, even though they know better intellectually. Often, the partners of rape victims need help in expressing all the emotions they feel, too. This is not something to try to handle by yourself.

All you need to do to receive guidance is to ask for it and then listen.

—Sanaya Roman

Get professional help alone if you can't bring yourself to talk openly about this to your wife. You both deserve to free yourselves from a burden you were unfairly given. With good treatment, a full recovery is absolutely possible.

ᕃ Am I Normal?

Q: I'm afraid that the sexual acts I really long for aren't normal and that this would come out if we started to really talk. Isn't it better to keep quiet about some things?

A: Perhaps, but keeping quiet about your wishes and fantasies means that you cannot have real intimacy with your partner. Also, your fears about being "normal" are very widespread and probably unnecessary.

Anything both you and your spouse want to do sexually is "normal" if it causes no harm or pain to either of you. Here are only a few categories of things that are absolutely "normal":

- *Any sexual position you both like.*

- *Touching any part of your body to any part of your partner's body.*

- *Fantasizing about sex with anyone, anywhere, including one or more of the most inappropriate, unlikely, and unavailable partners of either gender.*

- *Wanting to discuss your fantasies.*

- *Wanting to keep your fantasies to yourself.*

- *Having "sex" only on rare occasions.*

- *Having "sex" several times daily.*

- *Making lots of noise when you make love.*

- *Being very quiet when you make love.*

- *Touching yourself in any way that feels good when alone or with your partner.*

- *Using any kind of harmless sex toy such as a vibrator or a dildo.*

- *Having fears about showing all of your body.*

- *Being afraid you won't "perform" well.*

- *Being afraid you will come quickly, won't stay erect, or that you won't come at all.*

- *Enjoying watching explicit sexual acts on film or video.*

- *Worrying about being normal.*

If your secret desire is not covered by this list, consider it in terms of these guidelines: Is it loving? Is it safe? If the answers are yes, it's "normal."

It's always a matter of how you hold the act in question. If you see all of these behaviors as part of your sacred journey of sexual sharing with your partner, they can be enriching.

> *We need to be willing to let our intuition guide us, and then be willing to follow that guidance directly and fearlessly.*
>
> —Shakti Gawain

∽ Communication Exercises ∽

The following exercises offer you opportunities to improve or deepen your sexual communication with your partner. To do any of them, allow a minimum of fifteen minutes when you will not be disturbed. Put children to bed and turn off the phone and the TV. Begin with a few moments of prayer or meditation. Envision the beautiful spiritual being and the luminous child within yourself and within your partner.

∽ Interviewing Each Other

Interviewing each other can help you provide a foundation of understanding of each other's sexual reality. These guidelines are divided into three levels. Level I is for those millions who have never talked freely about sex with each other. Couples who do talk but who have been afraid to talk freely should continue through Level II. Level III is for couples who think of themselves as advanced communicators, to assist them in communicating even more deeply.

Level I

1. What would your ideal sexual relationship be like?

2. What do you think would help you feel that our sexual relationship is really a part of our spiritual growth?

3. Tell me one or two things you like now or have liked in the past about our sexual relationship.

4. If we included music or poetry or meditation in some of our sexual experiences, what selections would you make?

5. Tell me one thing you like about your body and one thing you like about mine.

Level II

1. What are your favorite sexual touches? Are there any touches you don't like? What are they?

2. What touches you the most spiritually? Can you imagine learning to feel that our sexual relationship is a holy part of our spiritual lives?

3. What is your favorite way to come to orgasm? When you give yourself an orgasm, how do you do it? Will you show me sometime?

4. What fears or worries do you have about spiritual sex?

5. Tell me one sexual fantasy that turns you on.

6. What keeps you from enjoying sex as much as you could?

7. Tell me one thing you really like about our sexual relationship.

Level III

1. Please tell me one secret sexual desire that you've never told me.

2. Tell me about a time when we made love that was one of the very best times for you. Tell me about the time you remember feeling closest to me. Was this the same time?

3. Tell me about a time when our lovemaking wasn't good for you, but you didn't tell me. What went wrong and how did you feel afterward?

4. If you could choose one or two intimate caresses that I could do for a much longer time than usual, what would they be?

5. Tell me the things that are hardest to say—the things about our sexual relationship that trouble you but which we haven't talked about.

6. What makes you feel closest to God, and how do you think we can bring our awareness of the divine more into our sexual relationship?

∾ Expressing Withheld Communications

In this exercise, you will practice the reflective-listening technique. Decide who will be the sender and who will be the receiver. The receiver begins by quieting his or her mind and preparing to listen well. During the exercise, do not respond to what your partner tells you except to reflect and validate. Your turn will come later.

The sender begins by offering one or more acknowledgments. The receiver listens carefully and then reflects, using the instructions above. When the answer to "Is there more about that?" is "no," the sender goes on to the next message.

Now both of you should write down or verbally share two sexual "withholds," that is, two instances in which you have felt something or wished something but have not felt able to say so.

Take turns communicating these withholds using reflective listening. As receiver, do not comment on the message—just reflect it. Discuss and respond only after each of you has had a chance to state two withholds and hear your partner reflect them.

When our hearts and minds are open to the energetic possibilities of sex, we can learn to channel the powerful transcendent forces that can be aroused.

—Margo Anand

ᔐ Affirming the Sacred

If you as a couple have already learned to talk about your feelings and your bodies and your lovemaking, you may be ready to deepen your shared sexual experience. Consider directly accessing your connection to God or your Higher Power as you define it, and bringing that connection into the bedroom.

The first step can be opening up your communication to include the sacred. Share with your partner your feelings and experiences of God, of Higher Power, of divine love. Share any mystical experiences you may have been blessed with.

Actively seek divine guidance in your sexual life with each other. Ask directly for blessings on every aspect of your sexual exchange.

Complete the following phrases for your partner's benefit and add any additional ones that come to you. Revise in any way you wish.

"I feel closest to God (or Spirit or Higher Power) when . . ."

"I thank God for you and for our love and I am especially grateful for . . ."

"I affirm my gratitude for our bodies and their exquisite pleasures."

The Joys of Sexual Communication: Vanessa

Vanessa and Ben, like most couples, had serious communication deficits early in their relationship. Here Vanessa explains how things improved.

When Ben and I were first married, Ben told me that sex was supposed to come naturally to married people who loved each other and that he didn't see any reason to have to talk about it. I took this to heart, because in those days, I thought my role in the relationship with my husband was to be the follower.

I was also afraid of hurting his ego if I complained about anything, or if I started being what I had heard him refer to as a "sexual traffic cop"—a woman who keeps telling her partner what to do instead of just enjoying things. Another rationalization I used for not talking about sex very much was that we enjoyed our sex life so much in our early years. Things seemed to be going well without much discussion.

As I mentioned earlier, I once wrote Ben a pretty revealing letter about our sex life. That led to a time when we really felt in sync for a few years. But that changed when I became pregnant the first time. While I was pregnant, I felt completely different about sex, and I didn't know how to explain it to Ben. He kept expecting me to feel and act the same way I always had, but I couldn't. I know now that he felt rejected a lot and hurt about it, but all I understood at the time was that he was pressuring me about sex and that he had no clue what I was feeling.

I'm really grateful that our doctor recommended sex therapy to us, because we never would have even considered such a thing. We didn't even know that sex therapists often concentrate on teaching couples to communicate about sex. Our therapist really helped us with that. She gave us verbal exercises to do at home, where we had to start using all the sexual words we had never been comfortable with. She helped me explain everything to Ben about how my body was changing and how my sexual needs were different now that I was getting very pregnant.

In other homework exercises, I had to tell Ben "seven facts about my clitoris" and he had to tell me "five ways I like you to touch my penis." Our therapist also had us tell each other the details of three sexual fantasies, using all the anatomical words involved. We also had assignments to talk very specifically about "what turns me on the most" and "what helps me to have the best orgasms."

We started to enjoy this kind of talk. We started laughing a lot, partly because we felt sort of ridiculous at first. After we got more comfortable, we continued letting ourselves be playful. We started understanding that we didn't have to always be so serious about sex.

The next time we had a conflict about sex, we were ready for it, meaning that we were able to discuss it. That time it was Ben who had a problem. He was getting a little older by then, and he needed me to touch him more on his penis when we were starting to make love. The old pattern of him getting erect as soon as we started kissing was changing. Luckily for us, we were able to talk about it and we already had books we could use to educate ourselves about what was happening. I really think we might have had a serious problem at that point if we hadn't been good communicators by then.

To love is to return to a home we never left, to remember who we are.

—Sam Keen

Our communication has really developed. It's a piece of cake for me to say the most specific things, like, "Please lick my clitoris for a while, sweetheart," if that's what I'm wanting. Ben is also really comfortable telling me what he wants. Usually, it's some experiment he's read about and wants to try.

I know we wouldn't understand each other as well as we do now—not even close—if we hadn't learned to really talk about the specifics of sex. It's made us true partners in a way nothing else could have done.

Connecting with the Light

Learning to communicate your deepest sexual desires, fantasies, and fears to your beloved is a gift beyond measure. We are alone on this planet until we connect with others and with the Light or Higher Power. Our ability to love often lies dormant until we learn how to connect on a heart-to-heart level. Skillful, full, and courageous communication is our best tool for bonding deeply with our beloved.

Believe in a love that is being
stored up for you like an inherit-
ance, and have faith that in this
love there is a strength and a
blessing so large that you can travel
as far as you wish without
having to step outside it.
—Rainer Maria Rilke

CHAPTER 7

Powerful Tools for Passionate Bonding

Learning to experience sex as sacred requires tools that come from a Source deep within us. We need much more than new ways to touch or thrust. We start with a new consciousness about the relationship between sex and spirituality, a basic understanding of male and female sexuality, and well-developed communication skills. Most important, we need the power of our own intention to grow sexually.

This chapter offers tools that can help you create a sexual relationship that is physically, emotionally, and spiritually fulfilling. These are self-development and relationship tools. They are useful in every area of personal growth, but here they are adapted for your use in sexual matters.

Tools for Opening to Spirit

～ Asking

Ask and ye shall receive. Knock and the door shall be opened. These words allude to one of the simplest but most powerful methods of accessing more sense of the sacred in all situations as well as of manifesting our dreams. All that is required of us is to ask. Ask in whatever way is meaningful to you. If you long for more spirituality but are uncertain how to move in that direction, asking is a good place to begin.

Your request can be as simple as: "Lord, help me to feel your presence in these precious moments with my beloved." Or, when beginning to make love, you might silently request, "Help me to feel the Mystery in this experience." In any situation, you might say, "Inner Self, in this moment I resolve to feel your depths."

Asking is even more powerful "when two or three are gathered together." In other words, you and your partner can ask in unison. Try this prior to making love. Simply sit together in silence and, with or without words, ask for guidance. Ask for Spirit to manifest in your shared experience. Ask also that your partner willingly share the sacred journey with you.

～ Praying

Someone has said that the only prayer we ever need is "Thank you, God." This captures the essence of a process that is meant to bring us more in tune with the divine.

If you are comfortable with a particular prayer tradition, use it daily, particularly prior to and during any event that you would like to experience as sacred.

If you don't know any prayers, creating them is simplicity itself. Sim-

> ～
> *I myself do nothing. The Holy Spirit accomplishes all through me.*
> —William Blake

ply acknowledge that for which you are grateful. Whether you address "God," "Higher Power," "Inner Light," or, like Sam Keen, "an unknown God," the acknowledgment itself makes the difference.

If composing a prayer seems difficult, try this one by George Herbert:

> *Thou that hast given so much to me,*
> *Give one thing more, a grateful heart.*

∽ Meditating

Prayer is when we talk to God and *meditation* is when we listen. Meditation offers a direct way to access our spirituality; it is focused concentration. It quiets the mind and allows the heart to open.

Meditation has been shown to have value in the treatment of stress and of many stress-related illnesses. This includes mental difficulties such as anxiety attacks and social anxiety, and physical problems like migraine headaches, high blood pressure, and irritable bowel syndrome.

Meditation has great value in allowing an individual or couple to move beyond focusing on the mundane aspects of daily life and come into contact with the spiritual dimension. Even five minutes of meditation can make a difference in your day.

If you have never meditated, how do you begin? There are many methods you can study, or you can develop your own. Here's one approach that you can follow or adapt:

In a relaxed state, sit comfortably in a chair or on the floor with your spine straight. Breathe deeply and allow your eyes to close.

You may wish to use a sacred word that serves to focus your attention on a higher reality and helps you maintain focus in spite of your mind's tendency to bombard you with critical or irrelevant thoughts. Choose a word which touches you. It can be an English word like *peace, love,* or *beauty,* or a biblical word such as *grace* or *Creator.* Some people prefer words from other languages such as Sanskrit, Hebrew, or Aramaic.

∽

What is necessary, after all, is only this: solitude, vast inner solitude. To walk inside yourself and meet no one for hours . . . .

–Rilke

Consider *ohm* (God), or *shem* (light) or *shalom* (peace) or *om namaha shivaya* (I bow to the inner self). Sitting quietly, breathing deeply, and repeating your sacred word can put you into a meditative state quickly.

Wayne Dyer, in *Real Magic*, offers this method for entering a meditative state. He advises visualizing a clock with brightly lit numbers from 1 to 24. In your mind, "see" the clock shift down, now lighting up the number 23. Continue down to 1, "seeing" each number light up in sequence. If at any time along the way you become distracted or a fleeting thought comes into your mind even for a second, you must start the clock over again at 24 and work it back to 1 without any intervening thoughts or mental distractions.

This discipline teaches you to concentrate on one thing and to empty your mind of all other thoughts. It takes a lot of focused practice to learn to get all the way to 1 from 24, and doing so is a great achievement! It can lead to a state of lightness, joy, and peace.

Other ways to meditate include meditation while running, walking, or cleaning house. Focusing attention and consistency of practice are the keys to experiencing the benefits meditation offers.

ᴄ Meditating with Your Partner

Whether you and your partner have similar or different belief systems about spiritual matters, you can become closer by meditating together. It's an experience that helps you to see each other with new eyes.

Experiment with a time of shared meditation. Make it your mutual intent to connect with each other's hearts. Breathing deeply, consciously send loving energy to each other. Visualize being in complete attunement and harmony with one another.

Cultivating Beginner's Mind

Author John Welwood helps us understand why loving relationships are so difficult in our time. He says it's because we have tremendous expectations for our romantic lives, but we don't have the spiritual and emotional maturity necessary to manifest our vision. In *The Journey of the Heart*, Welwood teaches us that considering our limitations, the best strategy is *beginner's mind*. This means acknowledging that the answer to many relationship dilemmas is "I don't know."

Facing the "I don't know" free of old stories and interpretations first causes discomfort. Acknowledging our uncertainty though, allows us to bring fresh perspectives to the relationship.

"The truth is that two people can never completely penetrate the mystery of their connection," he writes. Our most familiar relationships, in other words, have much undiscovered potential.

The renewal of a sexual relationship that has foundered on familiarity and conflict can begin with an acknowledgment of that new territory. When we put aside our stories and evaluations of our partner, the next sexual touch can be profoundly sacred, deeply meaningful, and *new*. When we learn to be fully present in *this* moment, we become more able to treat each sexual experience as if it were our first.

The practice of beginner's mind is simple and difficult at the same time. At each point of conflict or feeling of disagreeable routine, remind yourself that "I don't know. I don't know what to do about this problem. *I don't know*. But I am willing to stay open and see what happens."

> ◡
>
> *We must accept that this creative pulse within us is God's creative pulse itself.*
>
> –Joseph Childon Pearce

Creating an Inner Vision

What we think is what we manifest. As old adage says, "Be careful what you ask for–you may get it." Shakti Gawain, in *Creative Visualization*, teaches the essential elements of this proactive process. She makes clear that accomplishing anything starts with visualizing exactly what you want in vivid detail. Then focus on it, dwell on it, and *speak about it and experience it as if were already real.*

All purposeful human change begins this way. What we can "see" in our mind's eye, we can manifest in reality. Outcome studies of such diverse pursuits as peak performance in athletics and success in psychotherapy show that the common denominator of success is knowing what you want to achieve and visualizing it over and over.

Vague or nebulous goals are an invitation to get nowhere. Wanting to have a "better relationship" is an example of an unclear goal. Better than what? How will you know when you've reached that goal? Feelings are also poor choices as goals, because feelings change like the weather. Choose measurable objectives when possible.

Even in the case of spiritual or emotional concerns, try to establish a *behavioral* objective. For example, "My partner and I affirm our spiritual commitment by meditating together every day." Use a daily planner or other means of tracking your goals. Write them down and help each other keep a record your progress.

Visualization is not the same as having undesired thoughts cross our minds. We continuously generate a tapestry of thoughts, feelings, and fantasies. These come to us with little choice, the effects of a mysterious mix of childhood experience and current stimuli. Often, in fact, we imagine things we consciously fear or reject, such as accidents or illness. "Cancel, cancel!" is the best response to such unwelcome thoughts. Then return to the positive visualizing of what you do desire.

Take some time now to write down your vision of the sexual relationship that fulfills your deepest longings. As with all creative visualizations, write it in the present tense, as though it were today's reality. If making an audiotape is more comfortable for you, do that. Be sure to include comments on your acceptance of each other, your willingness to experiment, your deepening communication skills, and your affirmation of the spiritual.

I will share my own visualization with you:

"I now enjoy a deeply satisfying sexual relationship with my life partner. We are fully committed to each other and to our sexual and spiritual growth. We trust each other fully and we both treasure the sexual relationship that we share. We enjoy it in all its forms.

"At times, we are outrageously passionate. At other times, we are sweetly tender or so playful that we can't stop laughing. Sometimes, lovemaking is no more than a simple comfort after a hard day. Other times, we have peak experiences in which we feel closer to each other than we ever would have believed possible.

"My partner and I are courageous about sexual experimentation. We try things that seem strange and forbidden at times. Usually, when one of us has a new idea, the other will be willing to try it out when the mood is right. At the same time, we are both willing to be told no or to stop something if the other isn't enjoying it.

"We don't need a script for lovemaking. It doesn't have to go any particular way to be a joyful experience. If the erection or the orgasm we had in mind isn't forthcoming, we just shift gears and do something else. We have had some wonderful experiences this way. Other times, when we've realized we were feeling like we were working instead of playing, we've decided that sleep was better than more effort. It's all part of the process. We treasure each other and our sexual partnership so much that we both feel that there's no such thing as a failure.

"We give each other lots of affirmation. We enjoy each other's bodies and we say so. We accept each other's flaws and our own flaws as the imperfections of being human. We treasure our imperfections! We both pay attention to nutrition and exercise, and we try to give each other the gift of being as fit as we can, but we don't try to match Madison Avenue standards.

As bees gather honey, so we collect what is sweetest out of all things and build Him.

—Rilke

"The spiritual connection we share is the most important part of our relationship and of our lovemaking. We see the Light in each other's eyes and we often feel it when we make love. We agree that our mutual spiritual growth is the ultimate purpose of our relationship. We affirm our lovemaking as the vehicle for the expression of our spiritual connection with each other. At the same time, we affirm and appreciate our innate earthiness.

"Our sexual relationship improves with each year we are together, because we become closer and more intimate the longer we are together. Even when we become unable to make love as vigorously as we now do, we know that our love, and therefore our lovemaking, will be radiantly beautiful."

Share your own vision with your partner and then create a shared sexual vision, including all of your areas of agreement. Write it down, making copies for each of you, and store them somewhere that is private but accessible. Agree to reread this vision every few months.

Making Treasure Maps/Collages

Making a concrete picture of your desired goals helps to give them a new reality. For any area of your life, construct a colorful visual representation of your desires. You can do this by painting or drawing a picture of the new situation, or by making a collage.

Use magazines to cut out pictures of evocative scenes, such as one of a couple lying close together on a beautiful beach. Cut out large-print phrases or write them yourself or print them out with your computer. You may use phrases like: *You are never alone*, or *God is love*, or *We see each other's inner beauty*. Make a collage of your images and phrases—one that gives you vivid inner pictures of what you intend to create in your intimate life.

You and your partner can make a sexual treasure map together. This can be fun as well as offering a pleasurable creative venture that provokes discussion of your goals.

Treasure maps created in my workshops have been very imaginative. One couple used a large piece of gold posterboard. They pasted pictures of objects that were sacred to them around pictures of couples in loving embrace. They included some photos of themselves and excerpts from favorite poems and erotic writing. The result was a pleasure to both of them—one they kept on the wall near their bed. The caption at the bottom was *Walking the Path of Sacred Sex Together.*

Where love is, what can be wanting? Where it is not, what can possibly be profitable?
—St. Augustine

Using Affirmations

Repeat that which you wish to manifest over and over as if it is already so, and it will be. You are instructing your inner self and your body when you make a statement such as: "I now experience great inner joy," or "I feel deeply bonded and in tune with my partner." Affirmations are most effective when they are frequently and enthusiastically repeated. This is positive self-talk, and it is powerful.

Its converse is powerful as well. Become aware of your negative self-talk and change any destructive messages you are giving yourself. Here are some common examples and their positive replacements:

NEGATIVE MESSAGE	AFFIRMATION
I am too heavy to be sexually desirable.	*I am warm and sensual.*
My sex drive isn't as strong as it should be.	*I am open to love and joy.*

Rituals

Rituals have been used throughout time to remind the seeker of the divine. Use traditional rituals if they touch you. Otherwise, create your own.

Consistent practice is important for continuing growth of skill in anything. Regular observance of rituals is a direct path to the development of soulful sexuality. The purpose of these rituals is to remind you both that *you are spiritual beings having a human experience.*

Any ritual is an opportunity for transformation … inner willingess is what makes the ritual come alive and have power.
—Starhawk

It is important to have a daily ritual that you share. Although it will affect your sexual experience together, this ritual should be nonsexual so that you can practice it every day, not just when you're going to make love. It could be as simple as five minutes of silent meditation together, perhaps followed by a sacred poem that one of you reads.

The second kind of important ritual is one that you develop to begin your sexual encounters. Here are some examples of rituals that you can adapt for either purpose:

1. Sit quietly together in meditation for five minutes or more. Use this time to contemplate the larger purpose of your relationship and the depth of the bond between you. Consciously open your heart.

2. For about five minutes, consciously breathe together. Begin with several deep breaths taken simultaneously, and then switch to breathing in tandem—one breathes in while the other breathes out.

3. Listen to an evocative musical selection, alternately chosen by each of you.

4. Take turns reading a short prayer or selection of poetry or prose designed to open the heart. It can be powerful to seek out and share inspirational words such as these by Marianne Williamson (from *Illuminata*):

> *We surrender all the ways, both those we are*
> *aware of and those that remain unconscious,*
> *in which we block our love for each other. . . .*

Daily Connection: A Quantum Leap

For most couples, time shortages are the enemy of love. The twice-daily "connect" can transform your relationship if you practice it religiously.

Twice daily, rain or shine, friendly or not, come together in silence. Do not talk unless you have something loving to say. Sit or lie together for five or ten minutes, making as much body contact as possible. This is bonding, not foreplay. Place your hands on each other's hearts and stay in eye contact for several minutes. Even if you are angry at each other, use the silence to focus on memories of times when you felt deeply connected. Think about the deeper purpose of your relationship.

An even more powerful version of this practice is to make genital contact during these times of connection. Create just enough arousal to allow penis-in-vagina contact, *not* as a prelude to intercourse but as a symbolic, unifying act. On most occasions, do not have intercourse at this time, but instead use this opportunity to experience the loving bond you share.

The results of commitment to this practice will deepen your love in a powerful way. More harmony will result, providing more opportunities for ecstatic experience, both physical and emotional.

> *Many men and women mistakenly believe that if they experience their sexual energy, they must do something about it. . . . They can learn to contain it and to allow it to spread out to the whole body rather than to express it genitally.*
>
> —Jack Rosenberg

Tools for Emotional Readiness

✑ Anger and Forgiveness

Ecstatic lovemaking is impossible in the presence of unresolved anger. I have counseled many couples whose lovemaking has been deadened by unexpressed anger. But because occasional anger toward anyone we share a living space with over time is inevitable, it's good to know that the free flow of love between your partner and yourself can actually improve when you learn to express anger appropriately.

Some of us imagine that we can skip the expression of anger. We want to avoid or deny our anger and get on to the more comfortable state of forgiveness. It doesn't work. This is the mistake many of us learned in childhood. We were taught not to challenge our parents, or to "turn the other cheek" when hurt or attacked. We learned to sweep our anger under the rug.

Repressed anger comes out later in unexpected ways. It's better to accept that anger has value when we become skilled in expressing it constructively.

✑ How Anger Gets in the Way of Sex

In counseling, people who are aware of their anger often say something like the following: "I feel angry at my partner a lot of the time, and this makes me feel like I don't want to talk at all. When I feel that way, I don't want to be touched, and I don't want to say anything that will make that more likely. What should I do?"

My answer to a person like this begins with observing that it's important to let your partner know about your anger. Your anger offers valuable feedback. Not expressing it encourages your partner to continue behaviors that don't work. Any two people who want a passionate relationship need to learn to regard loving expression of angry feelings as a vital part of that relationship.

There are several parts to learning constructive ways to express anger:

1. Agree that anger is okay.
Partners need an agreement that expressing anger is okay and welcome when expressed honestly and appropriately. Give your partner the gift of permission to express all feelings. Make agreements about how and when anger will be expressed.

2. Agree to work on acknowledging and owning anger.
This means identifying it as yours and taking responsibility for it, rather than saying that your partner caused it. "I'm furious!" is better than "You make me so mad."

Knowing that you make *yourself* angry is key. *You* choose to respond with anger in a particular situation. Often you could have chosen some other response, such as sadness, indifference, or even amusement. In each case, you are the one choosing the feelings.

3. Use "I" messages when you express anger.
This means talking about yourself rather than the other person. Don't say "You're always late," or "You never clean up your own mess." Instead, say "I get so mad when I have to wait for you," or "When I see these clothes on the floor, I get furious."

This is not a small difference. This way of expressing anger shows that you accept responsibility for it. It also decreases the opportunities for escalation. If I criticize you by saying "You're always late," you're likely to feel attacked and to start defending yourself. But if I say "I feel angry," there's less to argue about. I'm talking about myself, not you.

∽

Once the realization is accepted that even between the closest people infinite distances exist, a marvelous living side by side can grow up for them, if they succeed in loving the expanse between them . . . .

—Rilke

4. When your anger is about a significant conflict, don't try to solve the problem while you're angry.

When you're in the heat of anger, stick to the use of "I" messages, yelling them if you like. You might yell: "I'm furious! I can't stand it; I hate it, hate it, hate it when this happens!" Later, when you have calmed down, make an appointment to discuss the problem.

5. For times when you may be overcome with more anger than you can express in the ways just discussed, learn one or more techniques for healthy ventilation of it.

Some classic techniques are described below.

The point is to fully express and clean out your anger in a healthy, nondestructive way. This is the only way to make room for love to flow freely.

Constructive, nonviolent expression of anger is holy work. Building a loving and passionate relationship is a sacred and complex task. Refusing to allow anger to poison the loving connection with your partner is a spiritual act.

⁓ *How to Express Anger Safely*

In advance, set up a place for this work. You need a quiet spot where you won't be disturbed and where you don't have to worry about someone hearing you.

Plan to use a tennis racket or whiffle bat and a floor cushion or pillow. Some people prefer to simply hit a pillow with their hands. Or, you may prefer an outside setting where you can safely throw old plates or bottles against a fence or rock. You may also hit a punching bag. The point is to have a way in which you can use your body and your voice to loudly express anger.

If you are not in touch with exactly what you're angry about, begin by yelling "No!" as you hit the pillow or throw the plate. Yell "No, no, no, no!" over and over as you continue to express with your body.

As you continue, the particular source of your anger will probably come up. If it does, incorporate that into your words as you continue. "I hate how you always criticize me. I hate it! I hate! It hate it!" If no particulars become clear, just express your feelings with sounds *("Ahhhhhhhhh!")* as you continue.

You may find that you experience anger toward *yourself*. Keep going, loudly expressing whatever is there. Maybe it's "I hate myself for being a doormat–I hate it, I hate it, I hate it!"

Scream, swear, and shout while you continue to beat on the pillows, and keep going for ten or fifteen minutes or longer. It's best to stay with it–keep going as long as you physically can or until you have no anger left. This may take an hour or much longer.

If you are physically unable to keep going this long, rest when you must, but try to continue some body movement such as hitting the pillow lightly. Avoid stopping altogether, as you may lose some of your momentum. Come back to it as soon as possible.

Get it out! This is a safe way to honor your God-given anger. No harm will come to you or anyone if you use this method. This is so much better than actually yelling at your partner. It's also better than expressing your anger through passive-aggressive methods such as the silent treatment or refusing to express affection.

When you have no more anger, stop and relax. Acknowledge your courage. Breathe deeply, stretch, and consciously relax your body. Prepare to do the next exercise.

❧ Forgiving Your Partner

This exercise should follow the previous one, because anger needs to be expressed fully before real forgiveness is possible. It is a journey that will help you to understand your partner more deeply. You can do this anytime you are free of unexpressed anger and when you feel the need to experience some kind of softening toward your partner.

Set aside thirty minutes or more when you can be undisturbed. Read through the following instructions a few times prior to beginning the meditation. If you wish, you may record these instructions and then listen to the tape with your eyes closed.

When you're ready, put on some emotionally evocative instrumental music if you can. Sit or lie in a comfortable position. Now begin to count from 10 backward to 1, telling yourself that at 1 you will be experiencing yourself in the skin of your partner as a nine-month-old fetus about to be born. Wherever you don't know the facts, just imagine events as they might have happened. Imagine yourself in the skin of that tiny baby as labor begins. Experience the birth—you are in your partner's skin, being born at the end of a long period of labor.

Imagine yourself being very, very small. You are in a dark, warm place where you have been for as long as you can remember. But now something is happening. You are being squeezed tightly, and you're starting to have trouble breathing. You are moving, but you can't see where you're going. Now everything is back to normal and you start to relax. Oh no, it's starting again—you're being squeezed harder than ever. Now something hard and cold is grabbing your head and pulling hard. It hurts!

Wham! All of a sudden you're in a bright light that hurts your eyes. You've come out of the dark, warm place and you're lying on something cold. A large, white creature is holding you and putting something that stings in your eyes. Another one is wiping your skin with some rough cloth. Now one of them is holding you upside down and hitting you on

Ask yourself, and yourself alone, one question—Does this path have a heart? . . . If it does, the path is good; if it doesn't, it is of no use.

—Carlos Castaneda

the bottom. You're petrified and you scream. Now one of them hands you to someone familiar. You recognize her smell and the rhythm of her breathing.

If you are a boy baby, experience yourself being tied down to something cold and hard. Then one of the white creatures reaches down and takes hold of the most sensitive part of your body. All of a sudden you feel a terrible, searing pain there. He has cut you and you're bleeding. You are terrified and in agony. The white creature now takes you back to the one whose smell and breathing are familiar. How does she treat you?

Is she awake? Is she glad to see you? Who else is there? What are they saying? Are they happy with your gender? Experience all that happens in your first hours of life as your partner.

Now you are a one-week-old baby, home from the hospital. Who else is in your family? How are your parents feeling about themselves, about each other, and about you? How well do they care for you? Are you well fed? Do you feel safe? Do you feel loved?

Now you are a baby who becomes one month old, six months old, a year old, and so on through childhood and up to puberty. At each age, consider these questions: How do you feel about yourself? How do the other people in your family feel about you? How much do you trust others? How lovingly are you treated? How skilled in communication is your family? What problems or traumas or losses occur?

By the time you reach puberty, what kind of person are you? How lovable do you feel? How able to love others are you? How skilled at expressing yourself are you? How able to trust others are you? What saddens you the most? What frightens you?

Now take three long, deep breaths and, as you do, allow your partner's body to begin to change back into your own. Count from 1 to 10, saying to yourself that at 10 you will be fully yourself, grounded in your own body. Experience yourself as having more compassion, more understanding than ever before. Feel your understanding of your partner growing.

Tell yourself that now you understand why your partner behaves in certain ways that have disturbed you in the past.

Think of three or more of your partner's past behaviors that you now understand and are willing to forgive. Say aloud "I now forgive my partner for . . . ," finishing the phrase with some behavior that you now understand and forgive. Do this a few more times.

Now, bringing this awareness into the present, recall the feeling of your weight against the chair or sofa, remember the room where you are, and slowly open your eyes.

To complete this exercise, take a few moments and write down any insights you received from this experience. Share with your partner the forgiveness you are now ready to offer.

> Man's endeavor should be to merge his will with the Divine Will, as far as he is able to comprehend it, and by obedience to the Divine Will to become an instrument through which God's power works upon the world . . . .
> —Howard Brinton on Quakerism

✲ Conflict Resolution

The essence of conflict resolution lies in finding the common ground two disputants may be unaware that they have. When you have an unsettled conflict with your partner, it tends to interfere with the free flow of sexual spontaneity between you.

Anger expression and forgiveness are the most important tools for resolving conflicts. Learn to know that most actions of your partner that seem to have malicious intent are really the actions of the wounded child within. Once you see your partner's actions in this light, it becomes easier to negotiate and compromise.

Vanessa's Story of Anger and Forgiveness

I grew up in a family where anger was expressed—too much anger expressed too often, I felt. My father lost his temper more or less daily and would yell and swear when he did. My mother would sometimes argue with him, but mostly she would cry when he yelled.

When I got to be a teenager, I followed her example. My dad would get mad at me, then he'd yell and I'd cry. It wasn't very healthy, and I hated it. I resolved that when I was grown, I'd never have awful fights like that with *my* husband.

When Ben and I got married, I was naïve enough to think that I could maintain this idea through a long marriage. For the first few years, I never lost my temper, but I did follow my childhood pattern of crying anytime Ben said something to me that I thought was mean. All he had to say was that the soup was too salty, and I'd cry. If he asked me if I had been gaining weight, I'd cry a lot. When he said we weren't making love enough, I cried for a week.

All this crying didn't solve anything. Ben would feel guilty (as I guess I wanted him to), and he'd be especially nice to me then. This encouraged me to act the same way the next time he got mad. Years later, I learned in therapy that we had a dysfunctional system set up. We both ended up feeling bad each time, but we never solved our problems.

It took a counselor to help us work this out. We went to see Dr. Reardon because some friends told us that he had really helped them to get over some hard times they were having. Now, they said, they knew how to reach an agreement when they had a conflict. This sounded great.

Dr. Reardon taught us how to express anger when it was really strong. He gave each of us a tennis racket and a big pillow and a timer. He said he was going to show us to different rooms in his suite and that he wanted us to beat on these pillows and express everything we were mad about. Even if we couldn't feel our anger right then, he wanted us to start hitting our pillows with the tennis racket and yelling "No! No! No! No!" while we were hitting.

When something we were angry about did come up, we were supposed to yell about that. He told us to "yell words or sounds or

Forgiveness is as necessary to life as the food we eat and the air we breathe. When an individual can cultivate an attitude of forgiveness, he helps to create a pocket of tranquility in the world.

—Jeffrey Moses

insults and swear to your heart's content—just keep yelling and pounding" until he came back. He told us we would be able to be more loving with each other if we did this.

While I was yelling "No! No! No!," things that I was actually mad at Ben about started coming up. He was critical and picky and hard to please and I was sick of it! I beat that pillow to death yelling about it all! I was almost sorry when the timer went off and I had to go back to the main room. But I felt a rush—a lot of energy was flowing through me.

When we both got there, Dr. Reardon didn't ask us to talk about what we had been dealing with in the separate rooms like I expected. Instead, he had us both lie down on separate couches while he did a forgiveness meditation with us where we went back in time and experienced each other as babies. I felt myself in Ben's skin as a baby, being born to parents who thought they had too many children already, and to a mother who was having a difficult birth.

I felt what it was like for Ben to be poor and to have critical, anxious parents who were never satisfied with him. I could really feel him—a little boy who kind of had to raise himself in some ways. I felt a lot of tenderness for him.

When Dr. Reardon brought us out of the meditation, I still felt that tenderness. Then he asked us to tell each other what we were ready to forgive now, in the present. It was powerful and touching. We forgave so much in each other that day!

Maybe it was even more important that we learned *how* to forgive. Understanding another person from the inside makes a big difference. You come to understand that everything the other person does and feels follows from how they were treated in childhood. It makes it pretty easy to forgive. And then it gets easier to forgive yourself too, realizing that you also were hurt in childhood. As the French say, "to know all is to forgive all."

Love means setting aside walls, fences, and unlocking doors, and saying YES. . . . One can be in paradise by simply saying "yes" to this moment.

—Pat Rodegast

All this made a big difference in our relationship. We saw Dr. Reardon for about six months, and by the end of that time we were pretty skillful at expressing anger safely and forgiving each other for all the little things that happen as you go along in life with someone.

We were both surprised to find out how big an effect this had on our sex life. Anger and passion don't go together. When we figured that out, we had a big incentive to get good at handling anger and reaching forgiveness quickly, so that we can get back to feeling our love for each other.

Choosing to Return to Love

Like Vanessa and Ben, please use these tools in a spirit of love and concern for your partner's best spiritual interests and your own. The act of choosing to learn new tools becomes a statement to your partner—a statement of intention. It says that although you may go off track on occasion, your intention is always to return to love and to soulful sex.

Here are some lines from a poem of mine, reminding us to let go and forgive:

> *The truth is*
> *forgiveness heals*
> *Telling my whole truth right now*
> *Dissolves the mountain of fear and pain*
> *Allows the miracle of love to flow*
> *Like melting snow in Spring.*
>
> *All healing starts with forgiveness . . .*
> *Forgiving myself, I allow myself*
> *your love*
> *our joy*

The truth of being known.
Forgiving you
the veil is parted
I see the luminous child
the weeping heart
the joyful lover . . .
All healing starts with forgiveness . . . .

When the heart is flooded with love
there is no room in it for fear,
for doubt, for hesitation.
And it is this lack of fear
that makes for the dance.
—Anne Morrow Lindbergh

CHAPTER 8

Heart-Opening Practices for Lovers

The road to ecstatic passion challenges the best within us. It asks us for courage and devotion.

Lovemaking can be sublime if your heart is fully open. Ecstasy is yours to experience if you are also willing to bring your higher self into the sharing of your emotions and your body. There are some wonderfully simple ways to do this. New attitudes come first. Then, practices done individually teach you a new experience of all-intimate touch. Later, shared practices with your partner can foster monumental shifts in your lovemaking.

Acceptance of Your Own and Your Partner's Body

Willingness to freely give your body to your beloved in sexual intimacy depends on feeling that your body is worthy and lovable. Therefore, whatever your size and shape, make it your goal to learn to love your precious body. This does not mean that you must look like a model or a body-builder. It does mean that *you* must accept your body if you wish your lover to accept it.

True love is not a feeling by which we are over-whelmed. It is a committed, thoughtful decision.
—Scott Peck

How can I accept my body when it is flawed? Most women and many men are preoccupied with this question. Women tend to ask such questions as: How can I love my body when it is "too" fat, "too" skinny, "too" short, "too" tall? How can I accept breasts that are "too" small, "too" big, sagging, or not symmetrical? How can I accept thighs that are "too" big, "too" small, "too" flabby, not "in shape"?

Men in our culture have fewer problems with body image than women do. A man's sense of self-worth is less identified with his body. A successful male executive rarely lies awake nights worrying about the shape of his thighs. Men do have their bodily concerns though, including feelings that their muscles are underdeveloped or that their bellies are too large or that they are too short or too tall. Concerns about penis size continue to plague many men.

In soulful sexuality, *the size and shape of body parts is unimportant in determining how much joy and pleasure you can bring to your lover.*

The road to sexual dissatisfaction is paved with questions about how many inches, how many pounds, how many minutes. The right questions are: How emotionally open am I? How sexually courageous am I? When making love, how aware am I of the divine within me and within my partner?

You Can Learn to Give Yourself Body Acceptance

Look into a mirror every day for a week, recalling some compliment that you have received and repeating it to yourself three times. Now focus on another positive aspect of your appearance and complement yourself three times. Notice your tendency to focus on your alleged "flaws," and gently revise your approach. Try an acknowledgment like this: My eyes are beautiful, and the inner Light that shines out of them is even more so; or, My arms are beautiful and their ability to hold and caress is a gift to me and others.

Do the same exercise with your precious genitalia. Look at yourself carefully in a mirror and learn to see your beauty. Practice positive self-talk here also. Tell yourself: My labia have a unique shape and so many beautiful colors; or, My penis is beautiful in all its states.

On another occasion, do the following exercise with your partner. Come together in a quiet room, wearing robes and underwear. Do five minutes or more of connecting. Then remove the robes and discuss with each other your feelings about your own and your partner's body. Share any negative evaluations you have about your *own* (not your partner's) body. Be kind to each other. Give three acknowledgments to each other of some aspect of each other's physical beauty.

Self-Love May Mean Body Change

Perhaps your inner self is calling to you to modify the size of your body. If excess pounds have been a barrier to emotional and sexual intimacy, perhaps you are ready to release them. Sometimes, being overweight is an unconscious message to an actual or potential partner that says: Before I can trust you, you must love me in spite of my appearance. Excess weight can also mean: You must love me before I can love myself. It can also represent an accumulation of unexpressed anger.

You know without being told whether your weight is physically and emotionally healthy for you. If it is not, make the decision to give yourself full health and pleasure in your body.

Of course, there are dozens of choices of diet books, programs, and support groups. If you wish, choose one that gives you support and nurturance and structure. The essence of weight loss, however, is startlingly simple: Limit your fat grams to 30 or less per day; eat lots of fruits and vegetables and moderate amounts of whole grains; minimize animal and dairy products, sweets, and alcohol; drink a lot of water; and exercise moderately for thirty minutes or more most days. A safe weight loss will result.

Have a sexual fantasy instead of a chocolate bar, and we'll call this "The Lover's Diet." You'll lose weight and gain libido.

Bodily delight is... a great, an infinite learning that is given to us....
—Rilke

Creating a Sanctuary

Creating an inner sanctuary is a marvelous gift to give yourself. It provides the possibility of solitude and deep communion with your inner self at any time you choose. It assists you in becoming receptive when you want to reconnect with your partner or with your Higher Power. It gives you a means of accessing awareness of your own deep sensual and sexual desires.

You can learn this technique in many seminars and training programs, but you can also do it by yourself. Put on meaningful instrumental music if you wish. Relax your body and go within. Imagine an ideal place that is yours alone. It can be indoors or it can be a protected site outdoors. It can be a castle or a cabin or a mountain that belongs only to you. Visualize this place as beautiful, tranquil, and completely safe. No one else can enter without your permission.

Design this place exactly to your personal specifications. Cost is no object. The size, location, colors, temperature, and textures are all of your choosing. Decorate or furnish it according to your personal taste.

This sanctuary is symbolic of your ability to create safety and peace at any time under any circumstances. Simply close your eyes, breathe deeply, and experience yourself in your sanctuary. Accessing your sanctuary is helpful when you want to relax your body or reduce stress. Use it to seek guidance and to create solitude when you need it.

Releasing Bodily Tension

The most intense physical pleasure you are capable of can occur only when your body is truly relaxed. Becoming aware of body tension is an important step on the way to full enjoyment of sexual pleasure.

Wilhelm Reich, Ida Rolf, Alexander Lowen, and others have written about "body armoring" and how it prevents full awareness of feelings. *Armoring* refers to muscles held so tightly that much sensation is prevented. This occurs because our natural tendencies to move and feel were limited in childhood. We were told to be quiet and be still. Most of us learned not to express or, eventually, not to *feel* the sexual sensations that permeated our pelvises from an early age.

Most of us have a lifetime of experience contracting the muscles around the anus in order to control elimination and around the genitals to inhibit sexual sensation. We hold tension in other parts of our bodies as well, such as our shoulders and lower back. Various forms of body work teach us that the keys to tension release are breathing with sound release, awareness, movement, and conscious, progressive relaxation.

The primary nature of every human being is to be open to life and love.

—Alexander Lowen

❧ Conscious Breathing

Breathing is key in all forms of body work. Most of us are not in the habit of breathing deeply. Learn the belly breathing that yoga teaches by inhaling through your nose. Breathe in so deeply that your belly expands. Then contract your belly and continue inhaling until your chest is fully expanded. Consciously release tension each time you exhale. Take a few such breaths first thing every morning, last thing at night, and several times during the day. This oxygenates your blood and nourishes your whole body.

If your environment permits, allow sound to accompany your exhalations. This keeps the flow of emotional release going, preventing it from being blocked and held in your body.

❧ Awareness and Release of Tension

Practice becoming aware of tension by lying down in a quiet room and focusing on one muscle group at a time. Feel the muscles in your neck. Move your head from side to side, noticing how tense or relaxed the muscles are. Turn your head slightly to the right and slowly and consciously release the muscles on the left side of your neck. Reverse. Continue on to your shoulders and throughout your body, becoming aware and releasing as much as you can.

❧ Movement

Muscles need to stretch and to move. Giving them what they need allows them to serve you better, especially in terms of increasing your sexual sensation and pleasure. Adopting the practice of hatha yoga is one of the best things to do for your body and your health. If this is not your choice, choose another system of stretching and moving your body four or five times a week. Frequent massage or other body work in which a practitio-

> *If an individual doesn't feel the tensions, rigidities, or anxieties of his body, he is ... denying the truth of his body.*
> —Alexander Lowen

ner moves and stretches your body for you is an important additional choice for health.

✑ *Progressive Relaxation*

Progressive relaxation can be used alone for stress reduction or to prepare yourself for any spiritual practice, including meditation and sacred lovemaking.

It may be convenient to make an audiotape of the following instructions. Or, if you do this with your partner, you may take turns reading them to each other, or just practice several times until the process is familiar. For maximum stress reduction, do a thorough progressive relaxation taking ten to thirty minutes. When time is limited, you can abbreviate the process to two or three minutes.

If possible and pleasing to you, turn on soft instrumental music. Lie down or sit in a comfortable position. Begin by breathing deeply and stretching your body. While sitting, do a short progressive relaxation in which you consciously relax each area of your body.

Close your eyes gently and focus on your feet. Relax the muscles in your feet by mentally telling them to let go. See the word *RELAX* in large black letters on the inside of your eyelids. Feel the subtle release as a wave of warm, relaxing energy spreads throughout your feet. Breathe deeply, breathing in the Life Force and breathing out tension with each exhalation.

Now bring that wave of relaxation up into your ankles and calves. Relax the muscles of your calves, knees, and thighs until both of your legs feel completely relaxed.

Bring that wave of relaxing energy up into your pelvis, relaxing your buttocks, your genitals, your belly. Then relax your back and shoulders, bringing the warm energy up your spine and allowing it to radiate out from your spinal cord to every part of your body.

Relax your chest and your arms, allowing the relaxation to flow down your arms and out your fingertips. Now bring it up into your neck. Relax all the muscles of your neck. Relax your scalp, your ears, and, finally, your face. Relax your forehead and let your eyes be soft. Allow your jaw to open gently. Breathe deeply, again experiencing the inflow of the Life Force and the outflow of tension. Relax your tongue.

I have spent my days stringing and unstringing my instrument while the song I came to sing remains unsung.

—Rabindranath Tagore

Now scan your body and notice any areas of remaining tension. Breathe into these areas, consciously relaxing them. Now breathe deeply three times, allowing each exhalation to be a little longer than the last.

Create and focus on a thought such as *I am deeply relaxed and content.* Breathe deeply and relax a little more. Focus on that same thought for a few more minutes.

In this relaxed state, you may choose to enter meditation or worship or a time of self-pleasuring or lovemaking with your partner. If, instead, you choose to return to ordinary consciousness, simply breathe deeply three times, stretch gently, and open your eyes.

Addictions Obscure Your Contact with the Divine and Undermine Soulful Sex

Sacred passion cannot flourish in the presence of addictions. If you have an addictive relationship to food, cigarettes, alcohol, or other drugs, you have less contact with the Light than you could have. Addictions mean having *less joy* than is available to you today and every day!

Do you pour yourself a drink as soon as you get home from work? On a lonely night, do you eat several servings of dessert? Do you tell yourself that the way to have pleasure and adventure is the daily use of cigarettes, alcohol, or recreational drugs?

These are the patterns of addiction. Your first impulse may be to deny your addictions or to blame and condemn yourself for them. Like blame of others, however, self-blame is destructive. Replace self-blame with awareness that you can choose a better path.

Addictions come out of pain and the desire to avoid it. Addictions do *not* mean that you are a bad person, but that *you feel less lovable than you are* and that you are not in touch with your God-given capacity to live in a state of joy and love for yourself and for the people around you.

Addictions also make it very unlikely that you have as much sexual joy and fulfillment as you could have. Mature sexuality includes awareness and expression of your wide range of feelings and the ability to be fully present with your partner.

If you medicate or dull your emotions with drugs or food, you obscure your awareness and cloud your ability to enjoy your feelings and use them for guidance. Even mild addictions rob you of the intensity of feeling you could experience.

Get help if you recognize or suspect an addictive pattern that you are unable to change on your own. Twelve-step programs all across the country offer free, loving support and a compelling experience that you are not alone.

Showing up at a meeting of Alcoholics Anonymous, Al-Anon (for loved ones of alcoholics), Overeaters Anonymous, Narcotics Anonymous, or one of the many other twelve-step groups can change your life forever. Call the local chapter of Alcoholics Anonymous in your area; they can help you locate a twelve-step group for your issue, or a group for partners and family members of an addicted person.

If twelve-step groups don't appeal to you, find a mental-health professional or clinic that specializes in eating disorders or the treatment of substance abuse. Do this not because someone else thinks you should, but because you want a life of joy and passion.

> ✎
>
> *A giant step is taken toward success and happiness when one becomes able to learn from the advice of others, not only from one's own successes and failures. Until that time, progress will be slow, and unneccessary suffering will result.*
>
> —Jeffrey Moses

Creating a Sacred Environment for Lovemaking

It's very desirable to have a space for lovemaking that is beautiful and tranquil and available when you want it. Design it together or alone as a surprise for your partner. Choose objects, colors, and sights that are pleasing to you both. A room that is exclusively for this purpose is ideal, but if you must use the room for other purposes, you can use objects, flowers, candles, and lighting to create a temporary environment for lovemaking.

Have a bed that is comfortable and sheets that delight your skin. Add a source of music if it touches you. Have unscented oil and a water-based lubricant such as K-Y Jelly at the bedside. Be sure that your room can be locked so that you can make love without fear of interruption.

An altar or meditation corner is a beautiful addition. Choose a special room if you have one, or simply choose a corner of any room, and place sacred objects there such as holy books, candles, and any other symbolic objects that please you. Light a candle any time you want to remember the Light within.

Take the environmental imperative just as seriously if you are making love alone. You deserve it, and the experience deserves it.

Developing the Sex Muscles: Kegel Muscles

You can increase your sexual energy and your mutual pleasure by strengthening your PC (pubococcygeus) muscle. This is the muscle between your genitals and your anus. It controls the opening and closing of the urethra, the seminal canal, the vagina, and the anus. It also contributes to erotic sensation through increasing blood flow to the genitals and through moving energy. The PC muscle contracts and relaxes naturally during intercourse and orgasm. Learning to consciously control this muscle expands orgasmic sensations and makes you a more powerful lover.

Courtesans in some Asian cultures know how to arouse the penis and even bring a man to orgasm during intercourse without pelvic movement. They use rhythmic contractions of a well-toned PC muscle. Males who learn to pump blood into the penis through rhythmic PC contractions experience an ability to sustain intercourse longer and to spread out the sensations of pleasure over a wider area of their bodies.

You can strengthen and tone the PC muscle by stopping and starting the flow while urinating or simply by consciously contracting and releasing the PC while sitting at a red light or in a chair. Inhale and pulse, inhale and pulse. Contract and release the muscle ten or more times. Work up to a hundred or more contractions a day. Practice "Kegels," quick pulsing contractions and longer, sustained contractions.

When making love and highly aroused, inhale deeply while pulsing your PC muscle. Contracting this muscle and inhaling while very aroused increases sexual pleasure and power.

You can also practice during self-pleasuring.

Self-Pleasuring: An Important Step
in Self-Knowledge and Self-Love

As we saw in an earlier chapter, most of us experienced much devaluing of our sexuality in childhood. Disparagement or outright condemnation of self-pleasuring was a prime example of this.

As an infant or small child, we discovered that certain parts of our bodies produce delicious sensations when touched. Most of us, unfortunately, were told that "nice" boys or "nice" girls definitely *don't* touch themselves.

Sam Keen, in *Hymns to an Unknown God*, describes what happened when he was caught masturbating as a very young child: "Right and wrong suddenly switched places as I was instructed that the good feelings in my penis were to be considered bad. . . . My sexuality would henceforth be hidden under the cover of darkness. . . ."

In an ideal world, the enlightened parent who first saw you touch yourself would have said something like: "It feels good to touch yourself there doesn't it? God gave us wonderful bodies that can feel so good when they're touched!" Later lessons could have taught you to do your self-pleasuring in private. You could have learned this as easily as you

> ～
>
> *Whatever else we may say about sexuality, we must begin by acknowledging that it is surrounded by a cloud of obsession, a thorn thicket of guilt . . . a double wall of dogma and taboo, and seven veils of romantic illusion.*
>
> —Sam Keen

learned that taking off your clothes was best done in your own room. No scare tactics or threats would have been necessary.

Parents like this would have known that the desire to touch our own body is normal, good, and universal. Informed parents would have known that touching our own bodies is a fundamental form of gaining self-knowledge as well as an ever-present source of pleasure when we want it.

Unfortunately, few of us had such knowledgeable parents. We touched ourselves anyway, but for many of us the experience has always been colored by our parents' negative attitudes. As adults on the path of soulful sexuality, we can decide to learn new ways to feel about pleasuring our own bodies.

> *The lover is looking in a mirror in which he is beholding his Self.*
> —Plato

An Attitude Change About Self-Pleasuring

You are a sexual being, whether with a partner or alone. You have a sexual relationship with yourself, and it is a holy relationship. Because you are a precious embodiment of divine energy, every aspect of your physical, emotional, intellectual, and spiritual being is a sacred gift.

Although educated people today realize that masturbation will not produce hairy palms or psychotic episodes, we still tend to feel vaguely uncomfortable about the fact that we enjoy touching our own bodies. Some of us suffer honest guilt after enjoying a self-produced orgasm.

Enlightened self-pleasuring means claiming your birthright. This means acknowledging to yourself that you enjoy the sensations your own touch can produce and that you have every right to those sensations whenever you would like to enjoy them. If you feel like giving yourself several orgasms in a row, please do so. If you wish to masturbate during or after lovemaking with a partner, it's your choice. If your spouse is too tired to make love and you want to spend time pleasuring yourself, enjoy!

In a way, all sexual experience is about deepening your relationship with yourself. Solitary or shared lovemaking can take you into the deepest parts of your inner being. Every aspect of being human is fully present within your own mind, heart, and soul.

In lovemaking, a partner's main function, in a way, is to assist you in experiencing your own feelings and your own self more deeply. It's true that a beloved partner may help you swing wide the gate, but the journey is into yourself. This means that although sharing lovemaking with a partner may be your preference, it is not a necessity. And even if your beloved is an active and fulfilling presence in your life, your spiritual and emotional and sexual relationship with yourself is ongoing.

A Self-Pleasuring Ritual

Ask for guidance as you meditate on the fact that you were given this precious body and that it has the ability to experience exquisite sensations through its own touch.

What does your inner guidance tell you about self-pleasuring? Proceed only when you have come to peace and a deep inner knowing that your body and all of its capabilities are sacred treasures—gifts to be celebrated. Proceed only when you know that moving in this direction is right for you.

Consider choosing a celebratory time such as the Sabbath or another holy or special day to pleasure yourself. Rejoice in your body's ability to feel pleasure. You do have to give something up—it's the perverse pleasure we sometimes take in feeling naughty or in being secretive. In enlightened self-pleasuring, there is nothing to regret; no penance is necessary.

Set aside a time when you can be alone and uninterrupted for forty-five minutes or longer. You deserve more than quick and furtive self-pleasuring. Find time to be alone and lock your door! Set up the scene as you would for a treasured lover. Put on music you like. Light a candle if it appeals to you.

Make love to yourself. Begin with strokes and caresses on your face

⌒

The effects of pleasure are wholly positive. . . . Spiritually, enjoyment enhances your appreciation of your blessings and contributes to a brighter outlook.
—Harold Bloomfield and Robert B. Kory

and scalp, then moving on to other places that feel good when you touch them. Touch your genitals lovingly; be gentle at first. Consciously begin to reprogram yourself. Caressing your own precious body is a sacred act, and you can learn to experience it that way.

Use fantasies if these arouse you, but be conscious of the importance of creating an experience that you treasure, rather than one that you feel is a guilty secret. Fantasizing intercourse with a sex-crazed paid lover is unlikely to help you access your spiritual depths. Consider replacing any self-deprecating fantasy with a positive one. Tell yourself how lovable you are.

Taking your time, give yourself the experience of deep arousal. Savor it. Enjoy it. If you feel like it, bring yourself to orgasm once or more than once. Consciously experience your orgasm as holy.

Whether or not you come to orgasm, complete the experience with a time of quiet appreciation of yourself. Give gratitude to God or your Higher Power for these marvelous abilities. Think of becoming comfortable and skillful at self-pleasuring as a valuable step in becoming a joyful participant in soulful sexuality.

> *The spiritual manifests itself not only in invisible forms but also in physical forms....*
> —Piet Mondrian

Sharing Self-Pleasuring

A demonstration is worth many words. That's why it's very desirable to become comfortable enough to pleasure yourself in the presence of your partner. It is invaluable for your partner to *see*, instead of just hear about, how you like to be touched, what arouses you most, and how you most easily reach orgasm. Pleasuring yourself in the presence of your lover is a great gift to offer.

Second, accepting self-pleasuring as your birthright enables you to practice various skills and emotions that can ready you for ecstatic shared sexual experiences. One of these is learning to stay relaxed in high states of arousal. This is one of the keys to transformative sexual experience.

For most of us, it's necessary to feel very safe before we could be capable of this. When you have achieved a sense of safety with your partner, choose an occasion when you have ample time to be uninterrupted. Be naked or partially clothed as you prefer. Deepen your contact by placing your hands on each other's hearts and looking into each other's eyes until you feel your hearts begin to open.

The one who is demonstrating should then lie down, breathe deeply, and consciously relax. Acknowledge any shyness or shame your feel as you begin to self-pleasure. The one who is watching should communicate acceptance and support and should watch carefully while the other goes as far as he or she is comfortable. Eventually, giving yourselves orgasms in each other's presence can be very informative as well as offering a statement of trust in yourself and in your partner.

Loving Massage

Learning and practicing massage can be a joyful pleasure for loving partners. Massage of all or part of the body can be an end in itself, or it can be part of extended foreplay or afterplay. Use it as one of the gifts you offer each other in times when you separate the roles of giver and receiver. In massage, as in love, it is truly as blessed to give as to receive.

Genital massage can be an exciting variation for lovers. By agreement, focus on the genital area alone and see how many ways you can find to give pleasure.

Bathing Together

Use water as a tool for washing away daily life when you are ready to share an intimate time with your beloved. Water has been a part of spiritual ceremonies since ancient times. By mutual decision, you and your lover can use the symbolic power of water for your mutual healing. A hot tub, swimming pool, mountain stream, or bathtub all offer possibilities of sharing a water experience with your lover.

At home, take turns drawing a bath for each other. As giver, clean the space, provide towels, fragrant soap, oils, and perhaps candlelight. Being available to give a massage or back rub after the bath can be an additional gift. In each situation, take the time to acknowledge your love to each other.

A Sexual/Spiritual Meditation

The following guided meditation can be used in one of several ways. You may make an audiotape of it and play it for use with your partner or for a small group. Alternatively, one of you may read it aloud while the other follows with eyes closed. Ideally, play emotionally evocative instrumental music during the meditation, if it pleases you and your partner.

Begin by standing and taking three deep breaths, allowing sound to accompany your exhalation... "Ahhhhhhhh," "Ahhhhhhhh," "Ahhhhhhhh."

As the sound fades away, become aware of your precious body and allow it to relax as you breathe still more deeply and more slowly ... inhaling the Life Force and releasing tension with each exhalation ... inhaling relaxing energy and exhaling tension ...

Now scan your body, sending love and energy to every cell. Acknowledge your gratitude for the gift of your body and its every sensation.

Tune in now to your feelings, gratefully acknowledging the wide range of your emotions.

Be aware of your thoughts, appreciating all of your inventiveness and your curiosity.

Now focus on your higher self, experiencing the constant radiance of that aspect of your being. And now, be aware of your Higher Power as you understand it—the Inner Light or God. Breathe in that loving Presence.

Ask this Presence to surround you now with protective, healing light. In this light, you are safe, *perfectly* safe. You are relaxed and peaceful.

Now, into this protected space, at your invitation, someone approaches. This someone is your partner in love, your partner in the most intimate relationship you now have or wish to have.

This person now approaches you, coming so close that you can see deeply into each other's eyes. By unspoken yet mutual agreement, the issue between you is your sexual relationship. In this sacred moment, you silently agree to seek answers to two questions about your sexual relationship.

The first question is: *What is the meaning and purpose of our sexual relationship?* The second question is: *How can our sexual relationship be all that we both long for?* In this sacred moment, as you stand near each other, you both silently pose these questions, asking guidance from the Light.

Standing there together, each deeply receptive, you both feel the Light infusing every aspect of your being—your emotions, your intellects, your higher selves, and your bodies. The Light of wisdom penetrates, bathes, and surrounds you both.

A two-part answer to each question now begins to take shape within each of you. Slowly, you begin to understand that part of the answer to each question will be given to you, and part you will discover for yourselves.

And now your own unique partial answer to the first question—What is the meaning and purpose of our sexual relationship?—begins to emerge. It comes to you as you wait in silent receptivity. Take a minute or two to allow your own new understanding of the meaning and purpose of your sexual relationship to become clearer. Know that over the next days and weeks, still more clarity will come to you, but now, silently and receptively await whatever wisdom comes to you in this moment.

(Wait ninety seconds.)

And now, the part of this answer that is given to you begins to emerge. Silently, it becomes written upon your heart and mind. This is the rest of the answer to the question of the meaning and purpose of your sexual relationship.

The wisdom that now emerges in your heart is this: Your sexual relationship is your most profound way to share your *spiritual* journey with your beloved. Lovemaking, in all of its miraculous *and* mundane aspects, is sacred and holy. It is the expression of your creativity, your joy, your laughter, and, *yes*, your God-given lust—lust for aliveness, for passion, for pleasure, and for connection. This lust, in all its aspects, is holy and divinely given.

Look into each other's eyes now and experience this sacred truth ... take it in with gratitude and with joy.

And now, you begin to focus on the second question: How can our sexual relationship be all that we both long for? The part of this answer that is your own unique wisdom now begins to emerge upon your hearts and minds as you wait again in silent receptivity. Again, know that over the next days and weeks, still more clarity will come to you. For now, take a minute or two to allow new wisdom on the question to become more clear.

(Breathing deeply, wait ninety seconds.)

And now the part of this answer that is given to you begins to emerge. Slowly, it becomes written upon your hears and minds. In understanding how your sexual relationship can fulfill your deepest longings, you see, hear, understand, and *feel* that lovemaking is best when you bring all parts of yourself to each sexual experience: Your body, fully present and treasured for the gift it is, regardless of its shape and size; your intellect, with all its curiosity and inventiveness; your emotions, with all their spontaneity.

Most of all, you must bring awareness of your higher self and of your partner's higher self to your lovemaking experiences. Bringing your spiritual self to lovemaking means that sexual intimacy offers the possibility of contact with the divine and the transcendent.

When both of you—with all of your complex and lovable selves—are present in sex, your experiences will fulfill the deep longings of your heart. Take in this holy truth. Take it in with gratitude and allow it to merge with your *own* unique truth.

At your request, an integration of your own answers and those that have been given now comes to you. Now you *see, hear, understand,* and *feel* that every aspect of your sexuality is a divine gift. Your lust, your sensations, your hunger, even your anxiety and the fear that can emerge when two fallible human beings are intimate and close—all these are gifts to be cherished.

You know now that you can affirm all aspects of your sexual experience. You know that these gifts of wisdom are yours forever—yours to deepen and to modify in harmony with your own unique path. These gifts are yours forever in your holy sexual relationship with yourself or with any fortunate partner you may choose. Breathe in these gifts now—breathe them in with gratitude.

And now, begin to be aware of the surface beneath you and of this room. When you feel ready, please open your eyes.

Vanessa: Growing Up Sexually

Vanessa now shares some of the lessons she learned using the practices of soulful sex.

To really grow up as a lover, I had to learn things that I didn't even know I needed to know back at the beginning. One big example is that I couldn't have imagined when I started out that learning to make love to myself was one of the most important ways to grow sexually.

Although my mother had been quite positive about sex when she told me about it, she never said anything about masturbation. I found out about it from a book when I was thirteen years old, and it took me a while to even learn how to do it. Once I learned, I did it once in a while, but I always felt kind of embarrassed about it.

It wasn't until Ben and I were seeing a sex therapist for problems that I really learned self-pleasuring. She actually prescribed it. She called it "conscious self-pleasuring." When I told her I was a religious person, she said she was religious herself and that she believed enjoying your own touch is a gift from God. She gave me a booklet about self-pleasuring and showed me an instructional video that said that most women enjoy touching themselves if no one has made them feel bad about it.

The video showed a married woman who had never had an orgasm learning to have them all by herself. It showed her learning to look at her genitals and experimenting with touching them lots of different ways. Her next assignment was to act out what she thought it would be like to have an orgasm. She was supposed to breathe hard and moan and be dramatic. I guess she had seen her husband come, so she had some ideas. The acting was supposed to help her get over her self-consciousness. It worked, because it wasn't long before she started having real orgasms.

I was encouraged by all this because although I had been having orgasms, at that point I wasn't having them as often or as easily as I wanted to. I figured if the woman in the video could go from none to some, I could go from some to plenty!

The sex therapist told me to practice self-pleasuring alone several times per week for three or four months. It seemed really weird at first, but it turned out to be really enjoyable. I really learned about my body and how it responded.

I learned exactly how to touch myself when I wanted to get really excited. For instance, I found out that if I squeezed and stroked my breasts and nipples for about ten minutes, I could almost get to orgasm just from that.

I also learned some new ways to touch my clitoris, and I found out that it took about fifteen minutes of steady, rhythmic pressure right on my clitoris before I came. After a while, I got better at touching myself just right, and I started touching my nipples and my clitoris and the same time—and coming in ten or twelve minutes or even faster if I wanted to.

I had some of my best experiences though, by taking a long time. I found out that it was great to excite myself several times before coming. That would usually make for a very intense orgasm when I did come.

It was only after I got very skilled at pleasuring myself that the therapist asked me to start thinking about sharing the whole process with Ben. I had been feeling too shy to tell him much about what I had been doing before that, but with the therapist's encouragement, I got brave enough to talk to him about it. He was extremely supportive and understanding. He didn't push me at all, but he let me know that it was all up to me. He was more than eager to experiment with watching anytime I was sure that's what I wanted.

I felt nervous about all of it. I was shy about having him watch me be naked when we weren't actually making love and even more worried about having him watch me touch my genitals. I thought he might think my vulva was ugly or that he might feel critical about my thighs. I thought I might get strange expressions on my face if I got excited or reached an orgasm. I worried about getting excited and about not getting excited. The therapist told me all of these fears were completely normal and that lots of other people had them. She said I should start small—choose something to do that I was almost certain I could do.

Very tentatively, I decided to try five minutes of demonstration with my clothes mostly on and with the understanding that we could stop anytime I wanted to. We ended up spending about ten minutes that time, and I didn't even try to come. My goal was just to start getting comfortable touching my genitals in front of Ben. With his help, I succeeded in that, and I was able to go further and further later on. Eventually, I actually became able to let Ben hold me while I gave myself an orgasm.

He was great about all of it—very supportive and never critical or pushy. I'm very lucky. He understood that I was going through all of this discomfort because our sex life was as important to me as it was to him. He was a willing student of my responses and he learned what I wanted to teach him. His attitude helped me to really believe and feel that touching my own body was truly right and beautiful, and even holy.

Another great thing that came out of it all was that it took a lot of the pressure off both of us about worrying that I might not come when we made love. Once I got comfortable stimulating myself, I could just do it anytime I wanted to get more aroused or to have an orgasm when we were making love. I guess the cliché is "taking responsibility for your own orgasms." I did that, and it was a good thing for both of us.

We've had lots of time since then to enjoy the lessons we both learned from those experiments. We started trusting each other more at that time and we learned that trust can get deeper when you venture out into uncertain territory together.

For one human being to love another is perhaps the most difficult task that has been entrusted to us, the ultimate task, the work for which all other work is merely preparation.

—Rilke

Choosing Your Own Path

The practices in this chapter can give you years of ways to enjoy the sexual joy that develops when you fully open your heart to your partner. Of course, you can also design your own experiments, once you and your partner agree to become full participants in the journey to sacred sex. When you commit to the creation of deep closeness and the opportunity to share spiritually as well as sexually, lovemaking will become an endlessly creative endeavor.

Ecstasy is characterized by extreme peace, tranquillity, serenity and radiant joy. [It is] a blissful, tension-free state, a loss of ego boundaries and an absolute sense of oneness with nature, with the cosmic order, and with God.

—Stanislav Grof

CHAPTER 9

Secrets of Soulful Sex: From Bread-and-Butter Sex to Ecstatic Lovemaking

We now turn to a lovely menu of passionate possibilities—tools for going further on the journey of passionate sharing. Use these at will and invent your own.

Creating Mutual Harmony

Because joyful sexual exchange can be ruined by feelings of anger or emotional distance, it's important to become skillful at coming back to peace and closeness. As soon as you have that intention, stop talking about your disagreement for now, and commit to re-creating harmony.

Begin by closing your eyes and consciously relaxing your body. Then face each other while sitting or lying in a comfortable position. Place your hands on each other's heart. Silently making eye contact, synchronize your breathing. Be courageous, allow yourselves to be *seen*. Now place your other hands on each other's genitals. In silence, continue to breathe together.

Consciously create harmony with each other in your thoughts, putting aside ego conflicts and remembering the deeper purpose of your relationship: your mutual spiritual growth. Feel your love for each other. Consciously create your awareness of erotic desire for your partner.

Honoring Rituals

Take the time to acknowledge and honor your partner most of the times you come together sexually. A simple statement can become a powerful tradition. An example might be: "I honor the spirit of God within you," or "I see the Light deep in your eyes."

Create your own statements, choosing words that express values you share. Use these statements as a way of creating an emotional space for loving, a space that is different from the practical aspects of life that you share, such as parenting or financial concerns.

There will be times, of course, when what one or both of you desires is lusty and quick. Enjoy those times!

Maintain Eye Contact

Was it Hollywood that taught us to close our eyes when we kiss? We learned our lesson so well that it seems normal to close our eyes as soon as our lips meet our partner's. It is sad but true that many couples in long marriages have never looked into each other's eyes at the height of passion.

When you want to experience the deepest contact possible, *maintain eye contact* most of the time when you are making love with your partner. Risk experiencing the powerful connection that comes when you look into your partner's eyes while exchanging intimate touch. It can be frightening to allow another *in* so much. Have the courage to try it.

At orgasm, resist the impulse to turn away or close your eyes. Instead, allow your partner to *see* you fully in these moments of surrender.

Like other soulful sex guidelines, this one is not meant to be a hard-and-fast rule, nor a way to evaluate yourself. Instead, just be aware that when you close your eyes, you have a primarily individual experience. To shift the balance toward shared experience, maintain eye contact frequently and most of the time when making love.

You can practice and experiment with eye contact while sharing massage or any kind of sexual play. Discuss any discomfort that comes up, and agree to assist each other in learning to risk this kind of deeper contact.

Conscious Sexual Breathing

Breathing together or in tandem can increase your feeling of connection and harmony with your partner. For five or ten minutes, come close together, make eye contact in silence, and breathe together, inhaling and exhaling at the same time. This creates physical harmony and allows you both to feel more connection with each other. Let your sense of unity grow.

Now breathe in tandem. One person inhales while the other exhales. Allow your sense of connectedness to get stronger as you do this.

Whenever you decide to make love, you can increase your concentration and feeling of being present in your lovemaking by focusing on your breath and breathing consciously. You will find that you can use breath-

'Watching over the breath' consists in letting the breath come and go as it wants, without forcing it or clutching at it. In due course its rhythm automatically slows down, and it flows in and out so smoothly. This is both a symbol of and a positive aid to letting one's whole life come and go without grasping.

—Alan Watts

ing to slow or speed your level of arousal. To slow your rate or movement toward orgasm, slow down your breathing. To speed it up, breathe faster. Pant if you want to maximize your speed.

Creating Sexual Energy Together

The sexual drive is instinctual, raw, unrefined energy . . . this same sexual drive can be transformed and refined into ecstasy . . . . Sexual energy is therefore to be accepted and respected as the raw material—the 'crude oil,' from which the high-octane fuel of ecstasy is produced. . . .
—Margo Anand

It's good to know that you can create your own sexual energy, rather than depending on your partner, your mood, or anything else outside yourself. You can create sexual energy alone through breathing deeply, through working the sex muscles, and through undulating your pelvis.

To consciously create sexual energy together, experiment with a few minutes of mutual undulation. You can do this naked or partially clothed if you like. Stand with knees loose and hands at your sides. Bending the knees slightly, raise your arms, inhale deeply and allow the pelvis to rock, back and forth. Exhale, lower your arms, and continue undulating your pelvis. Find a rhythm that you like and continue it for five minutes or more. Consciously energize your pelvic area.

Combine this movement with contraction and release of the PC muscle. Think of energy beginning to move and circulate in your pelvis and genitals as you rock the pelvis and contract and release the PC. Unlimited amounts of sexual energy can be generated this way.

Trust Building

This exercise requires mutual trust and builds even more. Choose a time when you can be uninterrupted, and go together into your sacred environment. Decide who will receive and who will give on this occasion. Disrobe partially or completely, according to the receiver's preference. Blindfold the receiver. The receiver's job is to surrender to being cared for and pleasured. The other partner will explore the delights of giving.

As giver, provide your lover with an adventure in which the territory is sensual delight of all kinds. Have prepared a group of objects and substances that can provide sensual pleasure. The list of possibilities is as long as your imagination. Consider the following:

- *Objects of taste, such as a ripe peach or berry.*

- *Objects of touch, such as velvet, satin, feathers, or flower petals.*

- *Objects of smell, such as incense and/or fragrances of all kinds.*

- *Experiments in sound, such as music, percussion, or poetry.*

- *Experiments in sight: Remove the blindfold and dance for your lover or show arousing pictures of lovemaking.*

For as long as you both wish, the giver presents these sensual delights to the receiver. Play. Be silly or serious according to your mood. Have no agenda. There is no goal.

Allow this experience to end any way you both like. Switch roles now or on another occasion.

Nights of Service: Separating the Roles of Giver and Receiver

Offer this when you feel like giving something very precious to your partner. It's also a great way to introduce soulful sex to someone who seems reluctant. Here are the instructions I recently gave a client who was searching for a way to make an impression on a husband who wasn't at all sure he was interested in anything spiritual:

"Make a date for a night when you can be alone and uninterrupted. When your partner gets home and has had a chance to relax from his day, begin to serve him with all the love and consideration you can find

Effortless awareness is the key. All your energies will be drawn upward, diffused throughout the body, and absorbed into increasingly more exalted energy centers. As this takes place, lustful tendencies will be transmuted into feelings of love and the need for conventional orgasm will lessen.
—James N. Powell

in your heart. Feed him, wait on him, massage his feet, rub his back. Be playful and affectionate. Look into his eyes and tell him how much you treasure him.

"When and if he welcomes it, begin to touch him intimately after explaining that this time you want him to receive only. Offer his favorite caresses and put aside your own sexual needs for now. Honor his body with loving touch, intending only his pleasure. Allow him to choose the ending of this special time.

"It's likely that he will want to reciprocate, but don't allow this until another occasion. When he does, the two of you will be launched on a new adventure of exploring ways of being together intimately that can be new and uniquely satisfying."

> *At the height of laughter, the universe is flung into a kaleidoscope of new possibilities.*
>
> —Jean Houston

Games and Toys

The use of vibrators and other sex toys can be perfectly consistent with the pursuit of sacred sexuality. Attitude is everything. When you know that play that bonds you further to your beloved is a gift to your family and to the planet, exploration of games and toys can be seen as a positive choice. Enjoy all the possibilities that appeal to you and to your partner.

Play supports the health of your relationship. Acting the role of Cleopatra or a movie actor can be fun. Making love outdoors or in unlikely indoor places can be exciting. When you apply the principles of soulful sex, all these activities can become interesting additions to your journey with your treasured partner.

Make love in swimming pools, on picnics in the country, and under blankets on airplanes! Make love in the kitchen and on the back porch. Dildos, vibrators, and blindfolds are the bare beginnings of a list of toys that sacred sex couples can enjoy. See Appendix A for sources.

Commit to Frequent Lovemaking

The path of soulful sexuality invites lovers to commit themselves to daily sensual contact and frequent lovemaking. When lovemaking has been redefined as joyful touching and mutual affirmation rather than the old-fashioned foreplay-plus-intercourse scenario, most couples find that the choice to make a priority of loving sexual connection becomes more appealing.

Making love this way *creates* energy, so the old "I'm tired" excuses needn't apply. Lovemaking becomes an activity that you seek not only when you are feeling excited and happy, but when you feel tired or needy. This kind of lovemaking fills all kinds of needs and it often fills them better than withdrawing and isolating yourself can.

Kissing as an Art Form

When was the last time you kissed your lover differently than you usually do? An experimental attitude toward lovemaking involves frequently reminding yourself to take a fresh approach this time.

Humans are the only animals who kiss. We kiss babies and lovers. We kiss the ground of our homeland after long journeys away. Kissing is using your mouth to caress that which is precious. Honor this marvelous ability by learning to kiss with as much heart as possible. *Great lovers are those who can connect heart energy with the body.*

Study and practice kissing as an end in itself just as if it were any other form of creative expression. Use the many modalities of lip touch—hard, soft, sustained, quick, up, down, sideways, and more. Kiss every part of your lover's mouth and tongue. Kiss each lip separately. Kiss gently, kiss hard. Kiss playfully, kiss with fervor. Be the master and mistress of the twenty-minute kiss. At times, kiss for the purpose of kissing alone.

Experiment with the modalities of pressure, timing, location, and wetness. Kiss with exquisite softness, placing tender kisses on your lover's eyelids, forehead, cheeks, and chin. Kiss hard on the hollow at the side of the neck, searching for new erogenous zones. Try short kisses—many kisses only two or three seconds long. Try long kisses—don't break the kiss for ten minutes.

Kiss unexpected places. Try kissing your lover's toes, knees, earlobes, and buttocks. Use your mouth on your lover's genital area only after giving attention to other parts of the body. Dry-kiss the shoulders and French-kiss the mouth and the genitals. Wet kisses have more impact if they come later rather than earlier. With every variety of kiss, honor the soul and beauty of your lover.

Oral Loving

As is clear from the many varieties of kissing, our mouths are miraculous, God-given instruments of expression. So much feeling can be expressed with the mouth—feelings ranging from great tenderness to overwhelming passion. In fact, disabled individuals whose bodies are paralyzed often satisfy their partners with a skillful mouth alone.

The path of soulful sexuality asks us to take a new look at "oral sex" and to see its potential as an instrument of honoring the beloved. Oral contact offers a unique kind of intimacy. A skillful oral lover can create some of the most exquisite sensations humans are capable of feeling. Orgasms produced this way can be the most intense possible.

Perhaps its most delicious aspect is the way oral loving seems to communicate fundamental acceptance. If we were to verbalize this feeling of acceptance, we might say, "If you love being in such intimate contact with the most personal, often hidden part of my body, you must *love* my body and me. You accept me in this very fundamental way. If you arouse me or bring me to orgasm this way, you make a statement of fundamental acceptance of my sexuality."

Enjoying oral sex with a sacred sexuality perspective adds something precious. *In sacred sex, we honor the beloved's body as a temple of love and divine energy.* We honor the genitals as the instruments of divine passion.

Select a time to honor each other in this way. Rather than simultaneous stimulation, decide who will be the giver and who will receive. Shower or bathe, perhaps together. Take a few minutes for meditation on the sacred nature of your relationship. Then begin to touch and caress each other until the receiver signals readiness for oral loving.

As receiver, lie back comfortably and enjoy the giving. Do not return the caresses at this time—just receive. As giver, first make some kind of a verbal statement to your partner, such as, "I honor the Light within you." Then begin to experiment with the wide range of ways to orally caress your lover.

As giver, make this experiment longer and more heartfelt than your usual oral loving. Honor your beloved with your tongue and mouth, paying close attention to the response, whether it is verbal or faster breathing or sounds of pleasure. To feel more connection whether giving or receiving, maintain some eye contact.

Become practiced and comfortable stimulating each other orally. Then, on the same or a different occasion, give yourselves the gift of taking turns bringing each other to orgasm this way. The giver of extended oral stimulation can learn and enjoy as much as the receiver does.

As giver, know that you are honoring the eternal feminine or the eternal masculine. You are giving caresses that can express a unique depth of love and acceptance. As receiver, practice accepting the tribute and the loving respect you are being given.

The Sacred Spot: Key to Ecstatic Female Response

If you are one of the majority of women who have not discovered the great gifts your sacred spot has to offer you, this experiment can revolutionize your sexual experience. This part of the vagina is mentioned in such ancient Eastern books as the Kama Sutra, but in the West, Dr. Ernest Graffenberg first described it in professional literature more than thirty years ago. Uninformed sexologists downplay the existence of this area, which they call the "G-spot." Some say that the G-spot doesn't exist at all. Others think it does exist in some, but not all, women. A third group insists that we have to wait for further research to find out.

I invite you to conduct your own personal exploration of what is better called the *sacred spot*. With a trusted partner helping you explore the hidden mysteries of your vagina, you will indeed find an area that is unlike the rest. Stimulation of this area can produce greatly increased arousal and it can act as a trigger to one or many powerful orgasms.

Some women find that some spots on the back wall or other areas of their vagina are sensitive. It is worth doing a thorough and loving exploration of this often unfamiliar territory. (See page 63 for a drawing of the female genitalia.)

∽

This is in the end the only kind of courage that is required of us; the courage to face the strangest, most unusual, most inexplicable experiences that can meet us. The fact that people have in this sense been cowardly has done infinite harm to life....

—Rilke

Finding Your Own Sacred Spot

To find your own sacred spot, empty your bladder and lie down or squat and put one or two fingers inside your vagina. Curling your fingers in a "come here" motion, feel the area of the front interior wall of the vagina between the pubic bone and the clitoris at approximately the twelve o'clock position. The sacred spot can be from about the size of a dime up to four times that size. It feels distinctly different from the tissue around it. Its skin feels rough and spongy. When stroked, it swells.

The first contact with the sacred spot may make you feel that you must urinate. This can be a sign that you are in the right area. Just breathe deeply and continue the stroking. You may also experiment with trying to contact the sacred spot with a dildo or vibrator or any long, smooth object.

Sacred-Spot Exploration with a Partner

A trusted partner is important for this shared journey, because although many women can find their sacred spot alone, few are able to stimulate it effectively themselves. Sharing the experience that sacred-spot stimulation can provide can be a deeply bonding experience for a couple.

Prior to sharing this exploration with a partner, it is important to know that the sacred-spot area seems to have the ability to act as a storage site for painful memories and sexual trauma. These painful memories can be triggered when the area is stimulated. This means that the partner who is trusted enough to share this experience must be prepared to be a healer as well as a lover. He must also be prepared to defer his own sexual needs and preferences during this crucial experience.

Set aside at least an hour or more when you can be uninterrupted. Bathe together or separately. Wear lingerie or nothing according to your preference. Be comfortable. Ideally, the man should prepare the room. Have candles, music, and poetry close at hand if you want them. Be sure to have drinking water and perhaps some fruit or other small snacks. Have plenty of lubricant close by.

The woman should empty her bladder before beginning. Then come together in a quiet room. Lie down, with the woman on her back. Exchange caresses until she starts to become aroused. When she seems receptive, the man should ask for permission to enter the sacred space. This request in itself can be healing to a woman who has often felt that she lacked control over her own body in sex.

When she gives permission, the man should apply the lubricant to the outside and the first inner inch of the vagina and then to his own fingers. Then introduce first one or two fingers into the well-lubricated vagina. Gently feel and stroke different areas. Then curl these fingers so that the pads touch the upper ceiling of the vagina. Using a "come here" motion, slowly pull the fingers toward the front of the vagina. Somewhere between the pubic bone and the front of the ceiling you may both become aware of the spot. Look for skin that is ridged and different from the skin around it. Watch her for any response.

The woman's place of power. . . . is dark, it is ancient, and it is deep.
—Audre Lorde

If she suddenly feels an urge to urinate, he has probably found the right place. With her permission, he should continue to stroke, varying the speed and pressure. She should breathe deeply and consciously relax. Usually, after a few minutes, the urge to urinate will give way to great pleasure.

If, instead, she begins to cry or speak of painful memories, it is important for him to be there for her emotionally. Continue the stimulation as long as she is willing, but allow her to cry or express anger or whatever she wishes. The healer's job, in moments like this, is to listen and receive—never to fix. It is also not the time to agree or disagree with her comments about the past. If she wants to talk or cry, this is a time when the reflective listening-plus-validation tool discussed in Chapter 6 will be invaluable.

Continue to focus on stimulating her sacred spot for an hour or more, if she is willing. Experiment with giving other pleasurable caresses at the same time, such as fondling her nipples or pressing on the clitoral area while you stroke the sacred spot. Think of the sacred spot and the clitoris as two poles of the same highly sensitive structure. Stimulating them simultaneously can be delicious to her.

Avoid the temptation to use the high state of arousal you may both feel as a springboard to your usual ways of lovemaking. At least avoid this until you have allowed the experiment to go on for an extended time.

Orgasm is not the goal. She may have several or none. Be sure to take long enough to get the value of the experiment, which is to explore the effects of sacred-spot massage and to give any needed healing to the woman.

Female Ejaculation Is Possible

When the sacred spot is fully awakened, a woman may release a light fluid the ancients called *amrita*—holy nectar. This may occur during orgasm or at other times. It is a pale and slightly astringent fluid that seems to originate in the Bartholin glands and which is expelled from the urethra, but is not urine. It may be expelled dramatically or as a mist that is hardly noticed and which evaporates quickly. Do not strive for amrita or fear it, but simply accept it as a gift if it occurs.

Exploring the Male Sacred Spot

Yes, males do have an analogous sacred spot. You can find the spot by looking or feeling for the slight indentation in the perineum, about halfway between the anus and the testicles (see drawing on page 83). You can stimulate this area by pressing firmly on the spot. Watch your man's reactions. He may enjoy this touch prior to or during orgasm or both.

Direct contact with the male sacred spot is done anally, if both partners are willing and if both are ready to observe several necessary precautions. First, for aesthetic reasons, the rectum should be empty and carefully washed. Even when this has been done, the anus harbors bacteria that can cause infection in the vagina. So a finger or penis or object that has been inserted in either partner's anus must not be put into the vagina without a thorough washing. It's best to use lubricated surgical gloves for anal contact and to wash your hands carefully after removing them.

Most serious of all, the fatal AIDS virus is easily transmitted through anal intercourse with an infected person. For this reason, and because it is difficult to be absolutely positive that your partner is disease-free and monogamous, the anal play discussed in this book is limited to digital contact.

Perhaps it needs to be said that many, many couples enjoy their sexual relationships greatly and feel no need to include anal play in them. When both want to forgo this or any other choice, that is fine. It is only an option and is included in the spirit of viewing all mutually desired sexual possibilities as divine gifts to be considered.

During a lengthy period of perfect control, the whole being of each is merged into the other, and an exquisite exultation experienced . . . the interchange becomes satisfactory and complete without emission.

—Alice Stockham

Making Love Without Orgasm

Letting go of orgasm as *the* goal of lovemaking is central to soulful sexuality. On this shared spiritual journey, it is important to have many lovemaking occasions when there is no goal other than to enjoy opening your hearts to each other. Creating your own ways of making love without coming to orgasm can be a great shared adventure. As you give up asking each other to perform a preconceived role, you will become increasingly able to share deep intimacy and ecstatic states.

A man does need good ejaculatory control to best enjoy soulful sex. Quick ejaculation causes sexual energy to be discharged before it has had time to flower. This may seem, at first, like a performance demand that is inconsistent with the sacred approach. An invitation to develop mastery, however, does not have to be seen as a demand. Ejaculatory control is a *skill*, not an inborn trait. Any man who has normal erections and is willing to practice enough can master it.

The discussion in this chapter assumes that a man has some ejaculatory control already, but that he is open to developing this still further. See Chapter 10 for help with erection problems and with how to apply these principles if you feel you have a problem with premature ejaculation.

Reserving Ejaculation: Key to Ecstatic Experience

In sacred sex, *reserving ejaculation* refers to the choice to defer male orgasm on certain occasions when you have intercourse. Several ancient traditions taught males to withhold ejaculation during many of their lovemaking experiences. They believed that this practice improved health, youthfulness, and longevity. Perhaps they were right; we have no scientific studies to evaluate.

What we do know today is that a man who becomes skillful at reserving ejaculation at times starts enjoying unusually powerful orgasms when he chooses to have them. He is also likely to have a deeper relationship with his partner, and that partner is very likely to feel sexually fulfilled.

Some sacred sex teachers recommend that a man reserve ejaculation at least 25 percent of the times he makes love. An older man may find that an even larger percentage of lovemaking occasions without orgasm helps him to maintain high levels of sexual energy and feelings of bondedness to his partner.

For a man to experience reserving ejaculation, he should carefully focus on his sexual sensations. Trying to distract himself by such ploys as mentally reciting multiplication tables is the opposite of what is needed. Ejaculating more quickly than desired is fostered by the *lack of awareness* of his level of sensation. Developing control requires that he *become* aware and *stay* aware of his sexual feelings at each moment.

As a man, when you are ready to try this, prepare your partner in advance. Let her know that you are working on this for your mutual benefit and that you need her cooperation. Explain to her that when making love, men have a point of ejaculatory inevitability—the point of no return, after which orgasm cannot be stopped. Tell her that you need to be able to reduce stimulation before reaching that point.

When you do make love, notice when you are approaching orgasm. Before the point of no return, slow down or stop all stimulation. Then

> *In the course of an hour the physical tension subsides, the spiritual exaltation increases, and not uncommonly visions of a transcendant life are seen and conciousness of new powers experienced.*
> —Alice Stockham

use one or more of the following techniques while connecting emotionally and with your eyes. Don't worry if your erection subsides somewhat. This is natural. When it returns, it will be stronger.

The first two of the following techniques have the advantage of not requiring the man to stop moving or withdraw his penis:

A man's semen . . . is the driving force in [his] love for his woman. Once he has ejaculated, it is like letting the air out of a balloon—he feels flat, especially so when he ejaculates frequently.
—Jolan Chang

1. Contract your PC muscle and hold it while breathing slowly and deeply. Arousal tends to match your breathing pattern, and your arousal will diminish if you slow down your breathing.

2. Before getting too aroused during intercourse, slow down your arousal by focusing on the *pull*, rather than the push of your thrusts. Relax your buttock muscles at the same time, and breathe slowly.

3. Another kind of pull involves squeezing the scrotum gently and pulling down on it for 15 to 30 seconds. The man can do it to himself discreetly, or the woman can do it while caressing this area. Be careful not to put pressure on the testicles, as this can cause pain. Instead, squeeze just above them, where the sac touches the penis.

4. Firm pressure on the male sacred spot will also interrupt the ejaculatory process. Either partner can use a finger to press for fifteen to thirty seconds on the indentation between the testicles and the anus.

5. Using "the squeeze technique," either partner can hold the penis at the frenulum—the ridge about an inch down from the tip. Squeeze firmly for fifteen to thirty seconds. This will stop the desire to ejaculate and reduce the erection temporarily.

6. The stop-start technique refers to stopping all stimulation the moment you recognize that you are more aroused than you want

to be. Have a one-word signal you've agreed on with your partner, such as "Stop!" The moment you say that, both of you should stop all movement. Be still and breathe. Resume when the man signals that he is ready to do so.

Female Orgasm Increases Connection

Female and male orgasmic responses differ. Women do not really need to forgo orgasms in order to remain connected with their partners and interested in more touch. Women, in fact, often become *more* responsive and more emotionally open the longer lovemaking continues. If they have one or more orgasms, this is likely to *increase* their feelings of desire for the partner.

It is equally important, however, for a woman not to be preoccupied with orgasm or to feel that lovemaking is simply a means to "achieve" orgasm. A woman who is confident in her orgasmic abilities, yet unattached to orgasm as a goal, also has more capacity for joyous sexual experiences.

Each stage of this learning process makes you more available and more in touch with your partner. As the two of you look deeply into each other's hearts during your learning process, may you experience your bond in a new and heartfelt way.

For each of us as women, there is a deep place within, where hidden and growing our true spirit rises . . . an incredible reserve of creativity and power. . . .
–Audre Lorde

Shared Peak

When you do include orgasm in your sexual activities, there are many ways to vary the experience. In a slight modification of the skill just discussed, you can invite intense orgasms by building up the excitement several times before deciding to go ahead with orgasm. In this "shared peak" orgasm, you learn to dance with your partner so that both of you build up several times before climaxing in sequence or together. When very aroused, both of you should stop all movement, contract your PC muscles, and visualize energy going up your spine. Then begin to move again. Repeat this process several times.

You will reach successively higher plateaus of arousal this way. Enjoy the closeness you may experience with your partner during this dance. When you do finally come, it will most likely be an explosive experience.

"Valley" Orgasms

A "valley" orgasm involves a delightful experience of sexual sensation spreading over your entire body, rather than being discharged in one, quick "peak" orgasm. There is no explosive moment here. To have a valley orgasm, stop moving just before you reach orgasm. Breathe deeply, and visualize your sexual energy spreading out and entering into every cell of your body. Be soft and still. Experience a deep sense of love and union.

Combining Techniques

Combining several techniques for delaying and spreading orgasm can result in a longer experience of orgasmic sensation. For men, when very near to orgasm but not yet at the point of no return, inhale deeply and hold your breath. Push your tongue against the roof of your mouth and contract and release your PC muscle. Visualize energy flowing up your spine and out of your heart to your partner.

When you are ready to come, enjoy a longer, stronger orgasm by contracting the PC many times first and then by inhaling deeply as soon as your orgasm begins. When you exhale, accompany it with sound— really sing out! More sound means more sensation and more letting go.

We ... need to understand lovemaking as an exchange of the energy which is constantly moving in our bodies.
—Margo Anand

Allowing yourself to express the sounds that are a natural part of lovemaking increases your pleasure, your partner's pleasure, and your partner's understanding of your responses.

For women, blended orgasms resulting from stimulation of the clitoris and the sacred spot at once can be overwhelming. Continuing the stimulation immediately after orgasm can result in one orgasm after another for many women. Whether or not they have developed it, women have virtually limitless potential for orgasm.

Whole books, such as the well-written *Extended Sexual Orgasm* by Alan and Donna Brauer, have offered complex programs for achieving longer and more intense orgasms. With a loving partner, well-established trust, and good communication, however, you may choose to discover your own path.

Varieties of Movement

On the soulful sexuality journey, the possibilities of variety are unlimited. Every kind of sexual movement can be done in hundreds of ways. The ancient Kama Sutra taught sixty-four noble arts, such as singing, dancing, drawing, writing, and martial arts. It advised studying the sixty-four aspects of sexual union as well. The *Kama Sutra* asserts that "An ingenious person should multiply the kinds of love-making after the example of many different kinds of birds and beasts."

Nine distinct varieties of male movement during intercourse were described. These include forward thrusting, holding the penis in the hand and churning it around in the vagina, pressing hard while deep inside the vagina, rhythmic movement without any withdrawal, and striking the vagina with the penis. Orgasm is said to be facilitated by moving the penis up and down rapidly and playfully while deep inside the vagina.

An End to Sexual Boredom

Another ancient text, the *Ananga Ranga*, dates from the sixteenth century. Its author offers women many suggestions for varied positions and movements. It tells male readers that through varied sexual activities, a man can experience one woman as if she were thirty-two entirely different women, thereby permanently avoiding sexual boredom! Many of the suggested positions involve ways of making genital contact and then moving very little.

Those who want to have a deep love in their lives must collect and save for it and gather honey.
—Rilke

To experiment, sit together facing each other. Use pillows to find a comfortable way for the women to sit on the man. When aroused enough, place penis in vagina and move only enough to maintain the erection. Spend the time quietly enjoying whatever sensations arise. Look into each other's eyes and hearts. After this, experiment with a variety of unfamiliar strokes and movements, expressing yourself and your love with each one.

To vary this, lie on your sides facing each other, or make genital contact with one and then the other on top. Take your time and have no goal other than experiencing whatever comes.

∾ A Weekend of Joy ∾

When you and your partner have used the practices given earlier to reach a place of understanding and forgiveness, consider giving yourselves the gift of a weekend of sexual exploration and pleasure. This can be a great adventure—a time when you can concentrate only on each other from Friday evening until Sunday evening.

One of the romantic myths to be set aside here is that making love should always be spontaneous. On the contrary, you will prepare well for this special weekend. Plan to go away together or to stay home alone. If you have children, arrange to have them cared for and absent for the weekend. If necessary, arrange an exchange with friends whose children you can care for at another time. If animals or other persons live in your household, arrange for them to be away during this weekend also. The first commitment of the "weekend of joy" is to concentrate only on each other for two days and two nights.

In advance, arrange to have the following supplies and any others you may think of: candles, colored light bulbs, clean sheets, flowers, jojoba or vegetable oil and other lubricant, and a book of favorite poetry or prose. Get a weekend supply of food for two. Include fruit, sweets, favorite beverages, and other foods that take minimal preparation.

Each of you may also plan a small, inexpensive loving surprise of some sort for your partner. Also, plan what you will each wear. Comfortable, partly transparent or revealing clothing is best. Consider costume jewelry, makeup, and even body paint, if it appeals to you. If you are going to stay at home for the weekend, prepare the physical space you will be sharing in advance if you can.

Arrange the use of some music on tape or CD. If possible, also take the time to make an audiotape of the sexual/spiritual meditation given earlier in this chapter.

Prior to the weekend, tell friends or relatives that you will be unavailable from Friday until Sunday evening. When the weekend comes, unplug the telephone or leave the answering machine turned all the way down. Similarly, agree to leave the television off for the entire weekend.

✑ Ground Rules

Agree in advance that either one of you may say no to any practice, instruction, or request during the weekend. Also agree that if conflicts come up before or during the weekend, you will defer discussion of them during this special time. During your weekend of joy, speak only of the here and now—not about the past or future. Also, agree on one of the great principles of soulful sexuality: During this weekend, *no mistakes are possible.* You will both make your best effort to follow the instructions given here, but if something happens that you didn't intend, you will accept and enjoy it. Unintended or delayed orgasms, lost erections, and the like are perfectly acceptable.

⟨ *Friday Night*

When the weekend comes, complete your preparations. Clean and beautify your bedroom, using clean sheets on your bed, adding flowers and candles and any other objects that please you. If possible, bring some objects that have spiritual meaning into the room, such as scripture or pictures of holy places. Set up a supply drawer or area in your bedroom, placing in it the lubricant and objects for pleasing touch. Prepare some light, delicious snacks and have them ready for sharing later.

Begin your weekend officially with a bath or shower, taken separately. Consciously relax from the day. Take your time. End with a dip in cool water to stimulate your energy. Put on clean, loose clothes such as robes or nightclothes. Use oil or fragrance on your body if it pleases you.

When you are both ready, come together and put on quiet music. Sit down together. Light a candle and spend several silent minutes gazing at the flame and at each other. Join hands or make other silent physical contact, spending a few minutes doing so. Ask for guidance and blessings in whatever way is meaningful to you. Use alternate-nostril breathing to help clear your minds. Close the left nostril with your hand while inhaling through the right. Close the right nostril and exhale through the left. Repeat for several minutes. Meditate together for a few minutes, thinking of all that you are grateful for in your life.

When either of you is moved to do so, look at your partner and make some kind of statement such as "I honor the divine in you," or "I acknowledge Spirit within your heart."

Bring out the food you have prepared, and offer grace or some acknowledgment of gratitude for it. At this meal and all your meals this weekend, lovingly feed each other. In the interests of experiencing the most pleasure later, eat and drink lightly. Take your time.

Lie down together now in the spoon position—one of you with your back to the other. The one behind puts arms around the one in front. Breathe together for a few minutes, inhaling and exhaling at the same time. Do not talk. Instead, concentrate on the sacred purpose of your relationship. One aspect of this purpose is that you are providing each other an opportunity to learn to love more deeply.

When you both feel ready, offer each other some loving massage and caresses. Take turns giving each other back rubs, foot rubs, or other touch meant to nurture and to release body tension. Do not yet touch each other's erogenous zones. Focus on nurturing touch rather than on trying to arouse.

At some point, when you both are really longing to touch more intimately, sit facing each other, and touch from this position. Use pillows to make yourselves comfortable. Use the seated position for as long as you wish. Change positions at any time you choose. Play and stroke and make love, but don't have intercourse right now.

Make love in other ways, and if either of you gets near to orgasm, slow down, be quiet, and allow some of your arousal to subside. Your goal here is to enjoy and experiment with arousal, rather than discharge it through orgasm. It may seem difficult to forgo orgasm at this point, but give yourselves the gift of doing so. Allow yourselves the opportunity to maintain rather than dissipate the intimacy.

Play and talk at will, using the opportunity to share intimate feelings. When the time seems right, share with each other a heart-opening poem, story, or piece of music. Or, if you prefer, simply make a loving statement to your partner. If you wish, you may choose to read the following quotations to each other. The first is by Harold Bloomfield, and the second is by Sam Keen.

Partner A: "The effects of pleasure are wholly positive. Physically, pleasure improves circulation and increases energy. The emotional effects include greater self-esteem, increased self-confidence, and a generally sharper mind. Spiritually, enjoyment enhances your appreciation of your blessings and contributes to a brighter outlook."

Partner B: "Practice the discipline of delight—Let no day go by without adding something to the music of your experience . . ."

After this time of sharing, begin to move toward sleep. Pray or meditate together for a time, and then settle in to cuddle. Talk softly if you wish, allowing sleep to come at will.

> ～
> *A good mar-*
> *riage is one*
> *in which each*
> *partner ap-*
> *points the other*
> *to be the guar-*
> *dian of his*
> *solitude. . . .*
> —Rilke

～ Saturday

Wake up to the deliciousness of a weekend day alone together. Whoever wakes first should make a simple breakfast in bed for the two of you. Begin by acknowledging your gratitude for your food. See how many mutual acknowledgments you can fit into one breakfast. "You're great to sleep with—a great cuddler!" one may say. The response could be: "Waking up to see you lying beside me is one of the great gifts of my life."

After breakfast, spend some time in meditation or prayer. Light a candle to symbolize the presence of the divine within each of you. Reflect on a holy book or some other object. Put on some music that tends to evoke consciousness of a larger reality. Holding hands or making other physical contact, listen quietly, allowing the music to touch you.

Now come together to connect. Hold each other silently, in the spoon or other position for a few minutes. Begin to make it a habit to reflect on the deeper purpose of your relationship when in this position. With compassion, visualize the wounded inner child of your partner—the little boy or girl who endured disappointment and suffering at times and who was also capable of laughter and joy. When you look into your partner's eyes, *see* that luminous child.

Move into lovemaking when you both feel so inclined, but continue to omit intercourse for now. Instead, experiment with touches and positions that are unfamiliar or new. *Make it your intention to stop short of orgasm,* but if an orgasm should happen spontaneously at this or any point, just enjoy it and continue.

Whether or not you have become accustomed to making eye contact while making love, include this now, for at least a little while. Allow yourself to *see* and contact the inner being of your partner. Allow your partner to *see* you fully.

After a while, by mutual agreement, take a break from lovemaking. Do some sort of movement or exercise. Include some stretching of each part of your body, doing yoga if you know it or making up stretches if you don't. Then spend some time doing any kind of exercise that appeals to you both. Exercise separately or together, indoors or out. Run, dance, swim, walk, or bike; especially if you have a beautiful outdoor area to enjoy.

Come back to your indoor space when you are ready, and prepare for the next event.

∽ Dance for Each Other

Take a few minutes to change into your chosen costumes. If you have no costume, undergarments and a scarf will do. Whoever is moved to begin puts on music of his or her choice, and starts to dance for the other. Be as outrageous or silly or serious as you wish. Dance from your heart, forgetting about evaluations and criticism. When the first one finishes, the other begins. Dance together at the end, if you wish.

Now have a light snack if you are hungry, feeding each other while staying in eye contact. When you are both comfortable, prepare to spend an hour or two or three on the next set of experiences. Put on quiet music you both like and sit down together in chairs or on the floor, facing each other. Make silent eye contact for a few minutes, allowing soulful contact.

Begin to touch when you feel inclined to do so. Have this be a time of experimental touch. Choose some of the following experiments to try:

∽

A spark of pure love is more precious before God ... than all the other works taken together....

—St. John of the Cross

- *Give each other hand and/or foot massages. Give each other ample feedback as to what feels good.*

- *Kiss experimentally for a long time.*

- *Choose a giver and a receiver, and experiment with oral stimulation.*

- *Invent your own experiments and try them out.*

- *After reaching a high state of arousal, hold each other close and breathe deeply. While the excitement subsides, consciously think of spreading it throughout your body.*

∽ A Time of Meditation and Reflection

Spend some quiet, separate time now. Read, write, think, or listen to music. Focus within. Do not watch TV or read newspapers or magazines, because being reminded of negative world events or anything that causes emotional distance would be intrusive. Reflect on the preciousness of your bond with each other.

Focus on your gratitude and your appreciation of your partner. Set aside any worries or dissatisfaction that you may have, not resisting them, but not giving them any significant attention. Make a mental list of all the positive qualities you appreciate in your partner.

ல A Ceremonial Meal

When you are both hungry, choose a time and a way to eat together. Prepare a simple meal together, or one of you can do it as a gift for both of you. Light a candle and decorate the table with flowers if you have them.

If you choose to accompany this meal with wine or champagne or any caffeinated beverage, be sure to drink only a little; more than a little will detract from the experiences to follow. In the same spirit, eat lightly.

Include tasting of fresh fruit in this meal. Feed each other fresh strawberries, mangoes, or other fruit. Savor the exquisite and subtle tastes. Do the same with other foods. Try tasting with your eyes closed. Then savor a tiny bite on your tongue. Swallow slowly. You are teaching yourself still another way of savoring sensation.

ல Resuming Intimacy

When the meal is finished, go back to the bed or couch. Use the various means of connecting that you know now to feel your bond deeply. When you are both ready, begin to make love again, this time going for higher and higher states of arousal.

When and if it feels right, the woman should invite some sacred-spot massage. For a half hour or more, she should receive, while he gives. He should ask permission to enter her sacred space. Use plenty of lubricant, and follow the instructions given earlier in this chapter. Try combining sacred-spot and clitoral stimulation. Have no goal except loving contact. Let orgasms occur or not as they will.

When you both wish to, experiment with different ways of having intercourse now, but do not come to orgasm. Try positions that may seem silly or impossible, or positions you have avoided because they don't lead to orgasm. Stop and rest when you get close to coming, and resume only after your arousal has subsided a bit.

Let this be a time of play and experimentation. Try things you've never done before. Have no goal other than pleasure, exploration, and connection.

After an extended period of sexual play, allow yourselves to settle down. Enjoy the period of coming down from a high level of excitement. Cuddle and caress each other, and when you are ready, go to sleep.

❧ Sunday

Waking up together, savor the prospect of another day to explore and enjoy each other. Have a light breakfast prepared by the one who was served on Saturday. After grace, feed each other, savoring your food.

Then have a period of stretching your bodies. Take an extended bath or shower together. Give each other some massage, communicating your wishes clearly to each other.

Rather than go out to worship on this special day, create a service of some kind at home. If you share a religious orientation, do a home version of the service you would normally attend. If you have different paths, create a service that honors both of them. If you have no religious affiliation, create your own way to honor God, the transcendent, the Light, or your Higher Power.

Take turns leading this service. One can say a prayer, the other can read from a holy book. Add some music and some silence. Contemplate and reflect on the deeper side of the human journey. End the service with many acknowledgments of all that each of you are grateful for. Take turns stating them.

Examples can include all kinds of gratitude, such as: "I appreciate having you as a partner to share the journey." "I acknowledge your courage in participating in this weekend with me." "I thank God for the beauty of the morning." "I deeply appreciate our lovemaking and the joy it brings me." Continue until you have each voiced many acknowledgments and much appreciation.

When your service is complete, turn your attention to each other. Connect physically through loving touch and long eye contact.

When you both feel ready, it is time for the woman to honor the man. The man should now receive for half an hour or more. This means not responding or giving back right now. Just lie back and allow her to attend and pleasure you. The woman should touch him in many ways, concentrating on caresses that he is particularly fond of. Suck his toes, brush his hair, stimulate him orally. Do everything you're willing to do except bring him to orgasm.

When you both feel ready, change roles briefly. The woman now receives again, until her heart is open and she feels moved to initiate a time of unrestrained lovemaking. *Do anything and everything now—no holds barred.* Approach everything with gratitude and openness to new experience. Enjoy making love without a goal or a script. Let orgasms occur or not occur as they will. Ask each other for anything your heart desires. Give and receive freely, noticing how in lovemaking, as in life, everything you give comes back multiplied.

∽ The Lessons of the Weekend of Joy

You can re-create and expand upon the experiences of this weekend many times in the future. It starts with setting aside uninterrupted time for love and loving, a choice that some couples in long marriages never make. When you don't have a whole weekend, set aside a protected evening.

The next steps require that you have the skills to resolve any anger and resentment between you, and to re-create closeness, intimacy, and connection. When you add sexual courageousness and the mutual inten-

Believe in a love that is being stored up for you like an inheritance, and have faith that in this love there is a strength and a blessing so large that you can travel as far as you wish without having to step outside it.

—Rilke

tion to *give* to each other, you have the recipe for unique and passionate soulful sex adventures.

Vanessa and Ben: Integrating Sex and Spirit

Vanessa and Ben now offer some very honest comments on how they learned to connect on a spiritual level rather than just for a few orgasmic moments. We begin with Vanessa.

By the time we had been parents for a few years, romance was a dim memory most of the time, and, without romance, sex could feel pretty dull sometimes. I remember once telling Ben that after a long day taking care of two little girls, what I looked forward to most at night was a chance to read a good book at last! I look back on that as one of the many times I hurt the man I love out of simple immaturity and unconsciousness.

The seminar I've mentioned before was a turning point for us. One of the specific techniques its leaders were very enthusiastic about was what they called "reserving ejaculation." This was a totally strange idea to Ben and most of the other men in the seminar. Most of them said that ejaculation was the main *purpose* for lovemaking, so it made no sense to them to leave it out.

The seminar leaders told us that two things would happen if we tried it. First, we would feel much closer to each other when we made love. Second, they said the men would enjoy the orgasms they did have far more if they didn't come every time.

They also said that the women would feel as if they were being given precious gifts. While a lot of us had experienced having a man want us to respond enthusiastically and have good orgasms because it makes him feel good about himself as a lover, none of us had experienced lovemaking that seemed to be primarily for our pleasure.

I was excited when Ben asked me if I'd be willing to experiment with these new ideas. I was a little hesitant at first, but we decided to enjoy exploring this new territory and not worry about where it led. Ben started practicing, and pretty soon he learned how to monitor his own arousal when we made love. That was the key to his learning to stop soon enough. Eventually, he got really good at arousing me and even bringing me to orgasm several times without coming himself. This bothered me at first, but eventually he convinced that he liked it this way.

I was really touched, just as our teachers had predicted. It was obvious when we made love this way that his main interest was in *giving* to me sexually. I was also impressed with him as a lover who could absolutely control his ejaculations.

Other times, Ben *decided* to come, and he was like a wild man! This was the other payoff our teachers had spoken of—these orgasms seemed to be *much* more powerful than usual! I enjoyed him tremendously. He was *so* passionate, and I was so touched, so moved by his giving and his love. I felt like I was falling in love with him all over again, and I realized that this was partly because I was experiencing our sharing of passionate moments much more as an expression of love than I ever had. I felt like I was receiving gifts from God.

Reserving ejaculation turned out to be far more than a technique for us. It opened the door to far more spiritual, emotional, and sexual depth than we ever had before!

Ben's Story

When I first heard about the idea of mastering my own ejaculations, I was pretty skeptical. The idea of making love for a long time without coming sounded a lot like being a frustrated high-school kid to me. I had pretty rigid ideas about how sex was supposed to be and how it wasn't supposed to be. A night of love with no orgasm definitely wasn't on my menu.

It was when Vanessa and I first started having problems that I started opening my mind a little. The old ideas weren't working. When we went to that seminar, I met a bunch of other guys whose stories sounded a lot like mine. The ones who had been practicing the new approach for a while told me that I'd be a lot happier in my sex life if I learned to be in control of my orgasms instead of them controlling me. They said my wife would also get a lot more out of it.

Over the next few months, I learned that they were right. It wasn't hard to learn to control my ejaculations. I had learned pretty fair control in my twenties, and this was just doing more of the same, except that I wouldn't come at all during these times. When Vanessa and I were making love, I would just pay attention to how aroused I was getting, and when I felt like I was getting close to the point of no return, I'd just stop moving and ask Vanessa to stop what she was doing, or I'd use the squeeze or the pull.

Then I would concentrate on her for a while. She started coming more than once in a session sometimes, which hadn't happened before. I got to watch and be with her in a new way in these sessions, and it was great. I loved it, and I loved her more than ever.

When we had an exciting session and I didn't come at all, I felt something new, just like the seminar teachers had said I would. I felt very affectionate and into her, and it didn't change the way it does when I come. After I have an orgasm, I sort of lose interest in touching and even in being close to my wife for a little while, which a lot of guys in the seminar said was true for them too. But this way, I didn't lose interest at all. I'd feel like I wanted to touch her and be close, and that would go on for a couple of days!

∽

Our work is being truly alive, and that is a challenging job.

—Robert Tucke

Well, you won't be surprised to hear how much my wife liked all this—she really liked it! At first, she said she missed coming with me or watching me come after her like we used to. She felt like she was supposed to "make" me come. She was really touched when she finally understood that I was doing this so that we could grow together sexually and feel more love.

At this point, I realize how lucky Vanessa and I are. We've had our ups and downs, but I really feel that our love gets better every year we're together. For lots of years now, our sex life has been full of fire and honey!

The Joy of Courageous Sex

In the end, lovemaking offers us the ultimate path for sharing the depths of our being with a beloved other. Through courageous lovemaking, we share our progress toward the Light.

There is nothing quite so fulfilling as the ecstasy
we experience in truly meeting and joining with
another person in the spirit of reverence for the
total being of that person. It is in such encounters
that we can know and love the God who is love.

—Georg Feurstein

ↄ

CHAPTER 10

Solving Common Sexual Difficulties: A Spiritual Perspective

Why are millions of us troubled with sex problems?
Why is it that if you are female, you are likely to have problems reaching orgasm at times? A majority of women, some studies show, never reach orgasm through intercourse alone. How can this be?

Why is it that if you are a male in the vicinity of forty or beyond, you sometimes have problems with erection? Why is it that as a male of any age, you probably sometimes have trouble lasting as long as you want to?

Why is it that most couples have some unsolved sexual problems, however committed and in love they may be? More deeply, why is it that sex is so often a battleground, or an arena for feeling badly about ourselves?

Why is it that many of us seldom or never feel deeply moved and in touch with the divine through our lovemaking?

Part of the answer to all of these questions is that we grow up learning a very limited appreciation of what sexual exchange can be. And the most important factor in this is that we forget who we are when we approach sex with our beloved. We have no models for remembering the divine and the unlimited, unconditional nature of divine love in conjunction with sexuality. We make love as if our sexual experiences and the Source of our being have no relationship.

Love is a process, not a destination . . . a holy interpersonal environment for the evolution of two souls.
—Daphne Rose Kingma

Couples find the best solutions to sexual problems when they learn an attitude often discussed in this book—that of beginning to experience their sex life as one of the most significant ways in which they experience the sacred in daily life. With this change in attitude, their feelings about each sexual event change and deepen.

Events that used to be seen as sources of conflict now become the challenges of a holy relationship. When conflicts arise, partners share the desire to resolve them quickly so as to get back to loving harmony.

If you are experiencing sexual difficulties such as erection failure, lack of orgasm, premature ejaculation, or lack of desire, it is a gift to yourself to seek the services of a licensed health professional who is trained as a sex therapist. I know that many readers feel unable or unwilling to do this, however. The tools in this chapter are offered in the spirit of the belief that human beings have divinely given abilities to heal themselves.

The sexual concerns discussed here are shared by millions of couples. The solutions ask you to think spiritually and act practically.

Many Sex "Problems" Result from Misinterpretations of Normal Sexual Variations

The first possibility to consider when you face a sexual difficulty is that it is actually a normal variation in sexual response. "Impotence," better referred to as "temporary erection difficulty," is often a case in point.

Let it be said first that many erection problems have a physical basis. In cases where there is no medical problem though, the most common beginning to an erection problem involves anxiety and/or alcohol. A man who has had a few drinks approaches his partner feeling quite amorous. When the erection he expects doesn't materialize, he is surprised and shocked.

A well-informed man in this situation says, "This happens to everyone sometimes; let's try again later," or "Let's see how much I can turn you on with just my mouth." With this kind of positive self-talk, the incident passes without consequence.

Unfortunately, many men in this situation fall into anxious self-talk instead: "I'm over the hill." "Maybe I'm losing it." "Maybe I won't be able to get it up next time either," and so on. If he worries enough the next time, his erection will be uncooperative again. Two or three disappointments like this are all that many men need to develop what they think is a full-blown case of "impotence."

Many common "sex problems" start this way. Something normal, but different than what the person hoped for, occurs during sex, and then that person begins to worry and engage in negative self-talk.

Garden-variety problems that sex therapists see every day include erection problems and premature ejaculation in men, and orgasm or arousal problems in women. Desire discrepancies between both members of a couple are also among the most common problems.

Here are some examples of the way problems like these can start with negative self-talk and be corrected by reinterpretation:

- *"I'm just not like other women–I hardly ever have orgasms."* This was the self-talk of an orgasmic woman who expected herself to have orgasms during brief intercourse with her husband after little foreplay. This woman began to solve her problem when she learned to give herself a more positive message: *"Every woman needs the right stimulation to come to orgasm. I should learn exactly what I need, and then teach my husband."*

- *"My sex drive just isn't very high compared to my partner's."* The woman who made this statement had a history of enthusiastic lovemaking with her husband earlier in their marriage. Their current conflict was the result of poor understanding of each other's preferred sexual activities.

  When they learned to communicate openly, their supposed difference in "sex drives" disappeared.

- *"I'm just not as potent as I was when I was younger."* This man misinterpreted the natural changes in his sexual responses that occurred between adolescence and mid-life. He learned to say instead, "I'm a more sensitive lover now, and I need more direct stimulation than I used to."

"Am I Normal?"

This is the most common sexual anxiety people report in surveys. In most cases, the answer is a resounding yes. Any sexual behavior that causes no harm and which is engaged in by consenting adults is normal. Each of the following very common questions is followed by its most likely answer.

- *Are my genitals the right size and shape?* Genitals come in a wide range of types and sizes, all of which are beautiful and functional. Unless your genitals make it unclear whether you are male or female, you probably fall within the normal range. Commit yourself to learning to love this precious part of your body.

- *Do I have as much sex as other people like me?* For people in their teens through sixties and even seventies, a wide range is normal. It's best to think in terms of time spent in loving sensual contact with a partner, rather than number of orgasms.

- *Is my desire for a particular act or position or sexual experience "normal"?* Virtually any desire is normal. Whether or not to act it out is a question that requires consideration of possible consequences.

- *Is it unhealthy that I fantasize about terrible things like rape or having sex with my best friend's partner?* No. Fantasy is okay and inevitable. To imagine something does not mean you would do it if you could. Enjoy your fantasies, *and* make careful decisions about your actions.

- *Is there something wrong with me because I have no interest in sex for weeks or months?* No. You are in good company. Periods of fatigue, pregnancy or breast-feeding, illness, mourning, and conditions such as financial stress can drive your sexual feelings underground for a time.

- *Is there something wrong with me because I think about sex constantly or want it every day?* No. Some studies show that having sexual thoughts or desires several times a minute is very common.

> The real news on this planet is love—why it exists, where it came from, and where it is going . . . .
> —Gil Bailie

These examples all point to the same principle of normality: *Normality is self-defined.* Sexual feelings and desires are God-given and holy. If you desire it, desiring it is normal for you.

When we learn to look at our sex lives as aspects of our spiritual development, we start thinking about sex as an experience in mysterious encounter, rather than as a linear set of goal-directed behaviors. This puts all of our "problems" and fears about being normal in perspective. In this life, *we are spiritual beings having a human experience*, and this is especially true in the arena of concerns about sexual problems.

There are times, however, when sexual problem solving is needed. In such times, the principles and tools that follow can be helpful.

Solving Couple Problems Takes Change on Both Sides

Every therapist has had the experience of a couple coming in with the preconceived idea that a problem that's bothering them is one person's fault. They may or may not agree on whose "fault" it is. Here are some examples in which both members of the couple were sure whose "fault" the sexual problem was:

- *Art, age 41, felt terrible because he often lost his erection after he and his wife Mindy began to make love. Mindy felt badly, too, because she feared that Art was losing interest in her. Both of them agreed that Art had a problem—he was "impotent."*

- *Jolene, age 34, never had orgasms with her husband, Joseph, though he was a patient lover who tried hard to please her. She was easily orgasmic with self-pleasuring. Both of them felt that there was something wrong with Jolene.*

- *Raoul, age 28, often reached orgasm within two or three minutes after beginning intercourse with his wife, Lena. He was deeply ashamed of this, and both Raoul and Lena agreed that he needed help.*

- *Irma, age 46, went for long periods with no interest in sex. She felt that she was "frigid." Her husband, Lester, wanted her to "get help with your problem before I go crazy."*

The truth is that all of these people had a couple problem, and the solution in each case required participation from both partners. The partner who was identified as having the problem often had poorly developed ability to let the other know what was needed.

Most important and least obvious, each couple was oblivious to the fact that the spiritual side of their relationship needed more development, and that addressing that need would increase their sexual pleasure.

Soulful Sex Perspectives

It's a Mistake to Have an Inflexible Plan for Lovemaking

Our mechanistic American idea of sex tends to be sequential and unvarying. We expect "foreplay," followed by "sex" (which to many of us equals intercourse), followed by orgasm, followed by a little cuddling until we drop off to sleep. After the late-night TV news in your area, you can be sure that a large percentage of sexually active couples are having experiences like this. If both people have orgasms, many feel that the encounter has been successful and all they can hope for.

Thinking this way about sex diminishes its divine possibilities. The opportunity for deep encounter—for seeing into each other's souls—is always present, if we are open to it. On a particular occasion, fulfilling lovemaking need not include intercourse or orgasm at all.

Mutual orgasm is another mirage—an elusive goal that many set up as a standard of success. When it doesn't materialize, many couples feel they have failed.

A better choice is to begin opening to the possibility of making love with no goal other than fully experiencing what you are feeling. Two people who learn to look into each other's hearts will discover in the moment what will truly satisfy.

Do not fear mistakes. There are none.

—Miles Davis

Solving a Sexual Problem Often Requires Temporary Postponement of Your Wishes

Americans expect quick solutions. We want thin thighs in thirty days and one-minute management expertise. We may not be prepared for the fact that sexual change takes time and patience. When we understand sexuality as a spiritual path, however, it becomes more clear that the patience required of us is that of being willing to surrender the demands of our egos and personalities. We often need to set aside those demands in the interest of a higher goal.

Most sexual growth requires this kind of patience. A man who wants to help his wife learn to have orgasms during intercourse, for instance, may well need to postpone his own preferences for positions that don't stimulate her well.

Similarly, a man who is practicing being able to last longer needs a partner who will assist him in doing the prescribed exercises, even though they may not provide maximum pleasure for her. It's not so difficult to make these choices when you realize that as with all aspects of a loving relationship, what each partner gives comes back multiplied.

Solving Common Sexual Problems

∾ Lukewarm About Intercourse

Jed and Marie came in for marriage counseling, saying that they were feeling out of touch and often angry with each other. Their sexual issues soon came out. Marie rarely had orgasms when they had intercourse. She was orgasmic with self-pleasuring, and occasionally when she and Jed made love in the woman-above position.

It was oral sex that really turned her on and satisfied her, though, and she preferred it to intercourse. In twelve years of marriage, she had never felt that she could let Jed know about this preference. She was afraid it wouldn't seem "normal" and that he might reject her if he knew. Marie did not realize that many women's favorite sexual activity is oral sex, and that it is not at all uncommon for intercourse to be something that these women do primarily to please their partners.

Like many women, Marie lacked assertiveness in sexual situations. She had withheld this information so long that some emotional distance had developed between her and her partner, and this tended to reduce her arousal even further when they made love. If Marie had felt able to tell Jed what she really wanted, she would have said, "I'm happy to have intercourse when that's what you want—and I enjoy it too—but when I want to get really excited and have an orgasm, I'd prefer that you give me lots of oral sex. I want you to lick my vulva and suck my clitoris until I come. I love the way you do that!" Jed would have enjoyed hearing this message.

Sex lies at the root of life, and we can never learn to reverence life until we know how to understand sex.
—Havelock Ellis

When, instead, Marie went along with Jed's agenda when they made love, she thought she was being a good wife and sexual partner. But Jed's experience of these times was that his partner was less responsive than he would have liked. When they stopped making love after Jed's orgasm, Jed and Marie were both disappointed, but neither knew what to do.

Thinking spiritually in such a situation means wondering what this conflict means on a soul level. Something more than a new way to touch was needed.

During one session, Marie brought up a dream she'd had the previous night. In it, a young girl was offering tea to a large man dressed in a robe. He was a royal figure, and the young girl was serving him. Marie then shared a recurring fantasy of herself as a servant girl, dressed in a maid's short, black uniform with lace at the low neckline. This fantasy often came into her mind when she was doing something for Jed's pleasure.

The image evoked a useful discussion of how Marie viewed herself in relationship to Jed, and how this reflected a subservient role she had learned as the youngest child in a German-American family where her father was king.

Jed, a well-educated political liberal who had once served on the board of a national women's rights organization, was shocked over these revelations and felt a great deal of compassion for the oppression Marie had experienced growing up. As Marie wept at the memory of her child-hood submissiveness, Jed realized how hard it had been for her to assert herself in intimate situations.

Resolving this couple's sexual problem came easily, once both Marie and Jed resolved to share their honest preferences and feelings with each other. With Jed's encouragement, Marie began to speak up and ask for the oral stimulation she craved. She was astounded to find out that Jed loved giving her cunnilingus and couldn't get enough of it. "Believe me, sweetheart, it's no sacrifice!" he said. "Knowing that I can please you that way is one of the biggest turn-ons you could ever give me."

Later, this couple experimented with seeing whether Marie could more easily come to orgasm during intercourse. One method that worked pretty well was for Jed to give Marie intense and lengthy oral stimulation until she was very close to orgasm, and then to switch to the woman-above position. Marie took the responsibility here for letting Jed know when she was ready for intercourse.

In this scenario, Marie would reach orgasm within a few minutes of beginning intercourse, sometimes almost immediately. Other times, Marie chose to return to her preference for oral stimulation. When she took an assertive role in letting Jed know what she wanted, her orgasms flowed easily and plentifully.

An even more important healing for Marie, however, was learning that, unlike her father, her life partner supported her in being her full and true self and in having whatever she desired, sexually or otherwise.

Jed also gained a great deal from the experience of giving such understanding and compassion to his partner. He felt good about himself when he experienced satisfying his partner more than ever before.

Jed and Marie felt more bonded after this experience. They could not regret what they had been through, because their soul connection had been so strengthened.

∽ Insistent on Intercourse

In contrast to Marie, Danielle loved intercourse and felt she couldn't do without it. Although she was orgasmic with self-pleasuring, she rarely enjoyed making love to herself. She felt that should be "unnecessary for married people." In shared lovemaking with her husband, Cliff, she usually reached orgasm during extended intercourse, but never by any other means. She enjoyed oral sex, but only as a prelude to intercourse. Because Cliff was able to last for fifteen or twenty minutes or more most of the time they made love, Danielle was usually satisfied.

This couple ran into trouble when Cliff, during a very high-stress period in his life, began reaching orgasm much sooner than before. Cliff's company was laying off employees in droves, and he feared that he would be one of them. He feared losing his home, his benefits, and his financial security in general. Cliff felt badly about himself for having these problems, and this self-criticism manifested in his sexual behavior. "I just can't seem to keep it up very long anymore," he said when he and Danielle consulted me.

To Danielle, this meant that she could not be sexually satisfied. She was very distressed. She was used to making love in their old way and she didn't want to change. She did agree, when I gently asked her about it, that her love for Cliff was far deeper that her expectation of orgasms. She was able to tell him that she loved him and loved their life together and that she trusted that they could work out this problem.

I presented this couple with several options. On the level of concrete sexual behavior, there were at least two possibilities. One was the obvious one of helping Cliff to regain his former ability to maintain his erections long enough for Danielle to come to orgasm. This was the solution both Cliff and Danielle had in mind when they called me.

Another possibility, I suggested, was for Danielle to learn to have orgasms in other ways such, as through oral sex, hand stimulation by Cliff, or by touching herself when they made love. I said that she might want to learn all of these ways of increasing her orgasmic options. "It's a good thing to know that you don't have to be dependent on your partner for orgasm," I told her.

I was pleased when this couple brought up the spiritual aspects of their relationship, because it meant that they had special resources to draw upon. They were devoted to meditation and were members of a large church in their city. They had heard of sacred sexuality and were curious about it. Because of their receptivity, I asked them to consider the current problem in terms of its spiritual meaning.

The next week, Danielle shared that she had experienced an important insight during meditation. She said that their sexual problem brought up her tendency to worry that she would not be taken care of. A part of her did not trust God or the universe to provide.

Cliff, meanwhile, had been reflecting on the emotional aspects of the problem. He said that he now understood that when he felt stress, he began to feel as powerless as he had as a child. Danielle helped him with this by telling him that she didn't blame him for his job situation. She reminded him that they had gotten through other rough financial times. She was ready and able to help out more financially and felt that this was fair to do because of all the years he had supported her while she went to school.

As this couple became aware of their mutual supportiveness, they softened. They became more receptive to each other and to new sexual possibilities. Together, we decided on a three-part approach to reconnect them sexually.

Cliff started on a program of self-stimulation and monitoring his arousal. He learned to slow himself down with the techniques discussed earlier in this chapter—techniques such as slow, deep breathing; the pull; the press; or the start/stop method. Because he had years of experience lasting a long time, it took only a few weeks for him to reestablish his staying power.

Danielle realized that having more options for reaching orgasm would, in fact, be a good thing for her. She did a series of home assignments in self-pleasuring that helped her understand exactly what her orgasmic needs were. She taught Cliff just how to stimulate her orally, and found to her great surprise that she had wonderfully intense orgasms that way. She went on to learn to come through hand stimulation or through contact with a well-placed knee or rubbing against Cliff's pubic bone even if he didn't have an erection.

With the pressure off, this couple soon came back into sexual alignment. In retrospect, they realized that going off track for a while had actually served them, because they now had many new tools, as well as a better understanding of their sexual bond and its spiritual meaning.

Vanessa: The Elusive Female Orgasm

Here Vanessa shares her experience in learning to be fully orgasmic.

One of the first challenges that plagued us for quite a while when we were first married was that I often had trouble getting to orgasm. I thought I was really "slow" and I think Ben also thought so, although he never said it in words. But sometimes he would stop stimulating me just as I was getting close to coming, and that made me think he was getting tired of "working on me." Most of the time it was obvious

that he was ready to come very quickly, so we both thought I was slow.

When I think now about that period in our relationship, I'm aware that my ideas about sex were quite immature then. We spent quite a few lovemaking occasions sort of watching and timing my progress to orgasm. I was like a jogger trying to improve my time!

The self-pleasuring exercises I talked about earlier had one very unexpected benefit. As I got more acquainted with my body and how much pleasure it gave me, I started to love it more than I ever had. It was so responsive to whatever I asked of it, and it served me so well!

My self-pleasuring and teaching him really paid off, and it also opened up the space for him to start teaching me things, which he has since done a lot of over the years.

> ∾
>
> *The meeting of two persons' abilities is like the contact of two chemical substances: if there is any reaction, both are transformed.*
>
> —Carl Jung

Female Orgasm: The Steps

This is the path to easy female orgasm:

1. *The woman needs to learn exactly how she needs to be stimulated in order to come to orgasm. Informing yourself through self-pleasuring is the most direct path to acquiring this knowledge.*

2. *Teach your partner what you learn, partly by discussion and partly by demonstration. Ideally, let him watch you pleasure yourself. If this is too much to consider now, write down a description for him to read and discuss it thoroughly. You could write it as if you were writing fiction, if that is easier. In either case, be clear about details of the stimulation needed.*

   For instance, you might say, "I need a steady rhythm of pressure on and off my clitoris for ten minutes. It needs to come from the flat part of your hand or three fingers together. One finger doesn't feel good for some reason. When we have intercourse, I like to be on top so I can rub

*my clitoris against your pubic bone. When you're on top, I can't
maintain the angle I need well enough." Explain clearly that this is just
what you need for orgasm, but that you may enjoy many other kinds of
sexual exchange as well.*

Orgasm Lib

All orgasms are equal in the sense that there is no way to achieve them
that is superior to any other. Reaching orgasm through oral or digital or
vibrator stimulation is just as "good" as through intercourse. Having orgasms through intercourse doesn't make you more of a woman, and not
having them that way doesn't make you less of one.

Similarly, simultaneous orgasms do not make a better sexual relationship than sequential ones. If there is really a "better" or "worse" way of
having orgasms, it probably has more to do with a soulful exchange than
anything else. That is to say that when your orgasm feels like a spiritually
based experience shared with your beloved, it's going to feel a lot more
satisfying than if you feel that your orgasm came from rhythmic pressure
that had no particular meaning to either of you.

Sensate Focus Helps Performance Concerns

Sensate focus is a tool every couple should know about. Sex therapists
often prescribe it for couples dealing with very common sex problems
that involve anxiety or performance fears. This includes erection problems, orgasm difficulties, and premature ejaculation, among others.

It is certain that many sexual problems come about partly because of
anxiety. Any sexual response that requires a relaxed body and mind can
become elusive when we worry: Will I be able to get it up? Will I be able
to stay hard long enough to satisfy her? Will I come too fast? Will I get to

orgasm this time? What if he changes positions just when I'm getting ready to come? Will he be disappointed if I don't come?

Sensate focus can help. Agree to make love with your partner for a while without stimulating breasts or genitals. Is that possible? Very much so. For many couples, it becomes the first time since their courtship that they have ever focused on the sensual and communication aspects of intimate contact.

Enjoy this lovemaking with no goal. Make love in any other way that feels pleasurable, including massage, kissing, and caresses of a hundred varieties.

Making love this way creates a good context for paying attention to the sacred aspects of your intimate contact. It can help you both to keep in mind the principle that in soulful sexuality there is no goal and there is nothing to criticize yourself or your partner about.

After a week or two, add breast and genital stimulation, but continue to skip intercourse and postpone having orgasms together. Be really creative in discovering options that you may not have paid attention to in the past. There are so many ways to enjoy loving touch.

After another week, add the option of bringing each other to orgasm, but still without intercourse. Many couples are pleased to find out that it's quite easy to do this. It's very freeing to experience that erections and intercourse are not required for sexual satisfaction. It's equally important to continue to focus on enjoying deep contact and closeness during these experiences. Orgasm is only a pleasing option, not the goal.

When you both feel that you have learned the lessons offered by each of the previous steps, incorporate intercourse again some of the times that you make love. When you do, it's a good idea to set things up so that you cannot fail. Say to each other, for example, "The next time we have intercourse, we're going to relax about it and we're going to agree that it doesn't have to turn out a particular way. Since we know other ways to satisfy each other, intercourse will just be one of the choices on a great menu of possibilities."

It's important to prevent intercourse from becoming the only main course in your lovemaking again. There can be times when intercourse is what you both want, but there can be many other times when what you really want is oral sex or mutual genital massage or deep emotional closeness. The spiritual journey you are sharing invites you to use times of physical intimacy to look deeply into each other's eyes and hearts to recall and honor the divine within yourself and each other.

You can use sensate focus whenever it seems needed. It can be useful anytime you find that you are becoming goal-oriented, or anytime that you are starting to evaluate and criticize yourself or your partner. Let sensate focus become a tool for redirecting yourselves back to the path of sexual sharing that focuses on closeness, not performance.

Erection Problems

Every man has times when his mind says yes and his penis says no. This happens more often as a man ages, but it can happen in youth as well. Men are often shocked and frightened the first time they expect to get an erection that doesn't materialize. Most men feel that they are worthless as lovers, "not a man," without an ever-ready erection. This is a fallacy. *It is energy, heart, and courageousness that make a lover—not a hard penis.*

When there's a problem with erection, it's important to identify the cause. The idea that it's almost always "in your head," has been discredited. Many erection problems have a physical basis such as hormonal imbalances, back problems, injuries to the pelvis or spinal cord, reactions to medication, alcohol or drug use or abuse, and diabetes or other diseases. Anything that interferes with the blood supply to the penis can be a cause.

A medical condition, of course, may act in combination with anxiety. That anxiety can result from performance fears or from unrealistic expectations, poor arousal, or lack of a lovemaking environment that feels safe and meets your emotional needs.

If a man's partner is critical or demanding, her attitude can make things worse. If she believes that her orgasms are dependent on his erections, she may feel very anxious and communicate that. If he internalizes his partner's concern, his anxiety will grow.

We cannot escape fear. We can only transform it into a companion that accompanies us on all our exciting adventures.
—Susan Jeffers

If a man has regular morning erections and no problems getting and maintaining an erection with self-pleasuring, his erection problems are likely to be based in emotional factors or relationship issues. In all other cases, evaluation by a urologist who specializes in sexual problems (not all of them do) is important. Ask a sex therapist or your regular doctor for a referral.

Whether the cause of the problem is physical, psychological, or a combination of the two, determining the best treatment takes professional expertise. Whatever the cause, the professional will assist with a decision for a noninvasive treatment like sex therapy on the one hand, or a medical treatment such as injections or even a penile implant on the other.

Possible medical treatments cover a wide range such as taking testosterone or yohimbine, taking papaverine injections, using vacuum devices, having arterial or venous surgery, or having a penile implant. Bernie Zilbergeld, in his excellent book *The New Male Sexuality*, covers the advantages and disadvantages of many of these treatments in detail. He also lists many useful citations of medical literature on this and other aspects of the treatment of male sexual dysfunction.

Sex Therapy

Sex therapy can educate and help relieve the anxiety associated with either partner's performance expectations. A neutral, knowledgeable professional may be needed to help you work out issues that are as emotionally loaded as erection problems.

A therapist can advise a woman how she can lovingly help a man who is facing an erection problem. Much of the information on sensate focus applies. Taking off the pressure and learning to allow an erection to be there when it comes, and willingly doing something else when it doesn't, can make all the difference.

A professional's message to a woman in this situation might be something like this:

"It can be difficult because you may feel threatened and worry about your own attractiveness. You may worry that you'll be doomed to a life that lacks sexual satisfaction. If you want to support your man in gaining better erection capacity, though, this is not the time to let your insecurities control you. It's the time to reassure him that he pleases you whatever the state of his penis, and also that what is happening is normal and experienced by every man at times. Being an understanding and supportive partner to a man facing this problem is a challenge and a great gift to him."

"Impotence" is better called "temporary erection difficulty." It can be a great teacher. It provides an opportunity to reaffirm a loving bond and to become creative in your pleasuring of each other.

But what if you both are frustrated and can't help thinking about this as a problem? Use your new skills to communicate and to express your feelings. Then use the tools you have just been given. The path of soulful sexuality offers a new perspective on this kind of problem. Joyful lovemaking is available anytime you can open your heart.

"Premature" Ejaculation

Inability to control ejaculation is one of the most common problems that sex therapists see. Until they teach themselves to last longer, it is natural for many males to reach orgasm quickly. Probably the ability to ejaculate quickly was once biologically valuable, when conception needed to happen under uncertain and unsafe circumstances.

Some studies show that the average length of intercourse in Western society is less than three minutes. Millions of men—perhaps a third of them—have difficulty waiting as long as they'd like before ejaculating. On the other hand, there are also millions of men who have mastered the skill of delaying ejaculation for long periods. As discussed earlier, a man who wants to share the delights of optimal sexual exchange with a woman will want to learn to be in the latter group. The following discussion is for men who are ready to acquire this skill.

It is best to begin your development of this skill with a period of practicing alone. Arrange to have a protected time to pleasure yourself. Set up a comfortable, pleasing environment and arrange to be alone for at least an hour. Lock your door. Put on some evocative music if you like and spend a few minutes contacting your deeper self.

Think about the divine gift of passion, and choose it for yourself. Notice any ideas coming up that say that self-pleasuring is somehow distasteful or childish. Consciously put those ideas aside as you claim your birthright as a human being whose body was made to experience exquisite sensations.

Begin slowly to arouse yourself, imagining that your sexual arousal is being measured by a 1-to-10 scale as follows: 1 equals the lowest possible level of sexual arousal, 5 equals moderate arousal, 9 equals the point of ejaculatory inevitability, and 10 equals orgasm.

As you stroke your penis and any other area of your body that feels good, maintain awareness of what number on the scale best represents

Inspired sexuality makes the burden of individuality bearable, and increases each person's momentum toward conciousness, compassion and communion.

—Sam Keen

your level of arousal at the moment. Slow down when you become aware that your arousal is at 5 or above. Don't wait until you get to 9, which is the point at which orgasm cannot be stopped.

As soon as you approach 5 or higher, stop or reduce the stimulation immediately. Breathe deeply. Visualize your sexual energy spreading throughout your body. Feel your ability to control your arousal level. Continue being still and relaxing until your arousal level has gone down to 4 or lower. Then start to stimulate yourself again. Repeat the preceding instructions several times.

What if you make a "mistake" and have an orgasm? Enjoy it! Expect to make mistakes. That's part of any learning process. After three or more repetitions, go ahead and bring yourself to orgasm if you wish.

Using this process, you can learn to last a long time. Practice three times a week for a month or longer, always with a sense of pride and pleasure in your own courage and willingness to grow as a lover. Practice reaching 7 or 8 before stopping the stimulation.

Keep practicing alone until you feel that the following apply:

- *You are now more or less constantly aware of your arousal level.*

- *Most of the time, you can allow yourself to reach 6 or 7 or 8 and then stop all stimulation.*

- *Usually, you can repeat the cycle of getting aroused to 6 or 7 several times before you come.*

- *You feel good about your growing sense of control.*

- *You can tolerate "mistakes" without giving up your feelings of progress.*

When the above conditions apply, you are ready to practice with your partner. The first thing to do in this new situation is to make a "mistake." Start making love with your partner and have a fast orgasm. Together, create as much loving acceptance about this as you can. At the least, laugh about it and agree that it's not a tragedy.

This desensitizing was proposed by Bernie Zilbergeld in *The New Male Sexuality* mentioned earlier. As he says, it helps you learn to worry less about "mistakes"—orgasms that happen in spite of your intentions to delay them. It's not necessary (or possible) to be perfect at every step of your journey toward mastery. In fact, mistakes in this, as in everything, offer you valuable learning opportunities. As Dr. Zilbergeld also notes, it offers you more awareness of when you are approaching 9—the point of no return.

Once you have made the requisite "mistake" with your partner, you have various options for proceeding. Whichever you choose, I recommend that you spend time together remembering the deeper purpose of your relationship. It is a spiritual journey, and any improvements in the sexual skills you have can be viewed as tools for making that journey.

Please also take the whole matter lightly in the sense that you maintain a sense of humor and laughter about the learning process. It is not necessary to approach practicing these new skills with a long face and the feeling that either of you is sexually inadequate.

After discussing your plans with your partner, spend intimate time together in which you monitor your arousal level, and stop the stimulation anytime you reach 5 or above.

> It is not easy to find happiness in ourselves, and it is impossible to find it elsewhere.
>
> —Agnes Repplier

Moving Toward Intercourse

Approach this systematically. First, do the monitoring with non-genital "making out." At a later time, do it with intercourse in which you simply insert the penis but do not move. Still later, move gently, continuing to monitor your arousal and to stop all stimulation when you reach 5 or above. Squeeze your PC muscle and breathe deeply until you feel your desire abating a bit.

Eventually, adapt this to gentle intercourse. To maintain a slow pace, focus on the pullback part of your strokes. Pull back, inhale, and relax the buttock muscles. Exhale during the push. Relax and breathe deeply. Only when this becomes easy should you proceed to vigorous intercourse, still using the same now-familiar method. When you reach 5 or above, stop, rest, and breathe.

Repeat this several times. When you can do repeatedly before allowing yourself to come to orgasm, you have mastered your own ejaculations!

With practice, you will be able to use this skill during times of extended lovemaking. Sometimes, you will choose to use this method to build up your orgasmic energy so that you can have an especially intense orgasm. Other times, you can make love as long as you wish, while reserving ejaculation. Concentrate on the especially delicious feelings you are likely to share with your partner on such an occasion.

Differences in Desire

Just as couples who want to eat exactly the same thing every day are nonexistent, no two people have exactly the same wishes about sexual frequency. The result of this is that "desire discrepancies" are one of the most common sexual issues couples face.

If you and your partner are one of these couples, start addressing your difference with good communication and by taking a spiritual perspective. How might you solve this problem in a way that supports spiritual growth for both of you? How can each of you be as loving as possible toward the other while being true to yourself? Can you come up with a shared vision of a solution? Perhaps your visualization might say: We have learned to meet each other's needs so well that both of us are usually satisfied with our sexual frequency.

You have taken a large step toward solving the problem as soon as you redefine *sex* as "loving physical contact that may or may not include intercourse and orgasm." When *sex* means "do something for me because I want it whether you feel like it or not," it's not very appealing. But when *sex* means "let me hold you and affirm you and touch you in any way you wish," a refusal is less likely.

Even though many desire discrepancies can be greatly improved by the use of the tools of soulful sex, concrete differences in physical desire still do exist. Differences in level of desire for emotional contact also exist. Add these together and you may find that one of you seems to be saying yes more often than the other.

It's worth checking out the possible effects of physical factors. This means having a medical examination and investigating such possibilities as hormonal deficiencies, medication side effects, stress, and fatigue. Any medical problems should be checked out, because most of them can affect desire. Clinical depression should be ruled out, as should the possible effects of certain antidepressants, as well as alcohol or other drugs.

Feelings, beliefs, and fears also can take their toll. Some examples include: believing that it's more "spiritual" to have infrequent sex, or that it's not appropriate to feel lustful toward a woman who has become a mother, or that your partner is interested in sex but not in you, or that you shouldn't initiate. All of these and many other beliefs can deaden desire. Communication makes the difference. Being in touch with your beliefs and attitudes and being willing to communicate about them gives your partner a chance to respond.

After all of the tools have been applied, there will still be times when one of you wants to make love and the other doesn't. Loving compromise and taking turns making the decision will handle some or most of these occasions.

Other Common Problems

The following questions are often asked by clients or by my lecture and academic audiences.

Painful Intercourse

Q: "I have pain almost every time I have intercourse with my husband. He tries to be gentle, but it hurts anyway. I feel that I'm not being a very good wife, but I avoid sex whenever I can. Can you help?"

A: Painful intercourse is common but not normal. It needs to be investigated by a physician. It can almost always be successfully treated, but may become worse if it isn't dealt with. The most common causes are physical, such as inadequate lubrication, yeast infections, abrasions, or tense muscles, or menopausal changes.

Check on whether you always have plenty of lubrication when your genitals are being touched. I have seen a surprising number of clients who were unaware that using a lubricant is well advised and no reflection on either partner. Without enough lubrication, many sexual acts hurt.

It is very important to deal with any kind of pain related to lovemaking. An association between sex and undesired pain undermines the pleasurable experience that makes people want to make love over and over.

Compassion is the ability to see how it all is.
—Ram Dass

"I Don't Like My Partner's Technique"

Q: "My wife never touches me in a way that feels enthusiastic to me. She's very gentle—too gentle. I can barely feel it when she strokes my penis. How can I get her to touch me the strong way I like?"

A: Many clients tell me that there's something about their partner's way of making love they don't like. The partner touches too tentatively or too firmly; the kiss is too wet or too dry; the partner won't learn to effectively give the special touch the other craves during orgasm; the partner won't engage in the particular sexual behavior the one complaining longs for.

Usually, each touches the other the way they wish to be touched, instead of giving what the other wants. What's needed is for A to be willing to teach B what A likes and for B to be willing to learn. Successful teaching requires a motivated student, clear information, often demonstration from the teacher, and supervised practice.

Beginning a time of problem solving with prayer or meditation can remind you both of the holy nature of the process of learning to meet each other's needs.

A female client of mine taught her husband how she wanted her nipples touched by playful demonstration. "Just lie back for the next fifteen minutes while I show you what I want. Then I want you to practice until you get it right."

> *Sexuality is not a leisure or part-time activity. It is a way of being.*
> —Alexander Lowen

Less Common Sexual Problems

Problems regarding orgasm, erection, lasting long enough, and desire discrepancies are as common as sunshine. There are other sex problems, however, which can be even more upsetting to people because they realize they are unusual. These people often feel that they are not normal and they bear a great deal of shame in addition to the pain cause by the problem itself.

Here is an incomplete list of some of these difficulties. These problems need professional treatment, but having a problem like this does not make you sick or bad. With the right help, these concerns can be successfully addressed:

- *Vaginismus, in which the vagina spasms shut and cannot be penetrated.*

- *Preoccupation with some unusual behavior such as cross-dressing, food-smearing, or voyeurism.*

- *"Retarded ejaculation," in which a man cannot reach orgasm with his partner even after long periods of intercourse.*

If you feel that you or your partner have a sexual wish that seems abnormal or strange, consider the possibility that you can find a way to address the desire with no compromise to your relationship or to your spiritual integrity. When faced with this kind of situation, you may wish to ask yourself the following questions:

- *Will fulfilling this desire cause physical harm or medical risk to my partner or to me?*

- *Will either of us feel guilty about it or condemn the other for it? If the answer is yes: Does my guilt point to a need to change some attitude? Can I change it by an awareness that loving sexual acts are divinely given and good even if I was taught otherwise as a child?*

- *Can the principles of spiritual sexuality assist me in the resolution of this problem?*

Spiritual Solutions

In the end, we see that the willingness to let go of attachment to our minds' ideas about how things are supposed to be is crucial to solving sexual problems. Above all of these, however, stands the principle that sexual problems can be best solved in the context of a loving understanding that any sexual relationship is the outward manifestation of the spiritual journey two people are sharing.

Many of us think age is so terrible,
so unappealing, so unsexy. . . .
Let's change our minds.
Let's remember that the longer we
live, the more we know, the more
beautiful we are.
—Marianne Williamson

CHAPTER 11

Sex and Aging:
Deepening Love and Passion as We Age

Contrary to the messages of Madison Avenue and Hollywood, sexuality is not the exclusive province of the young. Lovemaking need not be less of a pleasure when our bodies are less capable of the feats we used to strive for as young people. As millions of disabled people can attest, even a paralyzed or otherwise handicapped body can give and receive sexual pleasure. As we grow in love for ourselves as well as for our beloved, the joy of lovemaking can only deepen.

Consider what I have been talking about throughout this book: The essence of sexuality does not lie in the body at all, but in the spirit, the soul. From this perspective, the essence of the joy of sex lies in *bonding*—bonding with the human race through one beloved other, and connecting with the divine.

Aging is an embodied metaphor of human transience. Aging forces us, kicking and screaming, to face how impermanent every aspect of the life of the body is. We resist this in every possible way, from obsession with bodily fitness to the seeking out of much younger partners.

We tell ourselves that *we* will escape the march of time and delay our inevitable end indefinitely. And we use whatever means of escape are available to us. Successful men and very attractive or powerful women find that they can attract a partner whose body and age are comfortingly younger than their own. Some males shamelessly use their privileged position to devalue their female peers. In anxious response, women support the nation's diet centers, spas, and plastic surgeons in the endless pursuit of the illusion of youth.

To the extent that these acts are strategies for denying the fact of aging, they always fail. The younger partner is emotionally immature and doesn't remember the Kennedy administration. Daily working out, constant dieting, and having one's eyelids tightened may create the illusions of youth, but nothing reverses the clock. As far as the life of the body is concerned, you're *not* as old as you feel, you're as old as you *are*.

A spiritual perspective can give us great comfort in these struggles. First, learning the path of creating passion through sacred sexuality makes us more, not less, able to have exciting lovemaking as we age. Second, aging means growing closer to the Light, and to the time when we will merge with it. Through an inner awareness of this truth, we may find courage to face the inevitability of our bodily decline and to find in it the gift of joyous acceptance. In the end, it's all about letting go.

Aging Is Not for Sissies

Perhaps you are old enough to have experienced a decline in some physical ability, or some unwanted change in your appearance. Have you ever pulled out a gray hair? Do you have a laugh line that doesn't go away completely when you stop smiling? Do you run more slowly than you could at eighteen?

More painful, have you already suffered any of the ageist rejections we all face eventually in this youth-obsessed culture? Have you been the forty-five-year-old wife who was left for someone half her age? Have you been the man whose dedication and experience on the job was ignored while a younger man was promoted instead?

Although women often feel that ageism is primarily directed toward them, men also face a painful devaluing of themselves and of their worth as they age. For them, the changes in their age-related ability to "perform" sexually may be the most disturbing. The following not-so-funny joke was told to me by a client in her sixties who refused to consider making love with her husband whose "old penis" turned her off.

Q: "What did the senator give his wife for her birthday?"
A: "An antique organ."

Dubiously humorous jokes about older women in all of their social roles (mother-in-law, gray-haired wife, grandmother) are even more numerous and sometimes more cutting than those about men. For example:

Q: "What's the worst thing about being a grandpa?"
A: "Having to sleep with a grandma."
It's funny until the grandparent they're telling this about is you!

The ageist prejudices of a youth-obsessed culture land in the laps of older women. Unless they are extraordinarily youthful, women over forty and certainly over fifty cannot avoid realizing that many males, *including their peers*, view them as no longer worthy of sexual interest. This is unfortunate for both men and women, given the fact that some older women have great sexual energy and expertise—a reality that is well known in more mature cultures than our own.

So often I have listened to everyone else's truth and tried to make it mine. Now, I am listening deep inside for my own voice and I am softly, yet firmly, speaking my truth.

—Liane Cordes

For us, the Hollywood archetype of the desirable female is burned into our thinking. She is slender, youthful, fertile, and unwrinkled, and her hair is never gray.

Many of us are unaware of how influenced we are by decades of exposure to media that constantly present us with images that tell us who we should find attractive. We have bought into the message that although we *all* lose our sexual value as we age, *women* lose their desirability earlier.

Men, folklore has it, become distinguished as they age, whereas their female peers supposedly lose their ability to excite. Countless television shows and movies have made it seem normal for a middle-aged man to attract the romantic interest of a woman young enough to be his daughter, or even his granddaughter.

These images and stereotypes do not serve us. They cause all of us to feel even more anxious about aging than we already do, and they get in the way of the flow of love and passion that can and should deepen as we become more emotionally and spiritually mature. We must learn to notice and to be less influenced by the biases and self-serving fantasies of Hollywood producers.

Many women in midlife can identify with the following anecdote, told by psychotherapist Rita Ransohoff in *Venus After Forty*. Her patient is an engaging woman in midlife.

I got on the airplane feeling great and looking good. Next to me was a man my age and next to him a younger woman. He immediately turned to her and for three hours I could not avoid overhearing his conversation. Every subject he touched was an area of interest and excitement to me, certain books, parts of the world I knew intimately and loved, art, theater, food. It was a shock to discover that it was as if the seat I sat in was unoccupied. I realized that no matter what I might have been able to share with this man, it was all irrelevant to him. Clearly

his interest was in the other woman because she was young. And
without sex appeal, all of a sudden I felt dead, dead as a woman.

It is unfortunate that this woman internalized the apparent bias of an immature man and that she made no effort to assert herself. These two acts illustrate classic mistakes in aging: internalizing prejudice and allowing it to define us.

Although our spirits are ageless, our bodies do become older and weaker with the passing years. Our spirits grow toward the Light, but our bodies grow toward the time when they will return to the earth. This inevitable and universal process need not diminish our delight in the gift of sexuality.

Even if you are young or in your prime, you have probably already experienced some age-related sexual concerns. Perhaps, like a few of my treasured clients, you are well into your seventies or eighties. Perhaps you have written off sexuality for lack of a partner or lack of sexual communication with the partner you do have.

Wherever you fall on the continuum of aging, your sexuality, like the spirit within you, shines on at every age. Please reject the cultural messages that lead you to feel that there is something vaguely disgusting about passion in a grandparent. Not so! Sexuality flourishes throughout life unless we internalize negative messages. Babies still in the womb lubricate or get erections. Eighty year olds still enjoy sexual touch if they are fortunate enough to have it.

∽

The older I get, the less I must live up to society's definition of "women" . . . and more woman I become.

—Martha Cleveland

We Can Become More and More Sexually Free as We Age

The good news is that things can actually get better as we age. We all need encouragement in affirming this reality, because there are so many negative messages in the media and in our culture.

Most of us are made anxious by the societal stereotypes that imply, for instance, that a women who looks older than forty has nothing to offer as a sex partner. Surely a woman who has lines in her face, extra pounds on her hips, or a few gray hairs is history so far as romance is concerned. Surely a man who "can't get it up" as easily as he could at twenty has nothing to offer as a lover.

Wrong! The truth is that passion and joy increase as the heart opens. As we become more capable of experiencing the ageless spirit in each other, lovemaking can become more and more precious, even while our bodies show the inevitable signs of aging.

This response to aging is certainly not inevitable. It happens only under conditions of support, safety, and love. Under such conditions, a woman comes into her own sexually in her forties and continues to expand her potential as long as she is sexually active. As her body and face begin to announce the end of youth, her heart and her sexuality can blossom in new ways. Similarly, a man who is no longer young can become a more sensitive lover with an increased openness to emotionality and intense experience.

Old fears about sex may dissipate and disappear. A women who disliked oral sex because her mother taught her it was nasty may now have enough distance from parental training to try it with a new openness. A man who was reluctant to display his emotional vulnerability in youth may find the courage to do so in maturity.

Women have a unique journey, in that while their sexual capacities are growing, their fears of aging are likely to be rampant. Very attractive women especially may find the transition from youth to maturity difficult. An attractive woman in her twenties and thirties receives much attention and approval just for looking good. When she begins to show her age, this source of automatic approval dries up quickly. For women who are still looking outside of themselves for approval, this can be a traumatic loss.

To the extent that she is free from fear, a woman's sexual potential at this time is limitless! Some of the possibilities are multiple orgasms or spectacular single orgasms, overwhelming response to sacred-spot stimulation, making love for hours at a time, and enjoying sexual possibilities she would not consider earlier.

These female abilities can be frightening to a man if he thinks his own sexual power is significantly declining. In a way, men and women have opposite processes here. A woman who has focused on the emotionality of sex in the past may now begin to affirm and develop the physical aspects of her sexuality.

Whereas she once had to be "in the mood," she no longer needs flowers and poetry to arouse her interest. A man who was once preoccupied with his physical needs in lovemaking may now find that its emotional aspects have become crucial to him.

A partner can have an important impact on the experience of aging. If a mate internalizes and expresses the ageism of the culture, that person becomes part of the problem instead of part of the solution.

Bella, age fifty-two, illustrated this to her women's group. "Albert never looks at me anymore—not in that special way," she said sadly. "Sometimes I catch him sneaking a look at another woman. She's always young and thin. It seems to me he stopped looking at me that way when my hair started to turn gray five years ago. He doesn't seem to want sex with me very often anymore either."

This couple is facing a passage that has great potential for joy or pain for both of them. They need to learn to express the fears of aging and death which come up for everyone at this time of life.

Sexual love can flower as couples age, if they learn to communicate honestly when these difficult issues arise. Albert does not need to give up his admiration of youthful beauty. He simply needs to open himself to seeing another kind of beauty in the woman who has shared his life. Bella needs to learn to affirm and enjoy the blossoming of her own sexuality in a way that she may have been unable to do when she was younger.

Acceptance Is the Key

Perhaps it takes a lifetime to accept the fact of our own aging. For many of us, it is certainly a struggle that takes many decades. Madison Avenue has taught us well—taught us to strive for youth and beauty and "style" as the alleged keys to happiness. In this milieu, the only possible view of aging is that it is synonymous with loss.

Lovemaking, according to these same values, is best enjoyed when you are physically beautiful. The more you look like a model or a body-builder, the better your orgasms will be and the more your partner will love you.

The truth is quite different. The truth is that sex is best enjoyed when we are spiritually and psychologically developed enough to love ourselves—body, mind, and spirit. This must be our first aim. Second, we may grow more and more willing to love our partners fully. The more we can love and accept ourselves and our partners, the greater our joy in lovemaking.

At sixty, we may hope to be better able to love than at thirty; at seventy, we can aspire to love better than at sixty, and so on, as long as we are given the gift of life. It's never too late to finally gain self-acceptance and to learn to love well.

My Own Journey

Though I always expected to live a long life, I also planned never to age. As a woman who received a great deal of attention from men in youth, I have always feared that any small sign of maturity might bring a loss of the abundant approval that attractive young women receive from males of every age.

In my twenties, living in Washington, D.C., I learned how to create the look our culture admires—a young woman beyond the girlishness of

If I speak in the tongues of men and of angels, but have not love, I am a noisy gong or a clanging cymbal. And if I have prophetic powers, and understand all mysteries and all knowledge, and if I have all faith, so as to remove mountains, but have not love, I am nothing.

—Apostle Paul

adolescence but still at the peak of her beauty. Born with girl-next-door looks and slenderness that came naturally at that age, I learned that with careful hairstyling, "natural" makeup, and designer clothes, I could attract diplomats and neurosurgeons. I learned to think of myself as a "man's woman," and my audience seemed to like my combination of looks and educational ambitions.

For a small-town girl from Arizona, whose parents had felt she was pretty only when "fixed up," it was intoxicating. The world smiled on me. Men approached me on street corners and buses and in crowded restaurants. They offered embassy parties and trips in their airplanes and marriage proposals.

It's an experience known only by women who have been there. It's very easy to get attached to the attention and approval lovely young women receive. Like many of them, I made the fatal mistake of thinking I *was* that persona that attracted so much interest.

At thirty-one, when the first delicate line appeared in my face, I was horrified. That year I began to apologize for my age and never stopped. I could see the handwriting on the wall and I was not happy.

My own journey changed when I began to learn to love myself much more than ever before. Self-acceptance and self-love make a lot of difference. However, I would be less than honest if I said that my concerns with aging are all behind me. It can still sadden me when I see an attractive man of my own age look longingly at a twenty-five year old.

My experience as an attractive woman in midlife is that no amount of emotional maturity or personal accomplishment brings the same approval and acceptance from men as that which came to me automatically in youth. Sometimes, like the woman in Rita Ransohoff's story, I feel that my openness, my ability to love, and my deepened sensuality are invisible to a man who looks at me with the filters of magazine images on his mind.

Such a man sees a woman with several facial lines now, but one whose body contours, thanks to devoted exercise, are nearly as lean as when I was a high-school cheerleader. I know that I speak for many women when I say that at such moments, it hurts to feel unseen and disqualified at a time when I have more to offer than I ever did before time wrote its lessons on my heart.

The quality of the attention I do receive from men, however, has improved. When a man looks deeply into me now, there is more to see—more compassion, more understanding, more acceptance of imperfection than I was capable of before I came to know my own imperfections so well. A perceptive man can also see more love and more passion. In such moments—moments in which I experience my own inner self—I know that in spite of some outer signs that I am forever beyond twenty-five, I have a new kind of beauty now.

We who understand these issues are pioneers in the breaking of crippling ageist stereotypes. Some of us must have the courage to say to our beloved children and others who follow that joy can be found in midlife and beyond. I have chosen to do my part, so I am here to say that my own sexuality has become more fulfilling than ever in midlife. The words of treasured clients and friends who are older than I am assure me that this can continue indefinitely.

With maturity, lovemaking can become a newly treasured way of sharing love and play and spirituality. I am more sexually courageous than I was capable of being at thirty—and more inventive. It took some maturing to be able to understand that lovemaking is not about erections and orgasms and success or failure, but about closeness and joy.

... 'inner freedom' means that a love relation can no longer fetter us; the other sex has lost its magic power over us, for we have come to know its essential traits in the depths of our own psyche.
—J. Jacobi
on Carl Jung

The Gift of Soulful Sexuality

A spiritual approach to lovemaking can help us with age-related sexual concerns. When you see yourself and your partner in the radiance of the Light, your perspective shifts. The question becomes: How can I experience the Light most deeply and most often? If you happen to be looking for a partner, your question becomes: Who helps me to be most in touch with the Light? rather than, Whose thighs or shoulders have the most pleasing outline?

The intention to accept the natural process of aging can get distorted at times. I have seen people use it as a weapon against their partners or as an unannounced test of the partner's loyalty. The message can be: Love me, love my fat and my gray hair. If the partner displays a predictable cooling of sexual interest when his or her lover suddenly looks fifteen years older, the cooling is taken to mean a lack of love.

Meg, a fifty-five-year-old physician, gained twenty pounds and allowed her previously colored hair to go gray after her divorce. "Let them [prospective new partners] love me as I am or forget it," she said to me. Phil, a forty-nine-year-old attorney, who prior to his wife's death had been athletically active, chose a similar course. He gained weight and stopped exercising. Women he met socially often seemed interested in him "only as a friend," he complained, unaware that he was giving out signals of sexual disinterest.

As humans living on the physical plane, we must acknowledge the fact that most men and many women are visual creatures whose egos struggle with aging. A loving gift we can give is the commitment to maintain a pleasing appearance as we get older.

It's a matter of changing the things you can. It's kind to give your partner the gift of being as healthy, attractive, fit, and youthful as you can be. Ignoring weight gain and avoiding exercise are not the actions of a self-loving person. But once we have done that which is reasonable, it's time to focus on acceptance of that which is.

Accepting Our Partner's Aging

For some of us, accepting our own aging is easier than accepting our partner's. Our cultural stereotypes hold that males are more prone to this difficulty than females. Men are more likely, according to folklore, to think of "trading in one forty year old for two twenties."

In my clinical practice, I have seen it both ways. If the partner who has the most power in the relationship also has issues with his or her own aging, that person will be susceptible to impulses to run away from confronting the fact of a partner's aging.

Veronica, a forty-seven-year-old musician, expressed this kind of concern to me regarding her fifty-year-old partner. "Gerard won't dye his gray hair, and the slender body I've always enjoyed is changing. He's gaining weight around his middle. He talks about retirement and grandchildren all the time, and he doesn't seem to be as interested in sex as he used to be. A couple of times he's lost his erection, and when that's happened, he seems to avoid sex for a long time afterward.

"I feel just the opposite. I'm full of energy! I work out five times a week at the gym, and I've had a few cosmetic improvements like having an eye tuck and collagen injections. Now that our kids are grown, I have more freedom and more excitement about life than I ever did.

"If Gerard is going to turn into a grandpa and couch potato, I feel really tempted to have an affair. A really cute younger man at the gym has been flirting with me, and I think he's trying to tell me something. I'm not ready to give up on sex. Just the opposite—I'm more interested in exploring its possibilities than I've ever been."

Veronica speaks for many women and men who find that their partners are not adapting to aging in the same way they are. This couple was in desperate need of better communication. They were undergoing profound life changes, but they were not able to support each other because their communication was stalled.

The biggest surprise in my search for the inner self was finding that it could be experienced by any human being whenever his desire for it was sufficiently sincere.

—Tim Galwey

In therapy, they began to express to each other the fear and excitement they each felt about this stage of their life. Gerard had not lost interest in sex, but he needed freedom from performance fears. He needed to know that Veronica wanted *him*, rather than fulfillment of a list of sexual demands.

Veronica needed more consciousness of what was actually going on inside her. The answers to the challenges of aging were not going to be found in a secret affair with a body-builder. The answers, of course, were within. When Veronica became able to tell herself and then Gerard how fearful she was of losing her youth and her sexuality, it opened a channel of understanding between them.

As this couple became informed about sexual changes and how to cope with them, they found a new depth of love and connection. They recaptured their old joy in sexual touch and open-hearted exchange of feelings.

Eventually, Veronica was able to say, "I treasure my history with Gerard so much. Things have changed since I learned to show him how much I cherish him and how afraid of getting older I've been. Now I have a fellow traveler on this part of the journey, and it's wonderful. Sex between us has blossomed since I learned the courage to really open my heart."

Truly it is in the darkness that one finds the light, so when we are in sorrow, then this light is nearest of all to us.

—Meister Eckhart

Aging Means That There Will Be Changes in Function

Each decade of life brings changes in the functioning of our precious bodies. The journey of soulful sexuality asks us to become knowledgeable and accepting of these changes. Armed with this awareness and acceptance, we become able to affirm and exuberantly enjoy each stage of our growth. What follows are some of the most important changes to expect as we get older.

Young males tend to be in a state of perpetual sexual response and have almost limitless sexual energy. An eighteen year old may be able to have many episodes of intercourse, one after the other, ejaculating after each one and being quickly ready to start again.

During a man's twenties and thirties, the frequency of erections lessens somewhat, and the time it takes him to get a new erection after orgasm (the refractory period) lengthens. The extent of the gradual tapering off varies greatly from man to man. The quality of a man's lovemaking experience may improve as he becomes less controlled by sexual urgency.

Starting within a few years after age forty, however, a man's body lets him know that things are changing. Sometime in this decade, he may find that his erections are somewhat less reliable; they occur less predictably and they can be lost more easily. Unwanted erections are rare now. Instead, lack of erection when the mind says "Go!" may be more common. Whereas in the past, excitement occurred easily through sight or thought of an attractive partner, now a man finds that direct stimulation of his penis is important to his initial and continued arousal.

These are events that should be cheered, not mourned! One of the battles of the sexes is solving itself. Male and female are becoming more alike in their sexual needs. Men are starting to be more influenced by emotional events than physical ones. As a psychology professor I know said about this period: "When I was twenty, I wanted to make love to anything female and breathing. Now, at forty, even the desire to make love requires good feelings about the person."

Attitude change is crucial for and toward a man in his forties. It's time to welcome the advent of sexuality based strongly on emotion rather than on hormonal demand. A man who has felt like a sexual machine—push the *on* button and he was supposed to be ready to go—finds that things have changed. Making love to someone he is angry with or out of touch with emotionally has lost its appeal.

Male sexuality becomes more integrated as men age. Sexual response occurs when physical *and* emotional conditions are right, and not otherwise. Like his female counterpart, a man finds that only when *spiritual* conditions are right does he experience the most gratifying lovemaking. As he becomes more concerned with the emotional aspects of sex, a man is likely to become more able to meet his partner in that vast arena of feelings and spirituality.

As the sexual partner of a man past forty, there is a lot of valued support that you can offer. Encourage him to accept his changes. Make it safe for him to express his fears. Men, like women, deserve to be treasured at every age and sexual stage.

The first time he doesn't get or maintain an erection when he wants to can be traumatic, especially if his partner becomes upset. "Sex problems" can begin here if either or both of you believe that something is wrong. Help him not to feel anxious about it. It doesn't mean that he's "over the hill," as he may feel. It means only that his body, his feelings, and his relationship needs are changing.

You might say that men have fears about declining sexual performance that are analogous to the fears women have about looking older. Our culture tells us that we are useless if we cannot fill the socially approved roles of high-performance lover or youthful sex object.

It can also be difficult for a man to face the fact that whereas his own sexual powers seem to be diminishing, women of his age may be coming to awareness of their virtually limitless capacities. This fear often gets acted out in the form of rejecting women of his own age for someone who is less threatening.

Help your man to understand that his potential as a lover can actually be *enhanced* by his maturity. Teach him that you find him just as desirable as a lover when he has a "soft-on" as a hard-on. Lovingly remind him that becoming skilled at ejaculatory control can make an even greater difference now than before. The ancients, at least, believed that storing semen results in more erections and longer potency.

Teach him that you love the increased emotionality that may come easily to him now. Assume "beginner's mind" when learning how to please him sexually as he changes. Give him more direct stimulation if he wants it. Most men need this after forty. Stroking his penis while you lie together making emotional contact becomes more important as he ages.

Share the responsibility for directing the sexual scenario. Allow him to be passive at times. Help him to affirm this stage of his own growth. Hopefully, he will do the same for you.

When an inner situation is not made concious, it appears outside as fate.
—C.G. Jung

Skillful Communication: Now More Than Ever

Women and men who want to understand each other's differing experiences at this time need skillful communication now more than ever. If you love and want to assist each other, fine-tune your mutual ability to create safety. Help each other to know that you will not become rejecting as age-related changes occur. *Her* increased or erratic passion, *his* increased need for direct, genital stimulation, and *their* need for more reassurance— all these and more will be accepted.

Communicate that it's all right with you for her to violate the "rules" of female passivity and avoidance of sexual leadership that she was taught. Let him know that his desire for a lessening of responsibility for sexual outcomes is okay.

Reassure each other in your first experiments with throwing off old patterns. Remind each other that experiments don't have to have any particular outcome. They should not be thought of as opportunities to "fail," but as chances to *learn and enjoy*.

Encourage your partner to share those long-unexpressed feelings and desires about sex. Even if you've been together twenty years, be assured that your partner has secret wishes that have never been voiced: She hates French kissing, but never said so. He prefers orgasms through oral sex, but felt you would be devastated if he acknowledged it. She's embarrassed to have you look at her when she's naked because she's sure that her Cesarean scars will turn you off. He's always wanted to try anal sex but thought you would be disgusted. Create safety and open channels of communication and there will be many surprises.

The Fifties and Beyond

Biological changes are unmistakable by now. The post-menopausal woman has less vaginal lubrication and more tender genital tissues. Like her man, she needs certain changes in their sexual practices. The most notable of these is the generous use of lubricants such as Astroglide or K-Y Jelly, if these are not already a regular part of their lovemaking.

Problems with weight gain are also common at this time and may contribute to feelings of being less attractive and therefore less sexual. A combination of greater self-acceptance and more effective strategies for weight management are in order.

The parallel facts for males over fifty involve an intensifying of the changes already discussed. Extended stimulation of the penis by either partner becomes even more necessary to a man's full arousal. Even then, erections may be lost at times, and orgasms become more widely spaced.

For many men, the refractory period can increase with each decade. Remember that the capacity for deep experience may increase along with it.

Men who find that they are continuing to function well start to realize that their age does not have to be a sexual limitation after all. On the other hand, men who have interpreted the changes of their forties to mean that they are "over the hill" are likely to become even more frightened after fifty and to need extra encouragement and reassurance.

Some men give up on sex at this time. They can "no longer perform," they say to themselves; sexually speaking, it's time for the rocking chair. This kind of thinking brings about a great and unnecessary loss. The

Taking a new step, uttering a new word is what people fear most.

—Fyodor Dostoyesvski

journey that our Creator ordained offers us the great pleasure of sexuality at every age.

The counterpart decision in women is the idea that menopause means the end of active sexuality. Women who have accepted the belief that procreation is the only justification for sexual activity now find that they have no inner permission to be sexual.

Some women take to heart the cultural message that the truly sexual women is nineteen and looks like Miss America. A woman with gray hair and middle-aged thighs may see a grandma rather than a passionate woman when she looks in the mirror. So far, the fact that many grandmothers love sex remains a secret to many.

We need to develop some new images. Picture a woman with shoulder-length gray hair and a look of fire in her eyes making love passionately. Imagine a man with a receding hairline and the hands of a violinist caressing her breast. . . .

The Many Faces of Sexuality in Later Life

The range of sexual satisfaction seems to get wider for both genders throughout the sixties, seventies, and later. Some people of these ages report that they continue to enjoy their sexuality. At eighty, clients of mine have reported greatly enjoying partner sex and masturbation, though they may have fewer erections and orgasms.

On the other hand, more and more people give up on sex as they reach these ages. Many of these women and men have no partners, and most have no belief that they deserve to be sexual at this age. Some had such unsatisfactory sex lives when younger that they gladly use age as a convenient reason to put sex out of their lives once and for all.

The following stories illustrate the range of possibilities. The first tells us how difficult things are for some older couples. Hannah is seventy-three and has been widowed for ten years.

"I told my husband when I was fifty that there would be no more sex. We had three children and I had been putting up with intercourse for thirty years by then. It felt like rape to me every time, meaning it was painful and against my unspoken wishes.

"Neither of us knew anything about sex when we married in our late teens, and I guess we never learned. Jacob was a kind man, but he knew nothing about how to make love to me. I've learned from reading sex books that one reason sex was always painful was that I was dry when we did it. Neither of knew about artificial lubricants or about arousing me enough to produce my own.

"I've never had anything that seemed like the orgasms I've read about, and after all these years I've lost interest in the whole subject. I do miss Jacob since he died. I actually came to love him after we stopped having sex because he continued to be kind and loving to me for twelve years till the day he fell over dead with a heart attack.

"No one ever told me a single thing about sex before my marriage, and I couldn't bear to ever talk about it with Jacob. I've been blessed in many ways in my life, but sex is not one of them."

In contrast to Hannah's sad story, Earl, age seventy-eight, says: "Being a dirty old man doesn't bother me, if that's what some people would think if they knew that my wife and I still enjoy sexual intimacy. We've been married for 'only' forty years—a second marriage for us both. She's a little older than I am, though I'm the only person who knows that. I felt like she was a gift from God when I found her and I've never changed my mind, even in our worst times.

"Terry and I have always loved touching each other and we've gone through many phases in our physical relationship. Back in our forties, we had periods when we made love every day. Those were the first years of our marriage. She amazed me sexually. She could actually have orgasms from being touched on her shoulders or especially on her nipples.

"When we were first married, I thought I was incredibly lucky to

Take a risk a day—one small or bold stroke that will make you feel great once you have done it.
—Susan Jeffers

have found such a highly sexed woman. She said—who knows whether she flattered me or not—that it was because I was such a considerate and 'hot' lover.

"Things slowed down for us for a while when Terry went into menopause. She had hot flashes and she was tired and moody a lot for a year or two. She finally confessed to me that she was afraid I wouldn't want her anymore since she was going through the change. She thought I might want a younger woman. When I told her I didn't want anyone but her no matter what age she was, she relaxed and started acting sexy again.

"I started to love her more and more because she was so honest with me. No other woman had ever shared her bare soul with me like that—certainly not my first wife, who never would even tell me what she liked and didn't like in bed.

"I also had a period when I got nervous about sex. It was when I was about fifty-five. I started losing half of my erections—at least it seemed like that—and I couldn't stand it. We actually went to a sex therapist at that point, something I never would have considered if Terry hadn't brought it up and half-dragged me there.

"It was a lucky choice, because our doctor taught us that it was time for us to find some new ways to make love. That was when Terry told me that she liked orgasms just as much if I gave them to her with my fingers or my mouth or even if she touched herself while we were making love. She said she liked intercourse, but she liked other things just as much, so I found out I could relax about my erections. We found out that the sixty-nine position got her to orgasm even faster than intercourse did.

"Something even more wonderful happened after that. Once both of us really relaxed with each other—this was about seventeen years into our marriage—we started to have these wonderful, close experiences when we made love. Terry called them spiritual experiences. What I felt was so amazingly close to her, so much in love with her, so aware of how precious she was to me. I could tell she felt the same way, though both of us found it hard to find words for those special times.

"I don't want to make it sound like it was or is always that way. Lots of times it's just bread-and-butter sex, and that's fine with me. Also, we've had hundreds of disagreements and arguments during our forty years—we're just human, after all.

"In the past five years or so, things have changed again. Terry and I both have some health problems now, and we can't make love on the kitchen table anymore. Also, I don't care much most of the time now whether I get erect or whether I come. I just like to hold Terry and touch her any way we feel like. Every now and then, though, the old fire seems to come back and we feel young again for a few minutes.

"It's all beautiful to me now. I've learned to love myself and my wife and my God more and more and more as I've gotten old. I admit that sometimes I feel like George Burns' song—'I Wish I Was Eighteen Again.' But most of the time, I feel that getting old is not bad at all because it took me this long to learn to love this much."

Vanessa's Story of Aging

I had to reach my fifties to find out how fulfilling sex could be. In my twenties, sex was fairly unconscious. We did it when we had a chance, and it felt good. That was about as far as it went.

In my thirties, I was always thinking about how Ben felt about me. Was I good-looking enough? Was I thin enough? Did he like my body? Did he love my body too much but not really love *me?* Would having babies ruin my figure? Would Ben enjoy my passion or would he reject me for it?

In other words, was I lovable and was I safe? Those were my great concerns in my thirties. Lovemaking was usually very enjoyable,

I always traded my sexuality for something—more security in the relationship, more power, more approval.

In my forties, I started worrying more about my physical appearance. I worried about the lines in my face, and sometimes I would try to show Ben one side of my face (the "better" side) more than the other. I gained weight for a while and I started wearing nightgowns, pretending to have developed a taste for lingerie. Actually, I was wanting to cover up what I felt were my new figure flaws. I was no longer young and I was anxious about it. I still enjoyed sex, but it usually had a significant component of anxiety for me.

Now, in my fifties, I enjoy making love more than ever and more often than ever. I'm not trying to manipulate Ben or get him to promise anything. I don't have to worry about birth control, which makes everything easier. But, most of all, I finally love myself, and this affects what I have to give in lovemaking. Now I give love to be giving and because I am full of love inside. I no longer give just to get.

I accept my body now in a way that I never did when it was younger and more like a girl in a magazine. I *love* my body! It's given me so much pleasure and has served me so well. My abdomen stretched to bear my two children, so naturally it's not perfectly flat. But it feels good when it's touched, and I accept it as it is. I stay as fit and trim as I can, but I no longer obsess about it.

A really interesting development in our sex life has been that for the last seven or eight years, Ben has started to be more like me. *He* wants to be in the mood now, *he* wants to feel close, *he* enjoys lovemaking more when we are spiritually and emotionally intimate while we're being physically intimate.

This started in his mid-forties, and I love it. I feel closer to him than I ever did before, and I just want to keep learning to love him more and more deeply as we get older. I understand now that we are

The life which is not examined is not worth living.

—Socrates

on a spiritual path together and that our lovemaking is one of several important aspects of our shared journey.

I haven't mentioned the most important thing, because it's so hard to put into words. I guess I could say I've learned to experience God in our lovemaking. I've learned that when my mate and I give or receive loving touch, we are expressing the inner Light. We are expressing *divine* as well as human love.

Sometimes when I look into my husband's eyes, I see in him a pure and golden light. I have no need for him to be different in any way, including the ways I used to want him to change. In these moments, I see divine beauty in him and it's overwhelming.

For me, it took reaching my fifties to experience lovemaking this way. I look forward to lovemaking in my sixties and seventies and eighties because I hope to continue loving more and more deeply, more like the love I feel coming to me from God.

Soulful Sex as We Age

Here's a summary of the principles that assist us in manifesting a spiritual approach to sexuality and aging:

- *Greater compassion for ourselves and others is the gift aging can offer us.* As young people, most of us are unable to empathize with the pain and feelings of those much older than ourselves.

    We haven't had their experiences and we just don't understand how they feel. Empathizing with those who are much older forces us to experience some of their pain, and we may not feel able to do that. It would force us to confront our own mortality, not a choice we want to make as long as we are able to feel young and therefore not in danger of aging or death.

    When we ourselves age, we lose youth's illusions. We face the truth of human transience with no shield of denial to comfort us as it did in youth. If we allow our hearts to break open over this truth, compassion for ourselves and for all human beings results.

- *Acceptance of change is the key to joyful aging.* Acceptance of that which *is*—of that which we have been given—is a spiritual act. We must accept our own and our partner's aging as part of the gift of life. Aging is an opportunity to grow toward God.

- *Our sexuality is a God-given gift that continues to flower throughout life if we nurture it.* Although many people use aging as a rationale to justify getting rid of the sexual behaviors they never enjoyed fully, we all have the more fulfilling option of choosing to act on the fact that we are sexual beings for as long as we live.

- *Loving our bodies fully while not demanding that they reflect cultural stereotypes is another spiritual task.* When we experience our sexual relationship as sacred, we find that concerns about such superficial matters as appearance become less important.

- *Life is difficult, and aging well is one of its greatest challenges.* We must seek out all the support and love we can find to help us meet that challenge with as much daily awareness of the divine as possible.

The most important fact about sex and aging is that *our enjoyment of our sexuality can continue to grow for as long as we live.* At seventy, we are less agile than at twenty, but we are likely to have more love to give.

More than ever, the world needs what you have to give.
—David Viscott

To have a spiritual relationship is to
consciously acknowledge that above all
we are spiritual beings and that the
process of our own spiritual refinement
is our true undertaking in this life.

—Daphne Rose Kingma

෴

CHAPTER 12

The Sex Life of Your Dreams

A few years ago, I traveled thousands of miles around India by train. I was searching for wisdom, for more contact with God. Early one morning, I sat silently in a holy place in a village far outside Bombay. Suddenly finding the grace to surrender my ego and my doubts, I began to be flooded with images and with joy.

The vivid faces of everyone I have ever loved came to me, as tears of happiness streamed down my face. First my children, then my parents, then lovers and friends—all of their faces appeared one by one. I understood that God's love has been manifested in my life through these treasured beings, each one a precious embodiment of the Light. I understood that each of my actions has the potential to express this love.

Soulful sex follows from the understanding that we are manifestations of the divine. Loving sexual acts, then, are divine love in action.

A Summary of the Journey

Hopefully, you have taken from this book what speaks to your heart at this time, and left the rest. Understanding that you have your own unique experience of this process, I offer a summary here of what seem to me to be the crucial building blocks:

- *Overcoming the influences of mechanistic thinking about sex and beginning to build more safety and more trust.*

- *Affirming sexual receiving and sexual giving as ultimately spiritual acts which allow love and passion to flow more deeply.*

- *Coming to a greater understanding and affirmation of the eternal feminine and masculine. We honor the profound feminine need for connection and for a redefinition of sex. We understand and respect the masculine need for sexual acceptance and for the nurturing and contact that lovemaking provides.*

- *Accepting the sacred duty to become skillful communicators about sex. We become very comfortable with the vocabulary of sex and we speak our sexual truth freely.*

- *Mastering the tools of sacred sex. This includes emotional tools such as the healthy expression of anger and forgiveness, negotiation, goal setting, and visualization of desired outcomes, as well as sexual tools such as staying in eye contact, conscious breathing, massaging sacred spots, and reserving ejaculation.*

- *Experimenting freely and laughing easily at ourselves. Playfulness becomes a regularly shared experience.*

- *Opening our hearts and knowing that this is the key to sexual joy.*

- *Understanding that open-hearted sexual playfulness and close-ness can continue to deepen at every age so that fears about declining sexuality are minimized.*

- *Knowing when and where to get help when we need it and being comfortable doing so. This includes being knowledgeable about finding assistance that is sensitive to our spiritual as well as our sexual and relationship needs.*

Vanessa's Reflections on the Soulful Sex Journey

With much gratitude to the couple I have called Vanessa and Ben, I now include Vanessa's final words.

Looking back, I am so grateful for the many incredible sexual experiences I have had in my life. I'm even grateful for the times when it wasn't incredible. It's all been precious.

There have been times when I felt nothing less than the presence of God in the embrace of my beloved. There have been times when the sensations I felt were so powerful that I completely lost my awareness of my self, my ego, my name. We were so close that we truly seemed one instead of two.

For me, this could happen only because there is such love and trust between us. We have been together a long time now, and we have been through a hundred kinds of conflict and disappointment with each other. I say this because I don't want people to believe the myth of romance—that we're supposed to find the "right" person and then being in love will make sex thrilling.

That's not my experience. When I look back to the time when Ben and I were always talking about being "in love," it seems like we hardly knew each other then, and our sex life was erratic. We were afraid then—afraid of each other, afraid of knowing what was really inside us, and afraid of the incredible kind of passion we have today. We were worried about our appearance and our technique and about how our sex life compared with others'.

It took a long period of working things out, getting professional help, falling on our faces, and sticking with it to get to where we are today. And it's only now that I really give myself fully when we make love.

As a young person, I never knew that lovemaking was a way to share my spiritual depths. I thought sex was a physical and maybe emotional function; and for a long time I believed that feeling romantic when we made love was the way to make it good. Romance was a kind of mirage, though, because after a few years, it faded.

I understand now that the reason for that is that romance is based on fantasy—it's based on not knowing someone very well and imagining a lot of wonderful, unrealistic things to fill the gap. It's great being seen as a marvelous person with no warts, but only until those warts get revealed. When people really get to know each other, romance gets to be a less and less frequent experience.

The kind of passion Ben and I often experience now is very different. We know each other extremely well after all this time, and we know each other's many faults. Neither of us was ever perfect-looking, and now we have some gray hair and a few wrinkles and bulges between us. Can you believe that this makes our lovemaking even more precious than when we were slimmer and younger? It's true! We make love with the full knowledge that the "forever" we once spoke of is not as long now as it once was, and I think the facial lines and gray hairs make that more real.

We are far more courageous as lovers now than we were as young people. We want to experience everything possible while we can, and we go for it in a big way lots of the time. Sometimes we're completely out of sync, and we end up laughing ourselves silly, like the time we tried to do it on the beach at night and got sand in our lubricant and had abrasions instead of orgasms.

But other times, they could make movies about us. I treasure the sensations my body is capable of and the deep spiritual connection I regularly experience when we make love. I feel the Light when we touch each other, and I freely use my body to express a depth of love which is beyond words.

Advancing Toward Our Dreams

We may not reach our aspirations, but we can cherish them. We can open our hearts, our bodies, and our spirits to the pursuit of lifelong, soulful passion. We can choose the path with heart and learn to fully experience the sacred in the gift of human touch.

APPENDIX A

Getting More Help:
A Treasury of Resources

If you have opened some doors as a result of reading this book, you may wish to continue further on the path that you have started. This appendix offers you guidelines and resources.

The following topics and resources are covered in this appendix:

- *Committing to Growth*
- *Understanding the Differences Among Health Practitioners*
- *Psychotherapy: Its Value and Limitations*
- *Understanding the Different Kinds of Psychotherapy*
- *Treatment of Addictions*
- *Spiritual Emergencies*
- *Choosing a Psychotherapist or Doctor*
- *How to Find a Sex Therapist*

- *Sex Surrogates: A Cautionary Note*
- *National Sexuality Organizations: Education and Referrals*
- *Hotlines and Information Services*
- *Seminars, Training, and Workshops*
- *Audio and Video Resources*
- *Books for the Soulful Sex Journey*

Committing to Growth

Commitment to becoming all that we can be should be our gift to ourselves. For most of us, this means a lifetime of reading, practicing, counseling when needed, participation in a spiritual community, and seeking out opportunities to stretch ourselves as often as possible.

Should you consider the wealth of literature, videos, counselors, seminars, and training that is available? My advice is to say yes to the consideration of *all* of it. Why limit your opportunities to grow by telling yourself you don't need these things? Why follow old patterns from parents or peers who may have been afraid to expose themselves to new sexual information and new ways of thinking?

My objective here is to offer you assistance in knowing what could benefit you and in identifying books, products, and video and audio materials that are consistent with the intention to ground your life in the sacred.

Understanding the Differences Among Health Practitioners

Some sexual, psychological, and spiritual situations require more help than any book can give you. My purpose here is to help you see that it is a self-loving act to seek help if you have been subjected to any experience or family circumstance that has caused you to feel lifelong pain.

First let's decipher the maze of categories of psychotherapists and counselors. *Practitioners from any of these disciplines may or may not be trained and qualified as sex therapists.* You must ask them about their training and experience in dealing with sexual issues. *Therapist* or *psychotherapist* or *counselor* can refer to any of the following:

Psychiatrists have completed medical school and are qualified to prescribe medication. Those with the most training are "board certified," meaning that they have been carefully evaluated by highly qualified peers.

Individuals who have been diagnosed with clinical depression, bipolar disorder ("manic depression"), or any kind of psychosis are some of the categories of people who should consult a psychiatrist, so that medication can be prescribed and monitored.

Some psychiatrists do medication consultations for other therapists. This means that you see a psychologist or other professional for psychotherapy, but the psychiatrist prescribes and monitors medication for you. This gives you the benefit of two professionals instead of one.

A common example is that of a clinically depressed patient who sees a psychiatrist for the prescription and monitoring of Prozac or some other antidepressant while seeing a psychologist, social worker, or other professional for psychotherapy. Some psychiatrists prefer to do psychotherapy themselves and don't want to do "med consults." Don't hesitate to ask.

Urologists are M.D.s who specialize in the physiology and pathology of the urinary tract and of the genitals. Some but not all of them are experts in sexuality, and some are qualified sex therapists. Ask them about their background and areas of expertise.

Psychologists are required to have a Ph.D., to complete a supervised internship, and to pass difficult written and oral examinations. Many psychologists are skilled in psychological testing, qualifying them to give IQ and personality tests. Psychologists in private practice often have extensive training in psychotherapy and/or counseling.

Many psychologists have general practices where they see a wide range of patients, including individuals, couples, and groups. Some specialize in such areas as child psychology, industrial psychology, couple counseling, or group therapy. As with every other discipline, psychologists' experience with treating sexual issues is variable, so you must ask.

Marriage and family counselors hold a master's degree or higher in the discipline of the same name. Licensed MFCCs have completed a supervised internship and demanding examinations. Some have special training and experience in a particular clinical area such as marriage counseling, child therapy, or chemical dependency, to name a few. In states where there is no Marriage and Family Counseling license, practitioners should be certified by the American Association of Marriage and Family Therapists or another professional organization.

Social workers have a master's degree in social work (MSW). In many states, social workers who have completed supervised internships and passed challenging examinations become Licensed Clinical Social Workers (LCSWs). Those in private practice may have extensive training in psychotherapy and they may specialize in particular clinical areas. They are often especially skilled at helping clients to find and use community resources.

Clergy who counsel: Some members of the clergy have been trained in psychotherapy and counseling. They can be skillful at integrating the perspective of their faith with the tools of counseling. Many have decades of experience and a deeply rooted faith.

Others have no professional training in counseling, but feel they must respond to the frequent requests of their parishioners for help with spiritual or personal issues. As with every other professional, question your minister, priest, or rabbi about his or her qualifications as a counselor. Most will refer you to a licensed professional if you ask for that.

Psychotherapy: Its Value and Limitations

The inherent self-healing potential of human beings is activated when a therapist is able to give unconditional acceptance to the client. My friend Mary Ellen Edwards wrote a beautiful poem that includes the following lines. They capture some of the essence of what can happen:

> In my work
> I become a lover
> understand people better
> than their own parents do,
> know them in ways
> their lovers and children long for,
> learn their signs, their movements,
> discover what their facial lines reveal.
>
> I love them better
> than they love themselves. . . .
>
> The work is privileged.
> I've lived more lifetimes now
> than I deserve
> and know the anatomy of inner space
> like my own two hands. . . .

As a psychologist, my bias is that one should explore the possibility of psychotherapy with no more hesitation than you would have about consulting a dentist. The idea that psychotherapy is only for those who are deeply disturbed is, of course, completely incorrect. Everyone needs help at times, and healthy people often benefit the most from psychotherapy. Many psychotherapists have practices that focus not on disturbed patients, but on people with "problems in living," such as divorce, stepfamily concerns, the stress of life transitions, or relationship conflicts.

But what *is* therapy and when is it really a good idea? Here are some facts you should know:

Psychotherapy is "talk therapy," where for one or more hours weekly you talk about your problems with a trusted, caring person who has been trained to help you find your own answers. Sheldon B. Kopp, in *Guru,* suggests that psychotherapists are needed because ". . . there are only different kinds of unhappy childhoods, and remembrances of happy childhoods are merely illusions desperately held on to. . . . Children are, after all, inevitably helpless and dependent . . . Parents always turn out to be a disappointment, one way or another. . . . Each child finds ways of pretending to himself that he is not as powerless as he feels . . ."

The goal of psychotherapy is to heal some of the pain of childhood and to build self-esteem. It is meant to provide one place in the world where you don't have to meet anyone else's agenda or suppress any aspect of yourself. The therapist's job is to not to give you advice, but to provide support and acceptance so that you can find your own answers.

Many forms of psychotherapy focus on understanding how your childhood experience influences your current attitudes and behavior and on how you can change. Other models of psychotherapy, often called "cognitive" or "behavioral," focus on changing your behavior, without much attention to early roots.

Some of the varieties of psychotherapy are Gestalt, transpersonal, family systems therapy, many types of group therapy, hypnotherapy, psychoanalysis, Jungian analysis, transactional analysis, redecision therapy, cognitive-behavioral therapy, and therapy that focuses on women's issues, men's issues, or a specific problem such as divorce or substance abuse.

Counseling is similar to psychotherapy but has the connotation of including some advice or sharing of expertise by the counselor. Examples are vocational counselors and relationship counselors.

Sex therapy is a specialized blend of psychotherapy and counseling wherein the goal is to solve sexual problems and to teach you how to have the sex life you want. A good sex therapist knows how to *counsel* you about new sexual behaviors and how to switch the focus toward looking at childhood issues or personality patterns *therapeutically*, if that becomes necessary because progress is stalled.

Psychoanalysis is a particularly intensive kind of psychotherapy. In its classical form, it is lengthy, intensive, and expensive, because you may see the analyst several times weekly for years. Its proponents believe that it is the most effective or only route to deep personality change.

Psychoanalysts are unlikely to be trained to help you solve specific sexual problems or to support your spiritual life. Working with a skilled psychoanalyst over time, however, can dramatically improve your feelings about yourself.

Jungian analysis is a similarly far-reaching and intensive process, but it is grounded in spirituality. Jung felt that human beings have innate religious cravings. In *Memories, Dreams and Reflections*, he encouraged gaining deeper awareness of "the sorrow of the world, no longer a personal, isolating pain, but pain without bitterness, binding all human beings together."

Jung said that treatment involved four stages: catharsis, explanation, education, and transformation. He also believed that the therapist should drop all theories when encountering the magnificence of the human spirit. In practice, Jungians tend to be inventive, supportive, and interested in supporting your inner life.

Treatment of Addictions

Psychotherapy doesn't work if you are abusing substances or food. If you go home from a therapy session that has brought up some painful feelings and have three glasses of wine or eat a whole cake, you are unlikely to take the needed action in your life. In other words, addictions should be handled before insight therapy can be expected to help.

Not all therapists are trained to treat addiction. Some will begin therapy with a new client without even inquiring about use of addictive substances. Nor do most therapists recognize that addictions often have a spiritual basis.

If you have problems with food, alcohol, cigarettes, or other drugs, it's important to go to a treatment program that has been recommended by someone you trust, or to a licensed health professional with specific training in the treatment of that addiction.

Whether or not you can afford paid treatment, twelve-step programs such as Alcoholics Anonymous, Narcotics Anonymous, Smokers Anonymous, or Overeaters Anonymous are free and available everywhere. They offer invaluable support. If you are not sure whether you are an alcoholic or addict, go to meetings and hear others' stories. The only requirement for attendance is a desire to stop drinking or overeating or using drugs. Simply getting yourself to a meeting of the appropriate group can be a vital first step in turning your life around.

If you are the partner, child, or parent of someone who has an addiction, it's crucial to seek support for yourself. See a therapist yourself or attend twelve-step groups such as Al-Anon or Codependents Anonymous. This is a gift to the addicted one as well as to yourself, because you are likely to enable (support) the addiction if you don't get help in seeing how you do this.

Local twelve-step organizations are listed in telephone directories in most cities. If your preferred group is not listed, call Alcoholics Anonymous and ask for help in finding other twelve-step groups.

Spiritual Emergencies

If either you or your partner is suffering from a profound spiritual crisis, you need help from someone who is trained to recognize such emergencies. Spiritual crises are sometimes misdiagnosed as psychiatric episodes, because their outer forms can resemble each other.

People experiencing psychotic episodes tend to lack insight and may have delusions and hallucinations and bizarre behavior. Spiritual emergencies can mimic some of these conditions, but they are actually crises of personal transformation and have great positive potential, such as the healing of emotional and psychosomatic disorders and providing solutions to personal problems.

Consider this possibility if you or a loved one ever faces what seems to be a severe psychiatric disturbance. The best course is to seek assistance from someone trained to deal with spiritual emergencies in addition to getting psychiatric and medical help.

The Spiritual Emergence Network was founded by Christina Grof in 1980 to help people find knowledgeable help in distinguishing spiritual emergencies and assisting with them. To get in contact with the Spiritual Emergence Network, call (408) 426-0902, or call the Institute for Transpersonal Psychology at (415) 493-4430.

Choosing a Psychotherapist or Doctor

As a consumer of professional services, remember that you are the prospective employer. You have every right to ask probing questions about any health professional's training and experience. An appropriate and much too rarely asked question is: "How many people have you seen who have a problem like mine?" The second question you should ask is "How recently have you worked with problems like this?"

How to Find a Sex Therapist

The best way to find any kind of therapist is through the personal recommendation of someone qualified to judge professional competence.

Although there are training programs that award certificates to professionals upon completion, there are no state or national licensing systems for sex therapists at this time. This means that it's doubly important that anyone you see for sex therapy be licensed as a psychiatrist, psychologist, marriage counselor, or social worker. Licensing is important, because candidates must pass examinations showing that they have been properly trained and that they understand professional ethics.

Be sure that any professional you consider seeing for help with sexual issues also has had training and experience assisting people with such problems. The way to be sure is to ask questions.

Sex therapy, like other kinds of psychotherapy, is a professional relationship. Ethical sex therapists do not engage in any sexual activity with their patients.

Sex Surrogates: A Cautionary Note

Do not confuse sex therapists and sex surrogates. Unlike licensed psychiatrists, psychologists, marriage and family counselors, social workers, and clergy, sex surrogates do engage in sensual or sexual acts with a patient to assist with the patient's problems. An example of sensual rather than sexual acts might involve teaching an extremely fearful and shy man to be able to tolerate sitting with a woman and holding her hand. Another case could involve full intercourse with a patient who is trying to learn to control his ejaculations. Most surrogates are women.

There is no licensing for sex surrogates. This means that there is no professional organization that investigates and examines them. Many work under the supervision of a licensed, professional psychotherapist, however.

Use of sex surrogates is controversial among professionals. Some contend that when supervised by a professional, surrogates can be appropriate and helpful to patients who are extremely shy and socially unskilled, or whose real-life partners will not assist them in therapy.

Other professionals treat only couples or individuals who want to work on an individual concern. Many of these professionals look with disfavor on surrogates for moral reasons or concern about medical safety.

It is unwise to deal with a surrogate who is not supervised by a qualified professional. Such a situation would give you no protection against disease and no assurance that the surrogate was competent and interested in assisting you, rather than herself.

ᗯ *National Sexuality Organizations: Education and Referrals*

Write or phone the following national organizations to request a referral to a qualified practitioner in your area. The first organization listed offers one of the few certification programs for sex therapists:

American Association of Sex Educators, Counselors and Therapists (AASECT)
435 North Michigan Avenue, Suite 1717
Chicago, IL 60611

American Association for Marriage and Family Therapy (AAMFT)
1717 K Street NW, Suite 407
Washington, D.C. 20006
(202) 452-0109

Society for the Scientific Study of Sexuality (SSSS)
Box 208
Mount Vernon, IA 52314-0203

The Association of Sexologists
1523 Franklin Street
San Francisco, CA 94109
(415) 928-1133

Sex Information and Education Council of the U.S.
130 W. 42nd Street
New York, NY 10036
(212) 819-9770

~ Hotlines and Information Services

The following national numbers can be called anonymously from any state in the country. Trained people will give knowledgeable answers to a very wide range of questions about sexuality and sexual health. Some services will send you free information if you request it and give them your address. Large cities have local services whose numbers you can get by calling directory assistance and asking for "sex information."

National STD Hotline
(800) 227-8922   8:00 A.M.–11 P.M. EST, Monday–Friday
This free service provides the latest information on all sexually trans-

mitted diseases and how to avoid transmission. They can often answer other sexual questions as well, and may be able to refer you to services in your area.

AIDS Hotline

(800) 342-AIDS = (800) 342-2437   24 hours, 7 days

Call for complete information on Acquired Immune Deficiency Syndrome (AIDS) and AIDS Related Complex (ARC).

HELP (National Herpes Information Line)

(919) 361-8488   9:00 A.M.–7:00 P.M. EST

This informative service can answer all questions about herpes and refer you to herpes support groups in your area.

Planned Parenthood (for men and women)

(800) 829-7732   9:00 A.M.–5:00 P.M. EST, Monday–Friday

This national organization offers low-cost AIDS testing, birth control, and sex education. They will send you free pamphlets and refer you to the Planned Parenthood division in your area.

∽ *Seminars, Training, and Workshops*

A large number of seminars and training programs can help you make large strides in personal growth. The following list includes some of the best sources. All of the following have growth opportunities that are grounded in spirituality.

Esalen Institute

Highway 1
Big Sur, CA 93920-9216
Catalog requests: (408) 644-8476

Located three hours south of San Francisco in Big Sur, Esalen has for decades offered some of the most innovative personal growth opportunities available anywhere. Its beautiful setting on a cliff overlooking the Pacific features natural hot springs open daily around the clock.

A sampling of recent or current offerings gives an idea of the variety of topics: "Managing with Heart: Changing the Leadership Paradigm," "Big Sur Wilderness Experience for Families," "Choice in Dying: Toward a Good Death," "Transpersonal Medicine," "Midlife Crisis as Spiritual Emergence," "Keeping a Good Relationship Alive," and "A Massage Workshop for Women."

Workshops at Esalen last a weekend, five days, or longer.

∾ Holotropic Breath Work

Grof Transpersonal Training
20 Sunnyside Avenue, Suite A-314
Mill Valley, CA 94941
(415) 383-8779

Dr. Stanislov Grof and his wife, Christina, offer various valuable training sessions and workshops in their method of breath work in the United States and abroad. This is a method of reaching altered states without drugs. Participants often have profound spiritual experiences. If you want to deepen your spiritual awareness, this path is worth considering.

∾ The Hoffman Process

If you are interested in a healing experience that gives you permanent peace with your parents and which puts you in deeper touch with the spiritual side of your nature, I highly recommend the Hoffman Process. It is a deep, cathartic experience which can give you results which are difficult to equal in other ways.

For a packet containing information and articles on the Hoffman Process by Harvard Psychologist Dr. Joan Borysenko, contact:

The Hoffman Institute
223 San Anselmo Avenue Suite 4
San Anselmo, CA 94960
(800) 506–5253

Hoffman Institute-VA
5504 Ivor Street
Springfield, VA 22151
(800) 598-7778

Marriage Encounter
(415) 485-5220; (800) 235-1010

These weekend seminars for couples, held at various churches around the country, can greatly increase the intimacy and stability of your marriage.

〜 *Victoria Lee Associates*

For orders of audio products, or to arrange speaking engagements, professional training, workshops for the public, psychotherapy, or sex therapy, contact:

Victoria Lee Associates
Box 31212, Dept. A
Tucson, Arizona 85757
(520) 575-5432

Appearances can be scheduled around the country and abroad. Benefit appearances for charitable causes are available.

〜 *Audio and Video Resources*

The following audio and video tapes offer you specific training in the various subjects offered. The pamphlets provide consise summaries of the each subject.

All products can be ordered from Victoria Lee Associates, listed above.

Sacred Sex is a ten-tape set of audio tapes based on *Soulful Sex*. They are available for $11.00 each, or $87.00 for the entire set; prices include shipping and handling. No indication of contents will appear on the package.

Arizona residents, please add 7% sales tax. Please allow 3-4 weeks for delivery.

Send a check or money order made out to Victoria Lee Associates for the amount of your order. Specify "full set" or state specific tape numbers.

1. *Communicating About Sex*
2. *Understanding Sacred Sexuality*
3. *Enhancing Sexual Intimacy*
4. *Greater Sexual Arousal Through Soulful Sex*
5. *Becoming Orgasmic for Women*
6. *Learning to Last Longer and Enjoy Sex More*
7. *Tools to Open Your Heart*
8. *Loving Meditations and Exercises for Couples*
9. *What Do Women Want? (Pleasing A Woman Through Soulful Sex)*
10. *What Do Men Want? (Pleasing A Man Through Soulful Sex)*

Victoria Lee Associates Videotapes

Lee Associates Video tapes feature Dr. Lee, clergy, and other health professionals presenting exercises and discussions of the principles of soulful sexuality. Inquire about the following topics: 1. Achieving Soulful Sexuality; 2. Solving Common Sexual Problems; 3. Male Sexual Reality: Men Speak for Themselves; 4. Female Sexuality: More Passion Through Soulful Sex.

Victoria Lee Associates Pamphlets

The following short pamphlets can assist your learning by providing a consise summary of the subject. They will be sent in plain envelopes. For 100 pamphlets, send $84.00. Specify pamphlets by number. For individual copies, send $1.00. Both prices include postage and handling.

Arizona residents, please add 7% sales tax. Allow 4 weeks for delivery.

1. *Soulful, Joyful Sex for Couples: Getting Started*
2. *Your Sexual Relationship As A Spiritual Path*
3. *What Do Women Want (in Bed)?*
4. *What Do Men Want (In Bed)?*
5. *A Spiritual Guide to Female Orgasm*
6. *A Spiritual Guide to Lasting Longer*
7. *Lovers Getting Older, Getting Better*
8. *Sexual Secrets of the Sacred Feminine*
9. *Secrets of Ecstatic Sex*
10. *Communicating About Sex for Couples*
11. *Soulful Sex for Newlyweds*
12. *Soulful Sex for Long-term Couples*
13. *Frequency Conflicts; Loving Solutions*
14. *What Goes Wrong With Romance*
15. *Marriage Is For Growing*
16. *Successfully Single*
17. *Your Baby's First Year: How to Stay in Love*
18. *Non-Destructive Divorce*
19. *Safer Sex for Couples*
20. *What You Should Know About STD's*

Imago Productions Videotapes
The Institute for Imago Relationship Therapy
1255 Fifth Avenue, Suite C-2
New York, NY 10029
(800) 729-1121

Dr. Harville Hendricks presents a video workshop for couples based on his excellent book *Getting the Love You Want: A Guide for Couples*. The institute also offers audiotapes and information about couple workshops being held around the country.

ꞏ Tantra Workshops

Source Seminars
Box 135-C
Mill Valley, CA 94942
(415) 972-7214

For those who are comfortable with spirituality that is based more on Eastern than Western models, workshops in a modernized version of tantric sexuality can profoundly change your experience of lovemaking. One valuable set of programs for couples and singles is taught by Charles and Caroline Muir, who can be contacted at the Mill Valley address.

ꞏ Books for the Soulful Sex Journey

The following books have been invaluable to me and many others on the path of spiritual growth. Consult them with joy.

Spiritual Growth and Religion

Andrew, Frank, Ph.D. *The Art and Practice of Loving.* Los Angeles: Jeremy P. Tarcher, 1991.

Borysenko, Joan, Ph.D. *Fire in the Soul: A New Psychology of Spiritual Optimism*. New York: Warner, 1993.

_____. *Guilt Is the Teacher, Love Is the Lesson*. New York: Warner, 1990.

Campbell, Joseph. *The Power of Myth*. New York: Doubleday, 1988.

Dass, Ram, and Paul Gorman. *How Can I Help? Stories and Reflections on Service*. New York: Alfred A. Knopf, 1990.

Eckhart, Meister. *Breakthrough: Meister Eckhart's Creation Spirituality in New Translation*. Introduction and commentaries by Matthew Fox. New York: Doubleday, 1980.

Grof, Christina. *The Thirst for Wholeness: Attachment, Addiction, and the Spiritual Path*. San Francisco: Harper San Francisco, 1994.

Grof, Stanislav, M.D., and Christina Grof, eds. *Spiritual Emergency: When Personal Transformation Becomes a Crisis*. Los Angeles: Jeremy P. Tarcher, 1990.

Grof, Stanislav, M.D., and Christina Grof. *The Stormy Search for Self*. Los Angeles: Jeremy P. Tarcher, 1990.

_____. *Beyond Death*. London: Thames and Hudson, 1980.

Hoeller, Stephen A. *Jung and the Lost Gospels*. Wheaton, Ill.: Quest, 1989.

Jampolsky, Gerald G., and Diane V. Cirincione. *Wake-up Calls*. Carson, Calif.: Hay House, 1992.

Joy, Brugh. *Joy's Way*. Los Angeles: Jeremy P. Tarcher, 1979.

Keen, Sam. *Hymns to an Unknown God: Awakening the Spirit in Everyday Life*. New York: Bantam Books, 1994.

Living Bible, The. Wheaton, Ill.: Tyndale House, 1971.

Moore, Thomas. *Care of the Soul: A Guide for Cultivating Depth and Sacredness in Everyday Life*. New York: HarperCollins, 1992.

Nelson, James B. *The Intimate Connection: Male Sexuality, Masculine Spirituality.* Philadelphia: Westminster, 1988.

Roman, Sanaya. *Living with Joy: Keys to Personal Power and Spiritual Transformation.* Tiburon, Calif.: H. J. Kramer, 1986.

Ryan, M. J., ed. *A Grateful Heart: Daily Blessings for the Evening Meal from Buddha to the Beatles.* Berkeley: Conari Press, 1994.

Singer, J. *Boundaries of the Soul: The Practice of Jung's Psychology.* Garden City, N.Y.: Anchor/Doubleday, 1972.

Snow, Kimberley. *Keys to the Open Gate: A Woman's Spirituality Sourcebook.* Berkeley: Conari Press, 1994.

Steindl-Rast, Brother David. *Greatfulness: The Heart of Prayer.* New York: Paulist Press, 1984.

Tsu, Lao. *Tao Te Ching.* Trans. by Gia-Fu Feng and Jane English. New York: Vintage, 1989.

Warter, Carlos. *Recovery of the Sacred: Lessons in Soul Awareness.* Deerfield Beach, Fla.: 1994.

Wilbur, K., J. Engler, and D. Brown. *Transformations of Consciousness.* Boston and London: New Science Library/Shambala, 1986.

Wilbur, Ken. *The Spectrum of Consciousness.* Wheaton, Ill.: Theosophical Publishing House, 1977.

Inspiration and Poetry

Allen, Marc. *Tantra for the West: Everyday Miracles and Other Steps for Transformation.* San Rafael, Calif.: New World Library. 1992.

———.*The Perfect Life: Ten Principles and Practices to Transform Your Life.* San Rafael, Calif.: New World Library, 1992.

Bly, Robert, trans. *The Kabir Book.* Boston: Beacon, 1971.

Campbell, Joseph. *The Hero with a Thousand Faces.* Cleveland: World, 1970.

———. *The Masks of God.* New York: Viking, 1968.

Campbell, Joseph, and Bill Moyers. *The Power of Myth.* New York: Doubleday, 1984.

Castaneda, Carlos. *Teachings of Don Juan: A Yaqui Way of Knowledge.* Berkeley: University of California Press, 1968.

Gibran, Kahlil. *The Prophet.* New York: Knopf, 1969.

Hesse, Herman. *Siddhartha.* New York: Bantam, 1951.

Hirshfield, Jane, ed. *Women in Praise of the Sacred: 43 Centuries of Spiritual Poetry.* New York: HarperCollins, 1994.

Keen, Sam. *The Passionate Life: Stages of Loving.* New York: Harper and Row, 1983.

Millman, Dan. *The Way of the Peaceful Warrior: A Book That Changes Lives.* Tiburon, Calif.: H. J. Kramer, 1984.

Mitchell, Stephen. *Parables and Portraits.* New York: Harper and Row, 1990.

Mitchell, Stephen, ed. *The Enlightened Heart: An Anthology of Sacred Poetry.* New York: Harper and Row, 1989.

———. *The Enlightened Mind. An Anthology of Sacred Prose.* New York: HarperCollins, 1991.

Oliver, Mary. *New and Selected Poems.* Boston: Beacon, 1992.

Redfield, James. *The Celestine Prophecy: An Adventure.* Hoover, Ala.: Satori, 1993.

Rilke, Rainer Maria. *The Selected Poetry of Rainer Maria Rilke.* Ed. and trans. by Stephen Mitchell. New York: Simon and Schuster, 1982.

Roth, Gabrielle. *Maps to Ecstasy: Teachings of an Urban Shaman.* San Rafael, Calif.: New World Library, 1989.

Rumi. *This Longing: Poetry, Teaching Stories, and Letters of Rumi.* Trans. by Coleman Barks and John Moyne. : Threshold, 1988.

Teresa, Mother. *Words to Love By.* Notre Dame, Ind.: Ave Maria Press, 1983.

Viscott. David. *Finding Your Strength In Difficult Times.* Chicago: Contemporary Books, 1993.

Williamson, Marianne. *Illuminata: Thoughts, Prayers and Rites of Passage.* New York: Random House, 1994.

Relationships

Hendricks, Gay, and Kathlyn Hendricks. *Conscious Loving: The Journey to Co-commitment.* New York: Bantam, 1990.

Hendrix, Harville. *Getting the Love You Want: A Guide for Couples.* New York: Harper and Row, 1990.

_____. *Keeping the Love You Find: A Personal Guide.* New York: Simon and Schuster, 1992.

Johnson, Robert A. *We: Understanding the Psychology of Romantic Love.* New York: Harper and Row, 1983.

Leonard, George. *Adventures in Monogamy: Exploring the Creative Possibilities of Love, Sexuality and Commitment.* Los Angeles: Jeremy P. Tarcher, 1988.

Moore, Thomas. *Soulmates: Honoring the Mysteries of Love and Relationship.* New York: HarperCollins, 1994.

Viscott, David. *I Love You; Let's Work It Out.* New York: Simon and Schuster, 1988.

Vissell, Barry, and Joyce Vissell. *The Shared Heart: Relationships Initiations and Celebrations.* Aptos, Calif.: Ramira, 1984.

Welwood, John, Ph.D. *The Journey of the Heart: Intimate Relationships and the Path of Love.* New York: HarperCollins, 1990.

Sexuality

Alvrez, Alicia, ed. *On the Wings of Eros: Nightly Readings for Passion & Romance.* Berkeley: Conari Press, 1995.

Anand, Margo. *The Art of Sexual Ecstasy: The Path of Sacred Sexuality for Western Lovers.* Los Angeles: Jeremy P. Tarcher, 1989.

Barbach, Lonnie, Ph.D. *For Yourself: The Fulfillment of Female Sexuality.* Doubleday, 1975.

———. *Pleasures: Women Write Erotica.* New York: Harper and Row, 1984.

Barbach, Lonnie, Ph.D., and Linda Levine, ACSW. *Shared Intimacies: Women's Sexual Experiences.* New York: Anchor/Doubleday, 1980.

Bouris, Karen. *The First Time: Women Speak Out About Losing Their Virginity.* Berkeley: Conari Press, 1993.

Brauer, Alan P., M.D., and Donna J. Brauer. *The ESO Ecstasy Program: Better, Safer Sexual Intimacy and Extended Orgasmic Response.* New York: Warner, 1990.

Butler, Robert, and Myrna Lewis. *Love and Sex After 60.* New York: Ballantine, 1993.

Castelman, Michael. *Sexual Solutions.* New York: Touchstone, 1989.

Chopel, Gedun, and Jeffrey Hopkins. *Tibetan Arts of Love.* Ithaca: Snow Lion. 1993.

Comfort. Alex, M.D. *The New Joy of Sex.* New York: Crown, 1991.

Dodson, Betty. *Sex for One: The Joy of Self-Loving.* New York: Harmony, 1987.

Feurstein, Georg. *Enlightened Sexuality: Essays on Body-Positive Spirituality.* Freedom, Calif.: The Crossing Press, 1989.

———. *Sacred Sexuality: Living the Vision of the Erotic Spirit.* New York: Jeremy P. Tarcher, 1992.

Heiman, J., J. LoPiccolo, and L. LoPiccolo. *Becoming Orgasmic: A Sexual Growth Program for Women.* Englewood Cliffs, N.J.: Prentice-Hall Inc., 1976.

Henderson, Julie. *The Lover Within: Opening to Energy in Sexual Practice.* Barrytown, N.Y.: Station Hill, 1987.

Hite, Shere. *The Hite Report on Female Sexuality.* New York: Dell, 1976.

————. *The Hite Report on Male Sexuality: How Men Feel About Love, Sex and Relationships.* New York: Ballantine, 1981.

Kaplan, Helen Singer. *PE: How to Overcome Premature Ejaculation.* New York: Brunner/Mazel, 1989.

Klein, Marty. *Ask Me Anything: A Sex Therapist Answers the Most Important Questions for the '90s.* New York: Simon and Schuster, 1992.

————. *Your Sexual Secrets: When to Keep Them, When and How to Tell Them.* New York: Dutton, 1988.

Moore, John. *Sexuality and Spirituality: The Interplay of Masculine and Feminine in Human Development.* San Francisco: Harper, 1980.

Muir, Charles, and Caroline Muir. *Tantra: The Art of Conscious Loving.* San Francisco: Mercury House, 1989.

Nelson, James B. *The Intimate Connection: Male Sexuality, Masculine Spirituality.* Philadelphia: Westminster, 1987.

Ramsdale, David, and Ellen Ramsdale. *Sexual Energy Ecstasy: A Practical Guide to Lovemaking Secrets of the East and West.* New York: Bantam, 1993.

Reinisch, June M., with Ruth Beasley. *The Kinsey Institute New Report on Sex: What You Must Know to Be Sexually Literate.* New York: St. Martin's, 1990.

Schover, L. R. *Prime Time: Sexual Health for Men Over Fifty.* New York: Holt, Rinehart, and Winston, 1984.

Steinberg, David, ed. *Erotic By Nature: A Celebration of Life, of Love, and of Our Wonderful Bodies.* Santa Cruz, Calif.: Down There Press/Red Alder Books, 1988.

———. *The Erotic Impulse: Honoring the Sensual Self.* New York: Jeremy P. Tarcher, 1992.

The Starr-Weiner Report on Sex and Sexuality in the Mature Years. New York: McGraw-Hill, 1982.

Zilbergeld, Bernie, Ph.D. *The New Male Sexuality: The Truth About Men, Sex and Pleasure.* New York: Bantam, 1992.

Sexual Health and Disease Prevention

Barbach, Lonnie, Ph.D. *The Pause: Positive Approaches to Menopause.* New York: Signet, 1994.

Institute for Advanced Study of Human Sexuality. *The Complete Guide to Safer Sex.* Fort Lee, N.J.: Barricade, 1992.

Lark, Susan, M.D. *PMS: Premenstrual Syndrome Self-Help Book: A Guide to Feeling Good All Month.* Berkeley: Celestial Arts, 1993.

———.*The Menopause Self-Help Book: A Woman's Guide to Feeling Good for the Second Half of Life.* Berkeley: Celestial Arts, 1992.

Masters, William, and Virginia Johnson. *AIDS, Crisis: Heterosexual Behavior in the Age of AIDS.*

Richmond. *There's More to Sex Than AIDS: The A to Z Guide to Safe Sex.* Victoria, Australia: Greenhouse, 1988.

Sharan, Farida. *Creative Menopause: Illuminating Women's Health and Spirituality.* Boulder: Wisdom, 1994.

Other Valuable Books

Bradshaw, John. *Homecoming: Reclaiming and Championing Your Inner Child.* New York: Bantam, 1990.

Estes, Clarissa Pintola. *Women Who Run With Wolves: Myths and Stories of the Wild Woman Archetype.* New York: BBallantine Books, 1995.

Gawain, Shakti. *Creative Visualization.* New York: Bantam, 1979.

Keen, Sam. *Fire in the Belly: On Being a Man.* New York: Bantam, 1991.

Kopp, Sheldon B. Guru: *Metaphors from a Psychotherapist.* New York: Bantam, 1976.

————. *If You Meet the Buddha On the Road, Kill Him! The Pilgrimage of Psychotherapy Patients.* New York: Bantam, 1972.

Lee, John. *At My Father's Wedding: Reclaiming Our True Masculinity.* New York: Bantam, 1991.

Markova, Dawna. *No Enemies Within: A Creative Process for Discovering What's Right About What's Wrong.* Berkeley: Conari Press, 1994.

Ransohoff, Rita M., Ph.D. *Venus After Forty: Sexual Myths, Men's Fantasies, and Truths About Middle-Aged Women.* New York: Macmillan, 1987.

Simonton, O. Carl, and Reid Henson with Brenda Hampton. *The Healing Journey: Restoring Health and Harmony to Body, Mind, and Spirit.* New York: Bantam, 1994.

Viscott, David. *Emotionally Free: Letting Go of the Past to Live in the Moment.* New York: Chicago: Contemporary, 1993.

Woodman, Marion. *Leaving My Father's House: A Journey to Conscious Femininity.* Boston: Shambala, 1992.

APPENDIX B

Safer Sex and Disease Prevention

It seems irresponsible in these times to write a book on sex without including material on safer sex practices and on the dangers of sexually transmitted disease if these practices are ignored.

It's very sad that sexual experiences that have so much potential for joyful passion and for spiritual sharing can also be a means of contracting an incurable or even fatal disease. It seems tragic that children learning about sex today never have a chance to think about sexuality without awareness that sex can be life threatening.

We are all potentially at risk. AIDS has reached epidemic proportions and it is increasing the fastest in groups that used to be at low risk.

This appendix offers you some of the vital information you need to stay healthy. You can get more detailed information from the books, hotlines, and telephone information services listed in Appendix A.

At this writing, AIDS is a fatal disease which has no known cure. Herpes, though not a serious health threat in most cases, has significant psychological and relationship effects and also has no cure. HPV or genital warts usually are curable, but may increase cancer risk.

These three diseases will be discussed in this appendix, followed by a summary of safer sex practices. Consult sources listed in Appendix A to find out about other STDs, and see a physician if you have symptoms.

AIDS (Acquired Immune Deficiency Syndrome)

Caused by the HIV virus, this deadly disease has made impetuous sexual decisions potentially life threatening. Cases of infection by the HIV virus are estimated at one million as of this writing, and projections of thirty to forty million cases worldwide in the next five years have been made!

Since much has been made in the media of high-risk groups for HIV infection, it is important to acknowledge that HIV is also found among healthy-looking, well-educated college students, athletes, clergy, and professionals of all ethnic backgrounds, as well as among the poor and disenfranchised. It is found in frightening and growing numbers among drug-free heterosexuals.

Unfortunately, many nice, educated people have the HIV virus and don't know it. Many of these people were unaware that a past partner was infected. Others were unaware of risk factors, such as having had a blood transfusion before effective screening was in place. There are also people carrying the HIV virus who have never acknowledged risk factors such as having used intravenous drugs.

Achieving a balanced attitude toward AIDS is not easy. On the one hand, it's important to be aware of the risks and to protect yourself. On the other hand, you don't really have to worry about AIDS if you take the necessary protective steps discussed following.

How AIDS Is Transmitted

AIDS is transmitted in four ways: through intimate sexual contact, exposure to infected blood or needles, from an infected mother to her fetus during pregnancy or delivery, and to a baby through nursing on an infected mother. In every case, it is the exchange of contaminated bodily fluids that makes transmission possible. There is no sexual activity that creates the disease if the virus is not present.

AIDS is not transmitted by casual contact. Extensive research has failed to find any evidence that the virus can be transmitted by sharing food, water, toilets, or even toothbrushes and razors. There seems to be absolutely no risk of catching HIV at school, at work, in a restaurant, or in a theater.

Protection from AIDS

The most positive thing that can be said about AIDS is that it is fully preventable. There are only two paths to complete protection, however. They are (1) abstinence from any activity that exchanges bodily fluids, or (2) monogamy between two uninfected partners. Although HIV-negative status can be determined by laboratory testing, its continued validity depends on monogamy, and monogamy is extremely difficult to be certain about. Millions of men and women have extramarital activities unknown to their spouse.

Most physicians can arrange an AIDS test, or anonymous testing is available in every metropolitan area. Call your local Planned Parenthood for this or to get a referral. The national AIDS Hotline at (800) 342-2437 will also provide referrals in your area, as well as much information.

Valid testing requires a six-month waiting period. If both you and your partner are tested today, and if both are negative, this tells you that activities *prior to the past six months* have not infected either of you.

Then you must wait six months, having sexual contact only with each other, and then repeat the test. Abstain or practice safer sex during this waiting period; do not exchange bodily fluids with anyone who has not been tested. If both tests are negative again, you both are safe from AIDS so long as you are sexual only with each other.

Making exceptions to the above risks your life. We know clinically, however, that many people will take that risk in certain situations. If you do, it is vital to follow the safer sex practices discussed later.

Herpes

Herpes causes painful, cone-shaped sores that itch and burn and develop into groups of small blisters filled with a clear, very infectious fluid. Often, flulike symptoms accompany the sores and can last a week or more. The first outbreak causes the most severe symptoms. Recurrences are less severe and can be frequent or not.

Herpes is traumatic for some and annoying for all who have it. It carries some risk to any future babies a woman may bear. Any pregnant woman with herpes needs to seek the care of an obstetrician experienced with pregnancy management in women with herpes.

Other sufferers face no special risks that we know of, but they must deal with the feelings that come with having a disease they probably got while making love, and one that affects their sexual organs. Often, they feel a great deal of anger toward the person who gave them the disease, especially if they were not informed of the risk in advance. They are aware that they too will always face ethical issues about discussing the disease with any future sexual partner they may have.

The positive aspects of herpes are that it is rarely a major health problem and that careful choices can usually prevent its transmission. It is not the end of the world, and having it only means that you have caught a virus; it does not make you a sexual pariah. Many long-term, sexually active couples exist in which one infected partner has not transmitted it to the other.

Preventing Herpes Transmission

Herpes is transmitted when the virus is being shed. This happens mostly during an outbreak when sores are present and during the prodromal phase—the two or three days before an outbreak when many sufferers have a tingling or other sensation that means an outbreak is imminent. There is disagreement about whether herpes can be transmitted at other times.

You risk transmission if you come in contact with a herpes sore (or a "cold" sore), whether it is located on the mouth, the genitals, or elsewhere. Mucous membranes such as the eyes or genitals are especially vulnerable. Persons with oral herpes can even transfer the virus on themselves by touching a sore and then touching their genitals or eyes.

If you have sores, keep them covered. Wash your hands vigorously with hot water and detergent if you do inadvertently touch one. If you are trying to avoid contracting herpes, don't contact towels, sheets, washcloths, toothbrushes, or anything else that could have touched a sore. Wash these items with detergent and hot water. Defer sexual contact during prodromal periods and outbreaks.

The use of latex condoms helps to prevent transmission, *but only if the sores are fully covered.* The spermicide nonoxynol-9 increases protection. Any sore that is not covered by the condom can infect. Rarely, perhaps six days a year, the virus may shed without any symptoms. This means that using condoms all the time is the safest choice.

Treatment with the antiviral agent acylovir reduces the duration of outbreaks and shortens the time the virus sheds. In my clinical experience, however, it is the psychological aspects of herpes that clients often have the most trouble dealing with. Don't hesitate to see a therapist who has experience working with this issue. There's no need to be embarrassed to ask on the phone whether a therapist has such experience.

You may also contact the national organization HELP (Herpetics Engaged in Living Productively). They can provide very helpful support and information. They are listed on page 279.

Human Papilloma Virus–Genital Warts

Knowing about this disease is important, because *some* types of it have been associated with developing genital tract cancer in both sexes, and especially with cancer of the cervix in women. If your partner has genital warts, insist on the use of condoms and nonoxynol-9 until the warts have been eliminated.

There are at least sixty types of the papilloma viruses that cause warts, and some estimates put the number of Americans who have them at more than twelve million. The warts can appear anywhere on the genital or anal area. They can also occur inside the urethra in men, inside the vagina or on the cervix in women, or inside the rectum in both sexes. Because of this, some people have warts without being aware of it.

Transmission occurs through sexual contact in most cases, but it is possible to transmit it on towels or clothing. Transmission can take a long time, because warts can incubate for months. Having been exposed and not contracting warts does not mean that you won't catch them if you continue to expose yourself to them.

Since HPV can often be completely eliminated, it is important to seek medical treatment and to follow through on it until success is reached. Treatment is easier the earlier it begins. A variety of methods can be used, recently including laser surgery.

The risk factors for cancer are reduced but not eliminated by treatment. Frequent pap smears for women and physical examinations for men are permanently needed both to protect fertility and to protect against cancer.

Other Sexually Transmitted Diseases

There are many other common STDs. Some, such as chlamydia, can damage the reproductive tract and compromise fertility. Others, such as syphilis, are curable if found early but dangerous if left untreated. Still others, like yeast infections, are not particularly risky but have the potential to interfere with your sex life and make the sufferer very uncomfortable.

Inform yourself in more detail by use of the sources in Appendix A. You can protect yourself from these groups of STDs by following safer sex guidelines.

"Safe Sex"

The only really safe sex is with a person who is not infected with a sexually transmitted disease. There are methods of reducing transmission if you have sex with a person who has an STD, but there is no 100 percent guarantee of safety if you exchange bodily fluids or if you contact a lesion. If there is any possibility that you or your partner have a communicable STD, choose activities such as hugging, dry kissing, massage, or clothed body-rubbing at least until you know exactly what the situation is.

Safer Sex

This term that has been coined to clarify the fact that no sexual activity that could lead to an exchange of bodily fluids is perfectly safe, unless both partners are free of disease. Barriers like condoms and diaphragms help, but they are subject to human error and they can be defective.

You can be *safer*, though, if you use these protective devices. Because many people will decide to go ahead with sexual activities without certainty of safety, it's important to know how to be as safe as possible.

The exchange of bodily fluids can be prevented by correct and consistent use of barriers such as condoms. It's important to use latex condoms, because animal-fiber condoms have walls of unequal thickness and sometimes leak. Use latex condoms that are lubricated with nonoxynol-9 or use a lubricant with nonoxynol-9 in it. This spermicide kills the HIV virus and greatly increases effectiveness. It offers some protection if the condom breaks or comes off at the wrong time.

Safety with a condom and spermicide increases with use of a diaphragm or a cervical cap. Get advice from your doctor if you want to consider the new female condom. Safety decreases when genitals are dry or irritated, or when people use alcohol or other drugs which can impair their judgment or coordination.

Safer oral sex on a man should include use of a condom. Safer oral sex on a woman also should include the use of a barrier. Dental dams are sheets of latex made for this purpose. A cut up condom or plastic wrap can also be carefully used.

Never use oil or oil-based lubricants with latex. Latex starts to deteriorate in sixty seconds after exposure to oil. This includes baby oil, mineral oil, cold cream, Crisco, Vaseline, and natural oils. Use water-soluble lubricants instead, such as Astroglide, Probe, or K-Y Jelly.

The dislike many people have for condoms can be overcome. Anything, including a condom, can be eroticized. Experiment with your partner and learn to make applying the condom a part of your love-play. It's a small price to pay for safety.

A *Soulful Sex Perspective on Sexual Safety*

Perhaps you are now convinced that you should begin to practice safer sex, at least until certain questions have been answered. It can be difficult for a couple who has not practiced safer sex to begin doing so. Making love in risky ways when health issues are unsettled, though, sets you both up for an experience in which you hold back and perhaps resent each other.

On the other hand, taking care of your body and your health by refusing to engage in risky sexual behaviors if you are not certain of your safety is an act that will be respected by any loving partner.

Ecstatic lovemaking thrives only in an environment of deep trust. It is a loving act to communicate to a beloved partner that you prize and will protect their health and your own.

INDEX

KEY: A = appendix A; B = appendix B; Book titles are italicized.

Psychotherapists, choosing, 275A
Psychotherapy, description, 272A
Psychotherapy, poem exerpt about, 271A
Pubococcygeus muscles, *See*: PC muscles
Puritanism, effect of sexual attitudes, 13
"Radiant beauty," Einstein quote, 7
Rape
    need to discuss, 119
    survivors' need for treatment, 119
Real Magic, 132
Receptivity, sexual
    as spiritual act, 51, 124
    barriers to, 49–50
    experiments to deepen, 50-1
Recovering passion, case of Vera and Morris, 71
Redfield, James, ix
Regan, Kevin, 1
Reich, Wilhelm, 155
Reflective listening, 111
    validation, 112
    value for lovemaking, 113
Rejection, sexual, effect on male self-esteem, 81
Relationships
    spiritual needs in, 22–3
    unconditional love in, 23
Relaxation, progressive, 157–8
Religion
    contrasted to spirituality, 12
    validates sacred sex, 4
"Religious—not," 4
Resources, audio, 282–4
Resources, video, 284A
Rilke, Ranier Maria, 129
Rituals
    consistent practice, importance of, 138
    honoring partner, for, 176
    prior to sex, 138
    self-pleasuring, 163–4
Rogers, Carl, 103
Rolf, Ida, 155

Romance
    conflicts over, 69–70
    deeper meaning of desire for, 69
    limitations of, 11
Rules, false sexual, 45-6
Rusty, (case of): Learning the Value of Self-Pleasuring, 94
Ryan, M. J., ix
SSSS, *See*: Society for the Scientific Study of Sex
STD Hotline, National, 278A
Sacred, the, experiencing in everyday life, 5
Sacred spot, female
    controversy over, 184
    how to find, 184
    key to ecstatic response, 184
    lubricated exploration, 185-6
    male as healer, 186
    mentioned in Kama Sutra, 184
    partner assisted exploration, 185
    same as "G-spot," 184
    "south pole" of clitoris, 186
    storage site of memories, 185
Sacred spot, male
    access and exploration, 187
    location, 187
Safer sex
    bodily fluid exchange danger, 300B
    description of, 299–300B
    soulful perspective on, 301B
Safety, emotional
    creation of, 36
    hygiene, effect of poor, 65–6
Safety, medical, abstinence only guarantee of, 47
Sanctuary, 154
Scientific method, value and limitations of, 6
Secrets, sexual
    fear of revealing, 118
    divine guidance, need for, 118
Self-acceptance, increasing, 34
Self-esteem and sexual acceptance, male, 81